READING WITH WORDS IN COLOUR

READING WITH WORDS IN COLOUR

A SCIENTIFIC STUDY OF THE PROBLEMS OF READING

CALEB GATTEGNO

EDUCATIONAL EXPLORERS
READING · BERKSHIRE · ENGLAND

First published in Great Britain 1969
by Educational Explorers Ltd
40 Silver Street, Reading, RG1 2SU
© Caleb Gattegno 1969
SBN: 85225 512 8

All Words in Colour books and
materials described in this text can be
obtained in Great Britain from
THE CUISENAIRE COMPANY LTD
40 Silver Street, Reading, RG1 2SU Berkshire

Printed in Great Britain
by Lamport Gilbert Printers Ltd.,
Reading Berkshire.
Set in Monotype Baskerville

PREFACE

AFTER SIX YEARS of investigation in the classroom and in a reading clinic, and after meeting a large number of teachers of reading at seminars and workshops in many parts of the English speaking world, it might be expected that the author of a scheme like Words in Colour would have something new to say.

The context of this book could be recast in three levels. The first might concern itself with the study of reading as a challenge to the scientist, the second with a description of techniques that take a non-reader to mastery of the skill, while the third might look at what is happening to learners in relation to their mother tongue as a result of the techniques they are using.

As a scientist the author worked on the *act of reading*, as it is carried out by himself and others, and found components in it that had escaped earlier investigators. Some of these (e.g. that reading is in time; that in reading the medium is forgotten while the message is retained; that algebra plays a central role in the awareness of sounds in words and words in sentences) would naturally change the face of things. Indeed returning to the beginning of the apprenticeship of reading we find that those learning bring with them spoken speech, and therefore an arsenal of intellectual instruments, insight and know-how. To study the nature of this contribution is also the preoccupation of scientists.

To subordinate teaching to learning in the field of reading means that we develop techniques that make sense to the non-reader who has mastered spoken speech. These techniques are part of Words in Colour, and are new; their names (Visual dictation 1, 2 and 3, game of transformation, continuous feedback) illustrate the awareness that time and algebra, as well as consciousness, are essential to the act of reading.

Since stress is placed on consciousness and since the role of memory is reduced, learners behave very differently from those taught to read by any of the traditional approaches. They are responsible for their own learning from the start. This is possible because inner criteria are encouraged, in the field of reading, to function spontaneously as in the field of spoken speech. This is in turn possible now because reading results as a by-product of the various Words in Colour activities, and is not their end. Thus learners acquire much more than the ability to read. They watch, listen, isolate sounds, correct faulty hearing or reading, notice how words and sentences behave; in short they become linguists, aware of the medium as well as its message. An approach to reading that simultaneously educates learners as persons and as observers can only commend itself to the attention of responsible people, for it achieves what they have asked of schooling but have very rarely obtained.

New York City
October 1968

Editor's note: Regional pronunciation

Reference to the Mute r Edition is made throughout the text, and refers to the greatest single difference in spoken English between regions and countries in the treatment of the letter r. Where this sign is always sounded, or rolled, it has a separate colour on the Word Charts and Fidel. Where it is often left unsounded it should be given the colour of the preceding vowel. The Mute r Edition applies to this second mode of speech, to such places as Southern England and Australia, where *pore* is pronounced like *paw*, or where only the first r in river is sounded.

CONTENTS

Appendices

INTRODUCTION

THIS TEXT, in addition to presenting new material of a general nature, is also intended to serve as an adequate guide for teachers in the classroom application of *Words in Colour*; the original *Teacher's Guide* published in 1962 may be used as a complement to it. The six years of progress (1961–1967) in the study of this reading teaching programme have led to the development of new ways of working and have crystallised outlooks only suspected earlier; here these are presented in print for the first time. And while it was clear that the Pilot Edition of 1962 could not report on the future experience of the author, it was not clear then that life would permit distinct progress to be made in a variety of directions. The passage of time has actualised what could only be presumed at first, and luck has done the rest.

As a teacher the author found several opportunities for developing the approach while teaching very young children; others arose while working with children who had encountered various reading problems, and still others in intensive classes of adolescents and adults with differing backgrounds, who were non-readers or in serious reading difficulty. The learning by the author-as-teacher on these occasions was often witnessed by observers and later discussed with them. Certain remarks progressively became the focal points for further inquiry. This gave rise to remarkable insights which in turn either provided the proper foundation for the existing techniques, or proposed new techniques to serve some of the newly discovered purposes. During this time the study of reading developed into the study of people engaged in activities yielding skill in reading as a by-product. The shift from viewing reading as a separate activity—as is conventionally done—to viewing it as a by-product of the extension of intellectual and linguistic power, is perhaps the most important single item in all the findings of the author made so far.

The questions that were asked by the researcher were concerned with what the learner must do mentally in certain ways in order that he should find himself knowing how to read at the end.

Indeed, reading is a skill. One does not know *reading* itself; one knows *how* to read, as one knows how to walk, talk or drive a motor-car. Practice teaches us how to drive, not rules or instructions. The analogy between learning to read and learning to drive can serve us here, for the level of experience sufficient to obtain a driving licence is far inferior to that reached by most drivers of motor-cars. The licence indicates only that the person concerned has shown a degree of familiarity with some situations that are commonly encountered when travelling by car and that he can cope with them. Driving in all sorts of circumstances follows; and it is this that provides the fully-fledged skill of driving.

Beginners at school can be considered as having to qualify for a licence to read, which is termed here the 'first reading certificate'. It is only *after* achieving this level of competence that through practice the learner advances further and further into reading, meeting greater demands and some hazards. But at what stage is the level reached when this first certificate can be awarded, and what comes after?

It will be seen in Chapter 1 what the activities are that lead with certainty to the successful passing of the test to determine whether the licence is to be issued or not. These activities must cover, in a schematised but nevertheless natural manner, *all* the fundamental techniques that make reading as a smooth and proper activity possible.

Just as the environment for a learner-driver cannot be complete, so the language for which the first certificate is designed for the learner-reader will also be restricted, though the exercises on it will not.

The concept of a *restricted language* is an important one for teachers of reading and of languages. We call 'restricted' all sectors of a language which permit the display of some of the normal linguistic behaviours associated with the whole of the language, but which do not permit the display of others also pertaining to the language.

The language each one of us uses is restricted since so much even of our own mother tongue is not part of the language we understand and use either in spoken or written form. This does not make our reading skill necessarily at all inferior to the maximal.

So it will be with beginner-readers. Their skill will develop on the selected restricted language introduced in Chapter 1 and which is replaced by languages less and less restricted as the programme advances. For the learners there will be continual expansion of the field of experience and of what can be done with greater facility and experience at their disposal. After the first certificate has been obtained by the learners, the role of the teacher is to present challenges extending the newly acquired powers, or the newly displayed powers, to lead to an awareness that more can be gained by practising in situations and under conditions differing from the initial ones but which still make use of what has been mastered.

Another important concept is that of the *cumulative effect of learning*; this takes into account the fact that no-one performs equally well before and after mastering a skill. In other terms, this proposition states that, in skills, practice develops the skill to permit a more highly developed practice, which in turn increases the skill, and so on.

Once the first certificate is obtained, the learner can attack much greater tasks making him more skilled at reading, and hence more competent to read still more challenging texts, and so on. Chapter 2 describes how learners can be enabled to meet the set of all the sounds of English in far less time than was previously thought to be possible. Chapter 3 shows how the complete set of spellings for each of these sounds is encountered. Both these challenges are greater than that first met through the restricted language.

It follows that learners can, early in their study, be made aware of grammar or of the structure of English, which as a language presents additional challenges approached in Chapter 4. In this manner will the transition be made smoothly from the relatively simple activity of associating sound and sign to the very complex activity consisting in the study of texts for their linguistic and literary insights. There can be seen in this programme a comprehensive introduction to the study of English.

As this programme is concerned with introducing people to their language, we must ask ourselves questions that involve not only the language but people too.

Beginners bring with them a contribution in the form of spoken speech. This is, among other things, a flow of experiences concerned with the organisation of parts of one's body to produce definite sounds in a definite sequence in order to convey a meaning through them. Beginning-readers are thus already highly knowledgeable and skilled in a number of ways; this they demonstrate by being capable of translating meanings into adequate sequences of sounds (words and sentences) which include such elements as stress, emphasis, intonation, timbre, structure and other dimensions unconsciously brought in to serve the end of communication. It is the intuition or awareness of meaning on the part of the speaker that calls in the words adequate to produce the proper flow of speech. In speaking, meanings are translated into words and their accompanying supporting non-verbal forms of communication, and we all know how to do this quite well early in our lives.

In looking at recorded speech, i.e. writing, we must 'listen' to the sentence—as much as when hearing a voice—to reach meaning. Underlying all written material the spoken word and all of its characteristics must be somewhere. To read is to restore spoken speech to the printed page. This observation presents the teacher of reading with certain problems, the most vital of which can be stated as: *helping the learner to understand the connection between the temporal aspect of spoken speech and the spatial arrangement of print.*

To read, it is necessary (a) to introduce an order into the movements of the eyes so that the signs making up each word are scanned from left to right, as they were put down in writing; and (b) to observe that the order of the words in the sentence is in the same direction, and to wait until it is finished to extract the meaning that these words in this particular order were intended to convey.

The two-dimensional space of a page is not oriented in a specific direction, but a straight line, including a line composed of signs printed, is thus oriented, but it is reversible; *time*, on the other hand, is ordered but not reversible. For this reason different languages can choose to write or record speech from the left or from the right on the horizontal, or move to the vertical. But *all* recorded languages display the same respect for temporal order when writing and reading.[1]

Further, in some languages, writing is done above the line, in others below, and in still others both above and below. In certain languages (the phonetic) each sound is represented by a single sign,

[1]Including hieroglyphics and Chinese ideograms.

and conversely in others (the non-phonetic—as English) evolution has introduced certain irregularities, while in still others some sounds are not recorded at all and must be added by the reader (e.g. Arabic and Hebrew). But all these modalities of recording the various languages do not seem to present major problems to vast numbers of learners, who manage to master the operation of translating speech into print (writing) and print into speech (reading), common to so many languages.

Indeed, the problems are *not* in the correspondences between spoken and written forms—unique to particular languages—but rather in the relationship of teacher to learner, and in the techniques of teaching. If the teacher is aware of what a learner has to master in order to make the correspondence and knows techniques to help the learner achieve this, all goes quickly and smoothly. But if the teacher forgets that what is to be communicated is meaning through finding speech in print in a natural way, or that learning requires concentration and no distraction, then learners have trouble.

Below is listed what seems obviously necessary to enable learners to be able to bridge the gap between spoken and written speech, and the findings are ordered to produce a scheme of work that moulds itself to the reality of the requirements of this process.

1. The conventions of the written code for each language, being arbitrary, cannot be justified on rational grounds but need to be met as gratuitous suggestions acquired without reference to other material. And in this manner the left to right convention, the alignment of letters and words with respect to the horizontal, is met, and particular designs or sets of designs are seen to be associated with particular sounds.

2. Some languages use single signs to represent their syllables and such languages have been found the easiest to be acquired by native readers. English on the other hand uses vowels and consonants. In reality, consonants only sound when linked with vowels. So, though different signs are used for writing both vowels and consonants, only the vowels are sounded on their own—the signs that stand for consonants *never* being sounded by themselves. For multiple consonants that are part of the written words, there are techniques

making learners capable of sounding them blended—not in isolation—as they come naturally in speech.

3. Time is to be kept at the centre of the activity of reading. For this a pointer is used as a linking instrument between the signs that form words, or between the words that form sentences. The actual movements of the pointer reveal the temporal sequence to be followed, generating the instructions necessary for the learner to determine for himself the corresponding spoken word or sentence.

4. In addition, when words are uttered, only the complete statement with *proper intonation and rhythm* can convey the full meaning. This aspect of time, obviously present in speech, can be lost if one says words on a printed line as if each were isolated from the rest. No reading word for word is of any assistance to learners who can be induced from the start to retain a sequence of words they have scanned and say them naturally afterwards in the manner of every-day speech. Reading-as-talking is of fundamental importance from the beginning.

5. Anyone capable of hearing words does so by means of a highly sophisticated instrument (the ear), and one which can perform a number of operations at the same time; these include the sorting out of harmonics, discriminating between relevant and irrelevant noises, filtering some sounds, and so on. A living ear does this all the time. We are able to analyse sounds from the first months of life and this guides us in many occasions all day long. But the ear cannot normally operate independently of temporal sequences; sounds are in time, and so is the functioning of the ear.

The eye on the other hand is a scanning instrument which functions in time, but it is such that it is also capable of taking in, or photographing, vast expanses simultaneously. This indicates that space may be comprehended in one look, as one whole, time not really being consumed during this activity. But when reading, the eye is not employed to take in the whole page at once. Here all words save one, or one and its immediate neighbours on the right, are ignored. While scanning, the eye does not function panoramically. Indeed, words are simply retained in the mind until meaning is conveyed, the image of the words scanned in the sentence being dropped as soon as the eye has passed over them. Thus the eye does not operate photographically on words when reading, any more than the mind retains words when we speak, write or listen.

To use the eye panoramically is a specialised exercise when reading. This accounts for the multitude of slips of the pen, the typewriter, the typographic compositor, and the legion of unnoticed printing errors—all far more numerous than errors of the tongue. But the eye must be used panoramically as a photographic instrument to take in words as designs, particularly if no rational principle will generate the word from other elements that may be already in the mind. For correct spelling to be achieved, therefore, requires that words be 'photographed', not simply scanned, or uttered as in reading. Hence special exercises will be needed to induce learners to look at, take in, and evoke words as designs. *Colour* can help to convey a phonetic clue to words, as much as relief in the spatial arrangement of the area covered by words (i.e. their shape) eases the task of the eye functioning panoramically, as a camera. Consequently colour will be used; exposure of the eye to coloured designs while learning thereby reduces the chances of overlooking the spelling of each word.

Learning to read calls in opposite uses of one's mental instruments. Normally the eye is synthetic in its functioning (as required by spelling) and the ear analytic; but both are able to function in the other way since the mind that governs them is both analytic and synthetic by nature. Some special exercises and materials are all that is required to avoid the neutralising effect of one use on the other.

6. If one becomes aware of words as aspects of reality and starts being interested in them as such, there is no end to the observations that can be made about their structure, and the relation between sounds, forms and meanings. This can be extended to sets of words, to the analysis of sentences in order to observe what is a general behaviour and what is a particular one. To take one instance, the effect of reversing the orders of words, particularly of verbs, can be noted. More specifically, it could be asked: can 'is it' (for example) be said otherwise than as a question?

To be concerned with such matters is an indication of the freeing of the mind from other preoccupations deemed vital earlier and which required all the energies of the learners for their performance. It follows that we may move from purely technical matters to a linguistic study, and then pass from the linguistic to a literary level, when what one has previously been concerned with no longer spontaneously calls on all the available energy.

7. Embedded in the study of words and their individuality is the order of their component signs. What would happen were

—the order of the signs reversed?
—a sign added?
—reversing and adding both done?
—another sign inserted?
—the three operations carried out in succession?

The 'game of transformations' based on links suggested by the phonetic structures of words, not their meaning, results in an awakening in the learner to a reality that users of words cannot stop to perceive; that sounds in words are sounds that may have a life of their own; that the creators of words may have chosen particular forms for reasons lost in the past; that it is always possible to produce new words either arbitrarily, or by fusion of others, and by other principles.

Linguistic awareness is the reward of progress in the use and observation of words. This in turn helps further progress to take place in one's linguistic education, which in turn permits the meeting of deeper and more demanding challenges.

8. This linguistic awareness can take the form of *analysis of sentences* of which grammatical awareness is one side, and sensitivity to ambiguity, precision and rigour another. It must be understood that the possibility exists of meeting all the challenges within a restricted language and that it is not necessary to wait until a certain age or a certain stage has been reached before attempting to make awarenesses more clearly present. As will be shown later, the recognition of meaning associated with a change of intonation is as clear an indication of recognition as will later be the explicit statement of a rule.

Formalised grammar is the explicit stating of how language is used correctly and adequately.

Rejection of nonsensical or contradictory statements as useless is a sure sign of understanding that content, not only form, is carried by words.

9. In this whole approach the education of the *linguistic powers* of the learners *in toto* is achieved. This includes reading of books, preferably of books which bring valuable experience to the readers and make sense of the activity of reading, providing a channel for growth through *experience by proxy* as contrasted with growth through direct experience in its uniqueness when personally meeting what actually takes place. And it also includes expressing one's own inner experiencing of events and insights so that others may share in these by proxy.

Words in Colour is successful if learners understand that the successive certificates of reading acquired through the programme are merely stepping-stones towards independent and critical reading and creative writing, using a vocabulary which is expanding and increasingly sensitive and adequate to the meaning the writer intends to communicate.

Chapter One

THE FIRST READING CERTIFICATE

In this chapter the first challenges of reading and writing are met and a solution is offered which should be effective with all children except for the very small fraction of perhaps one in a thousand requiring some other treatment.

The classroom activities both of the teacher and of the pupils will be outlined. When definite recommendations are made and stressed, it should be recognised that if these are neglected by the teacher responsibility for any eventual trouble encountered must rest with her and not with the programme. The author can convey his experience only through words, diagrams and pictures, leaving the reader to supply the understanding and actual classroom performance. And it will be a rule in this text that the writer will not trespass by taking upon himself what only teachers in their classrooms can do safely and knowingly. To work together in this context is to leave to each what each can do better in the circumstances.

First the actual beginning of learning to read and write will be met, which aims principally at providing an insight into the conventions of recording speech in English. This will be accompanied by a study which should not be by-passed even though it could not be said that the material explored is part of the English language. While the pointer and its uses will have been met from the start, special sections will be devoted to this tool since its role increases constantly throughout most of the programme. In the sections explaining the uses of the pointer, material will be considered which when mastered permits learners to earn their first reading certificate.

Work with the pointer produces words which can now be recorded, and which appear in print on Word Chart 2 in colour, and on the pages of Primer 1 in black on white. With these words, sentences can be made. The primer book and the chart are introduced and used in conjunction with the remaining materials for this phase— the Word Building Book and Worksheet 1. The chapter ends with a note on the testing of reading and of some of its specialised aspects.

It should be remembered that restricted languages (as defined above) are the only ones involved, that they make it possible that nothing learned need be unlearned, and that nothing should absorb energies uselessly.

I.

Some Conventions of Writing and Recording English

1. English is written on horizontal lines from left to right, with parts of some signs (the descenders) going below the line, and parts of others (the ascenders) rising above the other signs. Conventions of reading, such as the first two, can best be understood if an arbitrary language is introduced first, having only *one* sign and *one* sound.

2. The sign chosen for this is *a*, which is produced on the board in the usual handwritten form rather than with the alternative shape 'a' of Roman print. The sound the learners are given for it is the one readers associate with the left-hand letter in the English word *at*.

Every time this sign is drawn the learners then utter the associated sound. The teacher writes it on the chalkboard a number of times and elicits the 'same' sound on each occasion. For this exercise a piece of white chalk is used.

The teacher now produces the sign in larger or smaller sizes as she pleases. Sometimes kindergarten pupils raise their voices when the sign is large and whisper when it is very small. This gift from the class is to be accepted without comment even if enjoyed. Pupils soon forget about this once the letters maintain an acceptable average size.

Since there is only one letter and only one sound there is neither danger of confusion nor reason to forget. Repetition of the sign is the only activity possible. Once

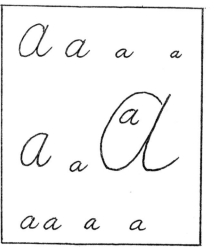

the game of repetition is played it is noticed that a new variable appears: the interval between two successive utterances. One can act on it by reducing it or extending it. Distinctions between the length of time taken between utterances can be given a conventional spatial representation through placing two *a* signs *contiguously* if the time is just sufficient to indicate that two separate *a*'s have been uttered instead of one:

aa

and a small distance apart on the horizontal line when some perceptible time is left between the two utterances:

a a

This is followed by:

(i) *Visual Dictation 1*, the teacher using a pointer on one sign *a*, pointing to this single sign as many times as seems fruitful—both increasing the speed of movement (resulting in sequences of taps on the chalkboard which are perceived by the ear rather than by the eye), and reducing it. Pupils utter what the rules of the game now make clear. It is a simple matter to hear whether or not what is produced by the learners corresponds to the succession of taps dictating, for example

a aa a aa or *aa a a aaa aa*

on the chalkboard.[1]

(ii) *Visual Dictation 2* in which the teacher writes several groupings of *a* on the board (such as *a a aa aaa*) and then records in horizontal lines what has been pointed at. This may, for example, look like

a aa aaa
aa aaa a aaa
a aaa aa aaa

This gives practice in seeing that the distance between signs indicates the time pattern for utterance and begins to make clear (1) that written 'words', put down from left to right, are separated from each other by a larger amount of space than the space which is

[1]In working with remedial groups (whether in the Primary or Secondary Schools, or adults) teachers may find that longer and more intensive periods can be worked. For this reason, and since the learners may need to experience rapid progress for their self-confidence, it is often wise to use Visual Dictation 1 only. This might be until five vowels and four consonants (the scope of Word Chart 2) or until six vowels and six consonants (the scope of Word Charts 2 and 3) have been introduced. With students who have a small sight vocabulary, or a little spelling or knowledge of the alphabet, this forces them to leave aside these inadequate guides and play an entirely new 'game'.

conventionally left between letters within a word, and (2) that reading is the decoding which must be executed from left to right to be correct and to correspond to what was said.

(iii) 'Reading' page 1 of Primer 1 silently by the pupils. Then after this some pupils may read aloud to each other, those not reading at any one time watching to see if they agree that what is being said aloud corresponds to what is printed on page 1.

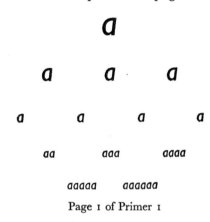

Page 1 of Primer 1

(iv) *Oral dictation* of such 'sentences' as

a aa	*aaa aa*
aa a	*a aaa aa*
aaa a	

Pupils may write on paper or on the chalkboard. Alternatively they may locate the correct writing on the chalkboard if it is there, or where it appears printed in Primer 1.

(v) Another exercise in which pupils may be given an opportunity to dictate their own 'sentences' (visually with the pointer or orally) to the rest of the class; or to create their own distinctive 'sentences' on their individual papers.

3. In a similar way the 'language of *u* (sounding as in *us*)' is introduced and the same game played. The sign *u* is written with a pale yellow chalk.

Page 2 of Primer 1 is now to be read.

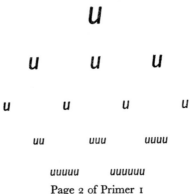

Page 2 of Primer 1

4. Up to this point, with 'single-sound languages', it has not been possible to use more than repetition as a procedure to follow. But now, with *a* and *u* used together, a 'two-sound language' can be imagined, for which a new tool becomes available: *combination*. Of the various ways in which one or more of each of these signs can be linked the most valuable is *reversal*: *au* can be distinguished from *ua*. First these are met in Visual Dictation 1 when the pointer reverses its direction, touching *a* before *u* (*a, u*) and then *u* before *a* (*u, a*). Then the reversals may be met in Visual Dictation 2 in spatial order of *au* and *ua* (and many more combinations) written with the white and yellow chalk.[1] It is thus made plain early in the programme that 'words' are read aloud by sounding the sign to the left first, followed by signs that are contiguous. This will remain the rule in all subsequent reading.

Page 3 of Primer 1 is used for such reading.

5. In like manner the signs *i* (pink), *e* (blue), and *o* (orange) sounding as in *pit, pet* and *pot* respectively are introduced and practised through the sequence of activities already outlined.[2]

Pages 4 to 9 of Primer 1 give examples of 'words' in the various successive restricted languages already presented: some words have one sound only, others employ as many as five vowel sounds. It is to

[1] Again with remedial cases the teacher may choose to integrate the new sound with *a* through Visual Dictation 1 only, and move on to introduce the next sound, leaving Visual Dictation 2, as well as reading from the Primer and oral dictation, until later.
[2] See above and also the schema on page 23.

be noted that when vowels follow each other rapidly their sounds merge, forming diphthongs and triphthongs, etc.

auieo	auioe	
oauie	oaoau	
iaoueo	aiouoe	
aioaio	eoioie	
ooiaooi	iiooaoii	
uoiuoia	uooiau	
ieoiouo	ouieauo	
oouuiieeaa	aouiauoiee	

```
a  a  aa  aaa
u  u  uu  uuu
au  ua  uau  aua
 i  i  ii  iii
aiu  uia  uiu  iau
 e  e  ee  eee
aei  eua  eaiu
o  o  oo  ooo
aaeeoo  ieoii
oaa  aoie  oou
```

Page 9 of Primer 1 and Word Chart 1

6. 'Word' Chart 1 is the permanent record in colour of what has been mastered so far, to go up on the wall *after* reading has been done with the aid of either

    a. the pointer used on the chalkboard by the teacher (Visual Dictations 1 and 2), or

    b. Primer 1 in which the pupils 'read' silently by sounding 'words' to themselves, or aloud by uttering them in turn in a small group.

It could of course now be used for the simplest form of Visual Dictation 2 which was first done on the chalkboard, if the needs of a few learners require this.

All this can be summed up in the following table of alternative directions:

a → *aa aaa aa aaaa . . .*

u ← *uu uuu . . .*

au ua uua aua . . .

i ← *ii iii . . .*

ia ai iu ui uuiii . . .

aui iua uia . . .

e → *ee eee . . .*

ei ie ea ae eu ue . . .

eia eiu eua . . .

auie eiua ieau . . .

o ← *oo ooo . . .*

oa ou oi oe . . .

oau oai oae oui oue oie . . .

oaui oaue ouie . . .

ouieo oeiua ieoau . . .

If teachers try systematically to utter the sounds that go with the signs just once and no more, they will in time become convinced that they help their pupils more than if they repeat the same thing once or many times. For it is the learner who must prove his mastery of the situation through his actions; it does not assist him if the teacher proves it again and again through hers. Rather than supply answers to their questions or encourage them to chant answers after her, the teacher can help her pupils by giving them a chance to sort out, for themselves, the problems confronting them. Allowed the opportunity to develop his *inner criteria* further and further regarding the reality he himself has met, the student learns to draw on his own resources to find answers and not to depend on outside authority. Silence and patient waiting are often the best means of assistance. Sometimes a simple silent movement of the pointer will alert the student to the factor of reality not yet taken into account by him.

II.

FIRST USE OF THE POINTER
WORDS AND SENTENCES THROUGH VISUAL DICTATION I

1. Teachers who have seen lessons of Words in Colour know that the common pointer—available in all schools—is an important instrument and will try to master its uses as early as possible.[1] In the hand of an experienced person it can work wonders. With it, teachers may learn how to help and not interfere in the process of learning. It enables them to remain silent and hence be the more effective. Through the pointer *time* is restored to its cardinal place in learning to read, and speed of reading is continually increased.

It has already been seen how the pointer and Visual Dictation I can help to achieve mastery of the five vowels (a, u, i, e, o) in their respective colours and representing five distinct sounds, and of their combinations and permutations. It will now be assumed that mastery in this field has been achieved.

---

[1] A rubber-tipped pointer for Visual Dictation is now included with classroom sets of Words in Colour materials.

2. In this programme *consonants are not sounded in isolation*: syllables are formed and sounded. The first consonant met has the shape *p* (coloured dark brown). Here is one possible arrangement on the chalkboard for all the signs introduced so far:

$$a \quad u \quad i \quad e \quad o$$
$$p$$

From the first, 'the brown one' is sounded only with one of the above vowels. With the first vowel, *ap* is produced (as heard at the beginning of the word *apple*). But this combination is not written down: it is formed by moving, or sliding, the pointer from *a* to *p*. Pointing at *a* the teacher says, 'Sound this'; and then, moving from *a* to *p* says, 'For the white followed immediately by the brown we say *ap*'. After forming this pair again rapidly and so as to be seen by all concerned, she asks, 'What is this then?' seeking the sounding of *ap* once more in order to have it put into circulation by the learners and not by herself. Then switching with the pointer from (a, p) to the new pair (u, p) and without sounding it herself, she tries to find out whether some of the learners can make the transfer, blending the yellow sign with the brown in the same manner as they did with the white and the brown. If the answer is obtained and all pupils say *up* on the second showing, a shift to the next pair (i, p) follows, and then to the remaining pairs (e, p) and (o, p).

It is most important to recognise that when the transfer is made to the combination of the consonant *p* with the other four vowels, a number of things have taken place:

a. The memory has not been loaded, since the learner is not required to retain anything; rather there is a reason which directs him to utter what he is doing.

b. Initiative at a level not too demanding has been passed on to the learners.

c. Judgment of correctness has been left to the learners.

d. Reward has been of the usual biological kind—the recognition that ability to do leads to further doing.

As to reward for the learner, teachers who before have found it necessary to provide adequate motivation by congratulating their students on each achievement will prove to themselves that in this approach—if they refrain from the usual reaction—the learners no longer need this praise and that it even interferes with, and distracts them from their learning. The excitement the pupils feel inwardly in meeting those challenges inherent in the intellectual game is more than sufficient motivation for continuing.

3. It is possible now to combine such syllables in different orders, but it is not recommended since in English unstressed vowels get distorted with the result that *apap*, for example, does not sound like *ap* repeated, any more than the beginning of *upon* sounds like the isolated word *up*.

4. Now another exercise may be introduced: *reversal*. The pointer may be moved from the brown to the white, or to any other of the five vowels, to form the syllable corresponding to the pair (*p, a*). When linking these two signs quickly with the pointer, some pupils may suggest the sound *pa* (as in *pat*). If they do not the teacher says, 'This is *pa*', and then continues, 'What do you say for . . .' leaving the syllable unsaid but indicating *pu, pe, pi*, and *po*. The order of presentation is immaterial but it is important that pupils who have already learned to reverse (*a, u*) into (*u, a*) and so on see these new syllables as the reverses of those met earlier.

Note that if *pa* is the reverse of *ap* the converse is true, and should be requested in a variety of ways:

a. By showing, for example, *ip* with the pointer and then, after the learners have read it, asking for its reverse;
b. and immediately after, asking for the reverse of the sound just produced by the pupils;
c. and immediately after that, asking for the reverse of any one of the ten syllables possible;
d. or for the reverse of the reverse of the reverse of them.
e. By asking a pupil to show (with the pointer) one of the syllables produced;
f. or to point at its reverse.

This type of game should further establish that each syllable has a reverse which can be thought of and sounded.

To strengthen the imagination, teachers and learners may play this game with the eyes shut, referring to the pairs by the colours found in the sequence of their signs. For instance one could ask, 'What is the reverse of the reverse of the sound for the pair *pink, brown*?' (or any other pair).

5. Of all the syllables available at this stage *up* alone is a word in the English language. It is not necessary to draw pupils' attention to this fact; there is no harm in their not noticing, in the midst of this gratuitous game with sounds and signs, that they have produced a 'word' they already know. Other more important things are taking place in the learners.

6. When words are being formed from these syllables it is important to avoid the distortion of sounds, explained above, caused by stress.[1] Thus only the *fusion* (or merging or blending) of reverse syllables can be used, starting with the syllable which begins with the consonant and fusing it with its reverse which ends with the consonant.

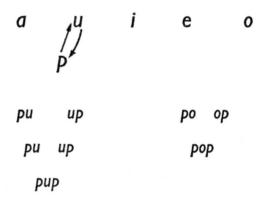

In this way *pap, pup, pip, pep* and *pop* are generated—all English words and most of them used by young learners. To achieve the blending yet without giving the answer herself the teacher can adopt either of two techniques. As the first example chosen is the one that will carry the rest, it is important to give all the necessary attention and time to it, and let the learners discover the answer. It is the writer's experience that pupils always accomplish the blending themselves if really helped by the teacher's silence. She may, however, speak in order to explain what must be done to produce this next step in the game.

(i) The pointer forming, for example, (*p, o*), or *po*, is stopped for a second at *o* to elicit the now familiar *po*: then is returned from *o* to *p*

[1]See page 27.

to form its reverse *op*. This is repeated a number of times in succession the pointer moving only when the right sounds are produced. By speeding up the rhythm until it goes as fast as could be compatible with the perception that *p* to *o* and immediately back to *p* is a continuous movement, the teacher can now request a single sound from the two syllables that have been uttered in increasingly rapid succession. Someone usually offers *pop*.

This is immediately followed by a transfer to these transformations:

$$(pa, ap) \quad \text{into } pap$$
$$(pu, up) \quad \text{into } pup$$
$$(pi, ip) \quad \text{into } pip$$
$$(pe, ep) \quad \text{into } pep$$

When this has been achieved the teacher may pause to enquire what meaning these sounds may evoke in anyone present. It is not yet the moment to give definitions for such words sounded or written, but it is reasonable, once so many have been obtained through the blending process, to spend a minute or so for making sure that the game is now oriented towards useful ends.

pop up can naturally be visually dictated by just making two of the combinations follow each other rapidly; it usually evokes a delighted response from most learners. (*pep up* is also possible.)

(ii) It may happen that some learners are still unable to blend the sounds after the teacher has used the pointer as above. She can then ask them to play a new game for the purpose of which one pretends that sounds can be held in the hand. Pointing at the syllable (*p*, *a*) or *pa*, for instance, the teacher obtains its sound from the class and suggests that they hold it in their left hand, closed.

'What have you got in your hand?' is a serious question in this context and is answered seriously by all as *pa*. The teacher then asks for its reverse to be placed in the *right* hand, closed. This is done and the teacher makes sure that the pupils understand by asking successively, in any order, 'What have you got in

—your left hand?'
—your right hand?'
—this hand?'
—that hand?'

Now the pupils are asked to do as the teacher does and put the sounds together by clapping the right hand on the left as if holding *pa* and pressing *ap* on to it. The noise of the clapping may cover the sound uttered for the result. A repeat will yield *pap* from some, who will be asked to say it loudly so that all the class knows that this is what the teacher desired. Reward for their efforts is in a transfer of their insight to the other pairs of reverses, not in compliments or approval from the teacher.

This clapping technique can be used several times and as the programme proceeds will be found to solve problems of blending again and again should they arise. All teachers will benefit from having mastered it.

7. The placing on the chalkboard of the six signs introduced so far is not a matter of concern for the learners if teachers ensure that the order in words, as they are formed by the pointer, is temporal and that the spatial order on the board is arbitrary and chance. Lessons could be given with the letters in any of a large number of different arrangements, four examples of which are shown below. Teachers could test which arrangement suits their classes best, or move to a new presentation at each successive lesson in order to maintain change at the centre of the work.

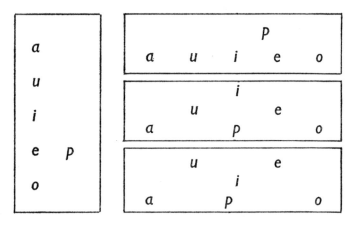

In the writer's experience such arrangements are more a convenience to the teacher at work than a problem to the learners, who in any case have so far been working mentally and on sounds rather than seeing words as whole designs, though visual imagery is being stimulated by the use of the individual signs.

8. Page 10 of Primer 1 can now be read. From among the many possibilities for producing syllables and 'words' with the six signs available, a restricted selection has been made. Several of these form words in the English language and are distinguished on this page and throughout Primer 1 by underlining.

9. Let us complete this section on the use of the pointer by introducing the sign t (which is coloured magenta). Since it is also a consonant it is not sounded alone; instead, when the pointer moves from the white sign to the magenta, the sound at is given.

a	u	i	e	o
		þ		
ap	pa	up	pu	
ip	pi	ep	pe	
	op	po		
pap	pup	pip	pep	
	pop			
papa	pupu	popo	pepe	

Page 10 of Primer 1

The chalkboard may now look something like this:

a   u   i   e   o

þ   t

Much of what has been established with the brown sign p can be transferred to the magenta t. The syllables

at, ut, it, et, ot

and their reverses

ta, tu, ti, te, to

can be formed. Thus two more English words are found—*at* and *it*. (*to*, of course, has the sound as in *top* and as such is not a word in the English language.)

Blending these new syllables produces the proper English words

tat, tit, tot and tut

and also the contrived

tet

31

10. Page 11 of Primer 1 can now be read.

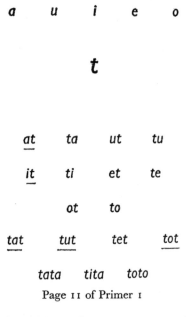

Page 11 of Primer 1

11. The merging of syllables to form words, now that two consonants are available for combining with the five vowels, can produce further 'words', some of which are part of the English language.

The pointer used as above on (*p, a*) and (*a, t*) to form *pa* and *at* will with blending produce *pat*, whose reverse is *tap*. The pointer in a single sweeping movement connects the brown, the white and the magenta signs to elicit the sound *pat*; a movement in the opposite direction creates *tap* in the minds of the pupils and they can then say it. If the pink sign instead of the white is included in this sweeping movement of the pointer, two other words and their reverses are obtained:

pit and *tip* or *tip* and *pit*

according to where the pointer has started.

Similarly *top* and *pot* are generated.

Since *tep* is not an English word, teachers may decide not to generate it and limit themselves to *pet*. But there is no harm in forming it, together with the 'words' *tup* and *put*. The latter is not an English word when it has this sound for the *u,* or the single spelling of the magenta sign. When the double spelling *tt* for the magenta is added on the board beneath the single spelling *t, putt* can be created to refer to a certain stroke or action in the game of golf.

12. After all this has been generated using the pointer and the technique of blending syllables, a number of new steps can be taken:

(i) Once the convention has been established that every time the pointer is withdrawn from the area of the seven signs it means that the formation of one word has been completed, pupils can be asked to hold in their minds the words formed by the pointer (either by touching particular signs individually or sweeping over them).

Thus these, and other, sentences can be produced in any order:

tap it	*top it up*
tip it	*pop up*
tip it up	*pot it*
pat it	*pet it*
tip it up pat	*tap at it pop*

After each sentence the teacher may turn to the class and ask, 'What have I shown?', if necessary showing it again to elicit the sentence, and at speeds that permit it to be a true challenge to the class. (With a little practice the teacher will become adept at selecting the signs quickly and without hesitation, after which words and sentences can be rapidly dictated with the pointer.)

Should the response be poor, each word could be sounded in turn, and then two uttered together after the manner of speech. Then the whole sentence would be recalled as the pointer indicates the remaining word or words, the learners saying the first two clearly now, followed by the last part. The teacher may want then to indicate the complete sentence again rapidly so it can be read as a whole.

(ii) Increasing speed in reading such sentences should be the aim. Pupils then come to know from the start that speed is one of the objects the teacher will be trying to achieve. Increases in speed are obtained by using the pointer with various rhythms—at first on words or groups of words that have been well established. For example if *tip it up pat* is considered, the sequence of quick alterations of the pattern of time could be:

   a. *tip, it, up, pat,* shown separately and made sure of as individual words;

   b. *tip it,* shown as two words in quick succession;

   c. *tip it up,* well sounded as a sentence;

   d. *tip it up* quickly shown, followed a moment later by *pat* to present the whole but with a slight pause to indicate there is to be a pause and special tone when it is uttered.

In the end, the only pattern acceptable is a well-expressed sentence uttered as in conversation with proper rhythm, pitch and intonation.

No writing has been shown so far. In the next section, through the extension of Visual Dictation 2, a type of work will be introduced where words are seen printed. Pupils will then see easily how to write words down. In Visual Dictation 1 words and sentences are formed as time sequences by the pointer and generate, within the mind of the learner, sequences of sounds which can be uttered since they have been heard and are known. The game involves auditory memories and in this way is more reminiscent of spoken speech at this point than evocative of printed words.

13. Page 12 of Primer 1 can now be read. On this page another spelling of the magenta sign is given: *tt*, as met in the word *putt* and in the surname *pitt*. It is found in the arrangement of signs at the top of the page, which accords with that on the chalkboard. Here *tt* has been introduced in the same colour as is used for *t*, to indicate identity in sound. The two words above can now be formed with the help of the pointer and can be sounded by the class.

14. At this stage Table 1 of the Word Building Book is

a	u	i	e	o
		p	t	
			tt	
pat		tap		apt
pta		tpa		atp
put	tup	upt	ptu	utp
		tpu		
pit		tip		ipt
pet		tep		ept
pot		top		opt
putt		pitt		

Page 12 of Primer 1

34

introduced.[1] This will be the first time this book is opened by the pupils.

$a \qquad u \qquad i \qquad e \qquad o$

$p \qquad t$

tt

Table 1 of the Word Building Book

Table 1 contains, in black on white and horizontally arranged, the vowels on one line and the two consonants on the lines below; this is equivalent to the first arrangement of the coloured signs used by the teacher on the chalkboard, and to that met without colour at the top of page 12 of Primer 1.

The use of the Word Building Book is shown to be similar to that made of the coloured signs on the chalkboard, a pointer being required to link signs to form 'words'. It will be found that the pupils' own pencils—held so as not to mark the page—serve usefully as pointers when working on the tables of the Word Building Book.

Each pupil can now produce words with his 'pointer' by touching the signs of the Word Building Book table. The teacher may at first give orally a few 'words' (some English, some not) and ask the class to move the pencil over the signs on the table in a way that produces what they have heard dictated, as any of them might have done at the chalkboard using the pointer to touch the signs there.

Pupils can now with their own Word Building Books create combinations of sounds in this way, uttering the 'words' after their own pointing just as they would when the teacher controls the pointer working at the chalkboard.[2] As vowels and syllables are the

[1]The numbers on the pages of the Word Building Book are table numbers, not page numbers.
[2]Later on Page 1 of Worksheet 1, they will have the opportunity to keep a record of these discoveries (see page 65).

phonetic units, not all 'words' formed can be sounded, as for example *pttptp*. But words such as *apt* or *opt* can be formed by substituting *ap* for *a* in *at*, or *op* for *i* in *it*. These two words can be uttered and can be recognised as proper English words even if the children concerned have not consciously heard them before or used them.[1]

15. The next step in progress towards the first reading certificate is the introduction of two sounds with the same shape. Thus the learners come to know even at this very early stage that in written English graphemes and phonemes[2] are not related in a one-to-one correspondence. The shape of the sign is *s*. The lilac *s* sounds as in the word *is*; the lime-coloured *s* sounds as in *us* or *sat*. Naturally the teacher gives the class these or other examples to put the new sounds into circulation and then continues with Visual Dictation I using an extended restricted language whose elements are now:

a   *u*   *i*   *e*   *o*

p   *t*   *s*   *s*

[1]Very occasionally two or three pupils may remain for whom there is still some barrier to full insight into how to combine signs to make words. Some teachers have found that they can assist in these instances by giving to these children pieces of black paper, one piece to each, on which the signs so far have been written in coloured chalk after the manner of the work on the board. But, following the suggestion on page 30 the arrangement of signs on the various pieces of paper differs each time so that no two children receive sheets with a similar presentation. Then the teacher dictates visually on the chalkboard sounds, syllables and words (and perhaps short sentences). The children are asked to indicate with their pencils, and on the pieces of paper each has, the signs appropriate to what has just been shown—exactly as has been suggested above with the Word Building Book itself for students who have no problem. Since the arrangement of signs is different on each piece of paper the pupils must sort out by careful thinking where to move their own pointers and can neither use their memory of the directions in which they saw the teacher point, nor copy the movements of their neighbours. The challenge of this new game is very great even with signs already met.

[2]A phoneme is considered here to mean first a single speech sound, whether vowel or consonant (e.g. either *a* or *t* in *at*), and second, strongly linked combinations—whether two vowels (as *oi* in *noise*) making a diphthong, or a vowel and a consonant (e.g. *ow* in *how*, or *qu* in *quick*, or even *o* in *one*), or two consonantal sounds (e.g. *x* in *box*.) Graphemes are what are elsewhere in this text referred to as 'signs'; that is, the writings for phonemes. The writings therefore include not only single letters of the alphabet—where these denote single separate sounds or single-letter spellings of strongly linked sound combinations— but also group spellings of sounds, like *ough* and *dge* (as in *dough* and *edge* respectively).

These signs, as has already been said, do not need to be presented in two parallel and horizontal rows.[1] Any arrangement would do and teachers will find it challenging to try others. On Table 2 of the Word Building Book and on pages 13, 14 and 15 of Primer 1 they are horizontally arranged as here, but there is no reason for this other than typographical convenience. Two more signs are also introduced in these pages because the lime *ss* and *'s* are part of the lessons as given in the classroom.

16. Practising Visual Dictation 1 further permits an extension of the scope of word formation and sentence formation.

sat, sit, as, is, set, sap, sup

are some of the words which can be generated now, yielding reverses that in certain cases carry meaning.

The following sentences can be formed:

is it,	*it is pat,*	*sit up pat,*
it is,	*is pat up,*	*set it up,*
it is us,	*pat sat up,*	*set it up pat.*

Such sentences are scarcely more demanding of the learners than the work done when only two consonants were in use. Still, the sentence

is it as it is

that is now possible represents a real boost since pupils are usually surprised to find that such short and so-called 'simple' words can produce so interesting a result.

17. With very young beginners (four or five years old) it *may* take a little time to get started on Visual Dictation 1 for they may not grasp the blending of syllables to form words, as was done earlier in this section. So the single-syllable words may provide the bridge to start them off. The two words *it* and *is*—the teacher's own examples given to introduce the magenta consonant *t* and the lilac consonant *s*—can be immediately used to form two different sentences carrying distinctively different pitch and intonation if sounded as in speech.

The pointer forms *it* and then *is* in a rhythmic way so that their sounds are elicited one rapidly after the other as in speech. If this rhythmic pointing is not successful, the teacher may tell the learners

[1]See page 30.

to hold *it* in one hand and *is* in the other, she herself doing it. When she holds out her clenched hand containing *it*, they do likewise and say '*it*' but she does *not* say *it*. When the other is put forward (and the original hand withdrawn), *is* is uttered. It is sufficient to present one hand after the other in increasingly accelerated movements and with the right speed and rhythm to achieve, in the successive utterances of *it* and *is*, the natural and customary intonation of speech when '*it is*' or '*is it*' are said.

What is worth watching is that when *is it* is said rapidly the learners are forced to raise their voices, as happens when a question is spoken. They do it without prompting. The intonation forces the understanding and makes it possible to establish a stepping-stone in the progress towards *functioning as readers*.

Then *as* is produced, leading to *as it is*, a sentence.

Now pupils 'take' *is it* in one hand and *as it is* in the other and their accelerated hand movements yield *is it as it is*. This is soon understood, the increasing speed of saying it introducing the proper intonation.

18. From this sentence and from those used to form it some feedback can be obtained about how the group of learners are entering into the game of visual dictation.[1]

Table 2 of the Word Building Book and the last pages of Primer 1 provide additional opportunities for making words and sentences and for seeing them in print in black on white.

From a study of Table 2 of the Word Building Book it becomes clear that not only have different sounds represented by the same sign (*s* and *s*) been met, but also three signs in a single column that correspond to the same sound. These signs must be practised through Visual Dictation 1 first on the chalkboard in classroom session and then by the pupils individually in the Word Building Book with a pencil.

Reproduced below is Table 2 of the Word Building Book:

pat's pet

is an example of the use of the sign on the bottom line;

pat's pup's top

is another.

---

[1]A teacher may want to do a simple form of Visual Dictation 2 here by writing words in coloured chalk on the board—see footnote on page 41.

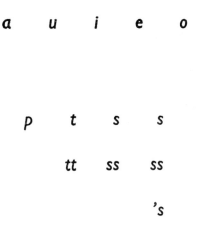

Table 2 of Word Building Book

pat's pets or *pat's pots*

shows a simultaneous use of two of the signs in this column of lime-coloured signs.

pat's ass stops and *toss pips at pop's pup*

are examples of more complicated forms to show similarities and differences between all the signs in this column. Other examples exist that are left to the reader to devise. When the names *tom* or *pam* appear on Word Chart 3, the lilac column of *s* will be used in a similar way, since in such cases as *tom's* the final sign has the same sound as the final sign in *is*.

The significance of this set of signs lies in its preparation of the learners for the realistic encounter with the truth about the way English is written. Pupils will know from the start that for various words and meanings different signs are used even when these signs sound alike; and conversely that like signs are sometimes used for quite different sounds. Although not explained explicitly, routine pointing to particular signs according to the words they are used in, or to which sound is heard, indicates that attention must be paid to both *sound* and *shape* and not to one of these elements alone. The successive tables of the Word Building Book never contradict this rule; to them signs are only added. The idea becomes as a result more and more established that, to build up a word correctly, one must know which columns are to be selected, and which signs within them.

It seems that creating this degree of awareness of the true nature of written English is much healthier than memorising rules and exceptions, particularly when exceptions will be numerous.

19. A number of techniques have now been met which make use of ideas not previously recognised as forming part of the exercise of reading. But beginners in these very early lessons will clearly have acquired an insight into sounds and their relation to signs that will serve them well in the coming work, which will be recognised as being akin to reading.

The materials that have been introduced include books for individual study, and a coloured word chart for classroom work; there has also been the first suggestion of the Fidel tableau from the content of the first tables of the Word Building Book drawn in colour on the chalkboard.[1] Insight in visual dictation has been achieved through the use of the pointer, but it is the books that give some substance to this very labile matter.

So far 'reading' has meant producing proper sounds with the proper integrating rhythm when the pointer passed over the signs used to represent those sounds. This is met again later when Primer 1 is studied for the recognition of spatial arrangements of signs that are in some way equivalent to the temporal sequences produced through Visual Dictation 1. These spatial arrangements of signs reflect the temporal sequences of sounds found in English speech.

III.

SECOND USE OF THE POINTER
SENTENCES THROUGH VISUAL DICTATION 2

STUDY OF SOME LINKS-BY-TRANSFORMATION BETWEEN WORDS

1. Now the learners are ready for an alternative course through the study of Word Chart 2, which shows in colour some of the words

[1] See the reproduction of the Fidel in colour on the loose card supplied with this text.

that can be (or have been) formed from the set of signs already introduced.[1] This chart is reproduced here.

pat	*pit*	*pet*	
pot	*at*	*it*	*up*
tap	*tip*	*top*	
pep	*pup*	*pop*	*tot*
as	*us*	*is*	
sat	*sit*	*set*	
stop	*step*	*toss*	
stops	*steps*	*spat*	
sap	*sips*	*test*	*pest*

Word Chart 2

2. The pointer is now used again, being moved from one word to another on the chart to form sentences. This activity is an extension of Visual Dictation 2, introduced earlier with 'words' composed solely of vowels when proper English words had not yet been met. This technique is employed only after words have been recognised for what they are—patterns in which the letters stand adjacent to one another from left to right on one level, representing the time sequence followed by the pointer in Visual Dictation 1. It is not necessary, or even useful, to go over all the words of the chart before beginners make sentences. But it is advisable to start Visual Dictation 2 with the small words—*it, is, up, as, us.* Some of these may be pointed to in turn to form a few sentences: *it is us, as is* and so on. The pointer is now being used to link complete words rather than merely the signs that form words.

3. The reason for the choice of words and their positions on the chart needs explanation. The placing of particular words and their reverses close to each other is deliberate. But the choice of *pat* as the first word was arbitrary. The aesthetic factor in making the chart has played a part here. Teachers should know that the charts are not intended to be scanned like a printed page. Indeed each chart has been produced so that it would *not* make any sense if this were done. But a large number of meaningful sentences can be made with the pointer using these few words simply by indicating different words in turn. Some of those which can be formed on Word Chart 2 are found on pages 14 and 16 of Primer 1; many others are, however, possible using the signs introduced so far on the chalkboard.

[1] Before introducing this chart, but after some of the signs it contains have been met through Visual Dictation 1, the teacher of *young* beginners may wish to write a few of the words on the chalkboard, in colour. The transition from temporal to spatial sequences can in this way be effected more gradually than through Primer 1. She can then employ a very simple form of Visual Dictation 2 (making sentences) by moving her pointer from one of these words written in chalk to another.

When teachers spend considerable time forming these sentences with the pointer on Word Chart 2 they begin to understand the full power of the exercise that has been called Visual Dictation 2 once it employs proper English words as its basis. The pointer, at first slowly, and when progress permits, more rapidly, indicates which words are wanted and in what order. In the beginning the learners say each word in turn so that they are sure of the particular word pointed to. But soon they are able to wait until all the words of the sentence have been touched by the pointer; then, as soon as the pointing stops, they say the whole sentence in one quick utterance, just as they would utter a sentence in ordinary conversation. Relating whole units of meaning to whole sentences is, by this technique, encouraged from the start and assures that reading is *never* separated from comprehension. Whether the movements of the pointer are slow or fast, it is Visual Dictation 2; but naturally as learners progress, the speed of the movement of the pointer approaches that of speech, or becomes even faster. Soon the learners are able to take in, in the same way, sentences that are long and complicated (once the necessary additional word charts are available).

This exercise must be witnessed in use for its power to be appreciated fully. Throughout the stages it will be noted that when one concentrates on increasing speed, the same set of words can be used so that there is no need for time and energy to be spent deciphering each one. So it is possible to view a part of a lesson as being concerned

    a. with making sure that such words as *step, it, up* and *pat* are known;

    b. with making every learner say *step it up* faster and faster until it sounds like the instruction it is; and

    c. with adding *pat* at the end so that the instruction is addressed to a person.

Whether the learners have developed the power to transfer can be tested at once either (1) by pointing rapidly at *set* instead of *step* and forming the sentence *set it up pat,* with the object of obtaining immediately the correct rhythm and intonation without requiring the successive stages of speeding up, or (2) by showing *pat steps it up* at a considerable speed.

This example, it should be understood, would not be a first exercise in Visual Dictation 2 but serves as well as any other to describe how the technique is used.

4. Word Chart 2 reproduced above does not include the most useful words, nor the most frequently occurring, nor even the simplest of those that could have been formed from the signs available. The words were chosen instead to introduce various ideas and concepts teachers of reading will find useful in assisting speakers to become writers and readers.

at and *it* are found close together, to serve as a reference indicating that it is possible to pass from the one to the other by the *substitution* of one vowel for another. And from *at* or *it* one may pass to *as* or *is* respectively on this chart by another substitution, this time of the consonant.

It is possible to pass, by *addition* of a sign, to either *pat* or *sat,* which are themselves linked through substitution. A similar exercise could be done with *it,* leading to *pit* and *sit.* These alternative beginnings help establish the transfers and reduce the burden on memory. With *at* known and the ability to carry out these transformations having been established, *it, pat, sat, pit* and *sit* can be found, and in a variety of different orders.

If *reversals,* already familiar as transformations, are introduced, *tap* and *tip* can be added.

The following schema shows in another way the links-by-transformation described so far:

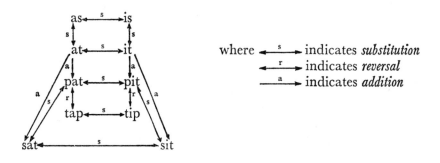

where ←—s—→ indicates *substitution*
←—r—→ indicates *reversal*
—a—→ indicates *addition*

5. A technique for obtaining words beginning with two consonants—as in *stop, spot* or *spits* and so forth—is the following.

Assume that it has been possible to obtain *top* and *sat* from the class. The learners can then be asked to play variations on *sat* by increasing the length of the sound they make for the first sign: *s . . . at*; or of the second: *sa . . . t*; or of the third: *sat . . .* This successfully done demonstrates that the learners are masters of their own throats; now they can use this control to help solve certain problems of learning to read.

They are next asked to 'hold *top* in their hand'. At a sign from the teacher they open their hand to release it, saying its sound as they do so. Now, while holding *top*, they return to saying *sat* with the length of the initial sound increased, as before (*s . . . at*). While they are beginning to say *s . . . at*, there is time for the teacher to give the signal that will release the sound *top* (and thus interrupt *s . . . at* after *s . . .*) and everyone hears *s . . . top*. This strikes one's ears as *stop* with the first sound prolonged. The same technique can at once be applied to *spot, spit* and *spat*.

6. The power shown by the pupils can be used again but in another way. They may be asked to evoke *top*; that is, to see it in their minds with their eyes shut. While their eyes are shut they can be asked to say what word they see if a 'curly green' (*s*) is placed

> on the left of *top,*
> or on the right,
> or at each end.

They can then be asked to reverse this last word formed in their minds

> and remove either curly green,
> or both;
> and reverse the new result;
> and then start again adding *s* at either or both ends.

This not only shows that *top* and *pot* are known as reverses the one of the other, but also that *stop* and *pots, tops* and *spot,* and *stops* and *spots* are so known as well. Developing an awareness of all these links within one's mind enables the memory to be still less burdened. The schema (opposite page) shows in another way the links followed in the above game with one's imagery.

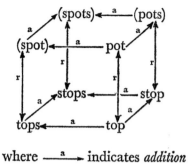

where ——ᵃ——► indicates *addition*

◄——ʳ——► indicates *reversals*

The words in parentheses in the schema are among those not appearing on Word Chart 2 but which may be created in the mind through this game, and through Visual Dictation 1 on the chalkboard.

7. *steps* can be obtained from *stops* by substitution of *e* for *o*. It can also be derived by starting with *pat*, making it *pet* by substitution of *e* for *a*, then *pets* by addition of *s*, then *step* by reversal, and finally *steps* by addition of *s*.

$$\text{pat} \xleftrightarrow{\ \text{s}\ } \text{pet} \xrightarrow{\ \text{a}\ } \text{pets} \xleftrightarrow{\ \text{r}\ } \text{step} \xrightarrow{\ \text{a}\ } \text{steps} \xrightarrow{\ \text{s}\ } \text{stops}$$

Word Chart 2 shows other words and their links, as follows:

pest at the foot of the chart, can be derived from *pet* by *insertion* of the 'curly green s' between the last two signs;

test can be found from *pest* by a substitution, or from *pet* by insertion and substitution;

spat may be found from *pat* by addition, or from *tap* by addition of *s* at the end followed by a reversal.

It is important to note that such transformations as from *top* to *toss* are permissible in a single move in this game since only one sound *ss* (considered as a single sign, not as two letters) is substituted for another (*p*). In this observation can be seen the beginning of the

45

discovery that in written English almost any letter of the alphabet can, in one word or another, be silent, or mute.

The schema below illustrates the links between words just described:

$$
\begin{array}{c}
\text{pest} \xleftarrow{\;s\;} \text{test} \\[2pt]
{\scriptstyle i}\Big\uparrow \\[2pt]
\text{toss} \xleftarrow{\;s\;} \text{top} \xleftarrow{\;r\;} \text{pot} \xleftarrow{\;s\;} \text{pet} \xleftarrow{\;s\;} \text{pat} \xleftarrow{\;r\;} \text{tap} \\
{\scriptstyle a}\Big\downarrow \qquad\qquad\qquad {\scriptstyle a}\Big\downarrow \qquad {\scriptstyle a}\Big\downarrow \qquad {\scriptstyle a}\Big\downarrow \\
\text{stop} \xleftarrow{\;s\;} \text{step} \xleftarrow{\;r\;} \text{(pets)} \qquad \text{spat} \xleftarrow{\;r\;} \text{(taps)} \\
{\scriptstyle a}\Big\downarrow \\
\text{stops} \xleftarrow{\;s\;} \text{steps}
\end{array}
$$

where $\xrightarrow{\;i\;}$ indicates *insertion*

8. If any pair of words on Word Chart 2 is chosen, is it possible to pass from one member of the pair to the other using the four operations of transformation? These are as follows:

substitution	$\xleftrightarrow{\;\;s\;\;}$
reversal	$\xleftrightarrow{\;\;r\;\;}$
addition	$\xrightarrow{\;\;a\;\;}$
insertion	$\xrightarrow{\;\;i\;\;}$

Since *subtraction* is not allowed in this game it will soon be realised that transformations are not possible in the case of all pairs. To pass from *stops* to *at,* for example, cannot be done. In such cases the pair can be reversed and the transformation attempted in the other direction. In the plan of the 'route', each 'station' is required to be a proper English word. This exercise is called the *Game of Transformations*.[1] That it can be played so early in the programme is a remarkable tribute to young children's word sense and linguistic powers. It is the experience of many observers of young children that, early in their lives, they already play with transformation of words when using them orally. If children learn now that written words as well can be transformed in this way, this knowledge will give their reading a dynamic dimension that pays high dividends.

[1]See page 70 and page 126.

46

Later on the game will serve in providing a test of mastery of the written language, in particular of spelling.

The comprehensive schema below makes clear all the links-by-transformation described above; most of the stations used are available as words already printed on Chart 2:

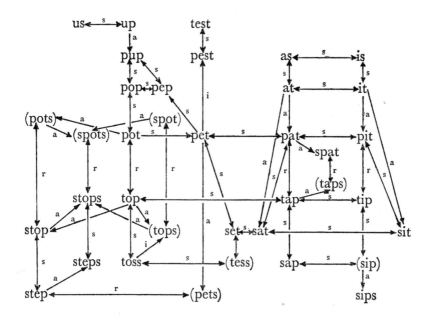

It is this 'fabric' of interrelationships—dynamic in nature—which, once it has become part of the mind of the learner through his use of the word charts, never allows any written word to be an isolated static entity held in the mind only by memorisation of its appearance. Each word is recognised to have so many supporting links with other words that it can always be decoded anew by the use of the understanding present because of these links.

9. The power of the pupils can be developed even further. It is already clear that even with this restricted language—and certainly later on—the word charts can contain only a very few of the almost unlimited possibilities for creating words and sentences. Therefore, besides using Visual Dictation 1, there is an additional technique

which can be used to make more words available for Visual Dictation 2. It is a development of the game, already played with the eyes closed, of evoking and transforming words.[1]

(i) In the beginning the teacher asks questions similar to the following, making the appropriate gesture with the pointer of drawing a sign while touching a certain word on the word chart. For example:

> *a.* What word do we get if we look at *pot* and in
> our minds add a 'curly green' (*s*) at the end?   *pots*
> or in front?   *spot*
> or at both ends?   *spots*
>
> *b.* What word do we get if we look at *pup* and in
> our minds substitute a pink (*i*) for the yellow
> (*u*)?   *pip*
> or substitute a 'curly green' for the first brown
> (*p*)?   *sup*
>
> *c.* What word do we get if we look at *step* and in
> our minds reverse it?   *pets*
> or look at *set* and reverse it?   *tess*
>
> *d.* What word do we get if we look at *at* and in our
> minds insert the brown (*p*) ?   *apt*

(ii) Then the teacher increases the challenge by asking the pupils to hold in their minds the word (or words) which has just resulted from the mental transformation and to say it when the one on the chart (from which it was just made) is touched. She visually dictates a sentence using *one* of these transformed words and thus elicits from the pupils the statement uttered in accordance with the rules of this new version of the game. For example:

pat spots us

is the correct response, after the transformations have been accepted, for the visually dictated words

pat pot us

(iii) Once these two techniques are understood by the pupils, teachers may find they can change a word as part of the visual dictation of a sentence.

---

[1]See above, page 44.

Thus, by stimulating the imagination teachers can create much more of the vocabulary of a given restricted language (here that of Primer 1 and Table 2 of the Word Building Book) than is contained in the word charts. Indeed the words on the chart, and the chart itself, seem to take on another dimension. More explicitly,

—not only is *pot* related to a set of words printed next to it:
pat, pit, pet, pop, top, tot
—it is also related to another set of words, each member of which can be imagined momentarily as replacing it on the chart:
pots, spot, spots, putt, putts etc. (not on the chart)
—and each one of the words in the imagined set is linked to others printed on the chart
as *spots* is to *stops*
(*stop* and *stops* are on the chart)
and as *pots* is to *stop*
and is linked to other imagined words
as *spot* (a member of the imagined set formed from *pot*) is linked to
tops (in the imagined set formed from *top*)

This seems a truly remarkable achievement considering all that is involved. Not only has positive use been made of a feature which is ordinarily regarded as a weakness—i.e. reading one thing for another—but the door has been opened for the imagination to control what is actually present in order to yield, by transformation, something both possible and new. Teachers who meet such proposals with uncertainty generally find their initial reservations turning to enthusiasm when they see for themselves how readily children accept these things.

This use of the imagination with the word charts—as its use in Visual Dictation 1—gives irreplaceable preparation for the games in the worksheets[1] since it helps to generate *in the mind* the dynamic and labile imagery necessary for meeting without difficulty these highly intellectual challenges.

10. As a whole, Primer 1 has set the trend for the programme, starting from the extremely artificial games involving the repetition and combination of signs, and moving to sentences read naturally

[1]See page 65.

as when spoken. This covers the ground opened up by the two forms of visual dictation.

The full extent of the vocabulary met so far, including that used in both forms of visual dictation and in Primer 1, is set out below (only the words in italics are printed on Word Chart 2).

—Two-sign words:
up, at, it, as, is, us (ass)

—Three-sign words:
pap, *pup,* pip, *pep, pop, pat,* pit, *pet,*
pot, tap, tip, top, tat, tit, *tot, sap,*
sip, sop, *sat, sit, set,* sot, pus, sis,
its, apt, opt, asp, pitt, putt, tess, *toss.*

—Four-sign words:
pips, peps, pops, pups, pats, pits, pets,
pots, taps, tips, tops, tats, tits, tots,
saps, sups, *sips,* sops, sits, sets, sots
pest, test, spat, spit, spot, *stop,*
step, opts, putts, pitts, tess's

—Five-sign words:
stops, steps, spats, spits, spots, pests,
tests, upset.

—Six-sign words:
upsets.

There are well over fifty common words, and over eighty in all. With these words at least one hundred combinations into sentences can be made.

It is characteristic of this approach that much is left to the learner's inventiveness and imagination.

The Word Building Book (whose use has been understood through Visual Dictation 1 on the chalkboard) indicates the signs available at this stage. On Word Chart 2 and in Primer 1 some of their possible combinations are presented. This flexibility in the use of signs increases as the programme advances. Eventually the full range of signs available for combining will be indicated on the Fidel[1], a tableau of eight charts in colour on which the work done

[1]See Appendix 6A, containing a miniature reproduction of Fidels.

on the chalkboard is extended to the level of the final table of the Word Building Book.

The number of words that are available and covered when the range of signs and sounds worked on is restricted to narrow limits has been presented above. It was also shown, when the field was still more restricted, that with the introduction of new signs many new words could be formed. As the programme advances and the restrictions gradually relax, the vocabulary count increases rapidly. Analyses of the more advanced stages of the programme are not included in this text since the expansion in the area of the language covered makes these tedious and unwieldy. For this reason an analysis of the simpler first stage of Words in Colour was prepared in detail and included here, to show what is achieved at this stage— where it can be demonstrated clearly that even a few new signs and sounds bring whole new areas of the language under control—and to give some indication of the rate of progress and the expansion of vocabulary that is to be expected.

Primer 1 is very brief and is completed almost at once (perhaps in a week with five year olds)[1] but its slimness is not to be mistaken for emptiness. On the contrary, in this thin volume is proved just how much can be done with so little. This is possible because children or other learners already have the ability to use speech, so that our function is to lead them to master the codification of it in its written forms, as these have evolved.

11. This section concludes with a summary in diagram form of the ground covered this far. And yet, even with the language restricted as it is in Table 2 of the Word Building Book, the approach is too complex to indicate all its dimensions in this way.

So in what follows only several of the various directions possible for the alternative introduction of words[2] and sentences by Visual Dictation 1 are shown. The italics indicate which of the words are printed on Word Chart 2, and which sentences can therefore be given on this chart by visual dictation.

---

[1] When working with remedial groups (as mentioned on page 20) it may be that nothing but Visual Dictation 1 at the chalkboard is used until the programme moves beyond the scope of the restricted language of Primer 1. In this case, because the work is moving ahead so rapidly into less restricted vocabulary, it is often best to omit Primer 1 altogether, or to read only the last page of sentences, and then to begin with Primer 2.

[2] See the list of these words on the following pages.

1 —it is (r)
 —is it up—it is

2 —it is as it is
 —is it as it is—it is

3 —it is us
 —is it us—it is

4 —pop up
 —pep up

5 —pep it up
 —pop it
 —up it

6 —pat pop it
 —pat it *pat*
 —pet it *pat*

7 —pat is up (r)
 —it is pat (2r)

8 —pat is apt
 —pat is as apt at it as pitt is

9 —tap it
 —top it *pat*
 —tip it
 —tip up
 —tip it up *pat*
 —pat is top
 —pat is up top
 —pat is tip top
 —it is tip top

10 —pop putts
 —pat tips it up
 —pat pets pup (it)
 —pat peps up
 —pat peps it up
 —pat is tops
 —it is tops
 —its tip is top

11 —sit up *pat*
 —pat sits up
 —pat sat up
 —set it up *pat*
 —pat sets it up
 —pat is upset
 —pat upsets tess (us)
 —pat is as upset as pitt
 —sup it up *pat*
 —pat sups

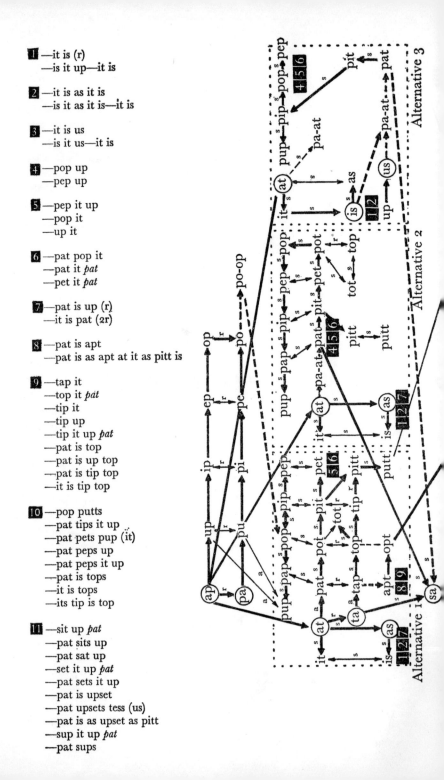

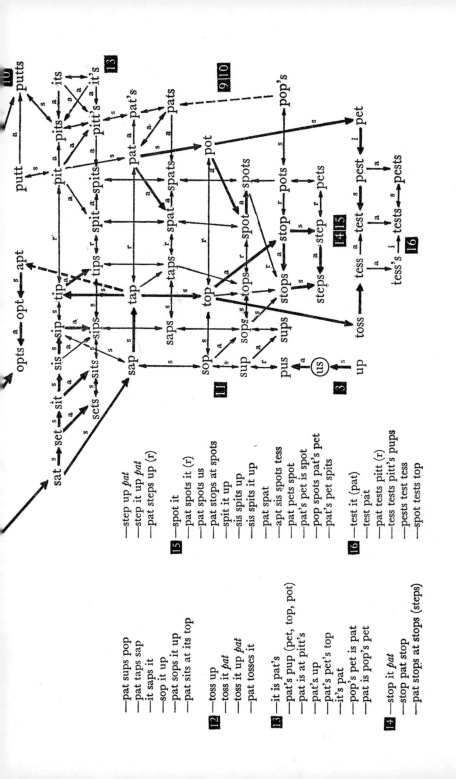

15 —spot it
—pat spots it (r)
—pat spots us
—pat stops at spots
—spit it up
—sis spits up
—sis spits it up
—pat spat
—apt sis spots tess
—pat pets spot
—pat's pet is spot
—pop spots pat's pet
—pat's pet spits

16 —test it (pat)
—test pat
—pat tests pitt (r)
—tess tests pitt's pups
—pests test tess
—spot tests top

12 —toss up
—toss it pat
—toss it up pat
—pat tosses it

13 —it is pat's
—pat's pup (pet, top, pot)
—pat is at pitt's
—pat's up
—pat's pet's top
—it's pat
—pop's pet is pat
—pat is pop's pet

14 —stop it pat
—stop pat stop
—pat stops at stops (steps)

—step up pat
—step it up pat
—pat steps up (r)

—pat sups pop
—pat taps sap
—it saps it
—sop it up
—pat sops it up
—pat sits at its top

Of course, as has been intimated above in §9, if the teacher and pupils learn to use their imagination fully in order to transform words, all the words needed beyond the scope of those printed on the chart can be generated from them by gestures with the pointer; and according to the extent this is done, many or all the suggested sentences can also be done by Visual Dictation 2. And all of these and others too may be used in oral dictation[1] and in writing one's own compositions.

I. Words Linked to Each Other by Transformations of Sound (and Sign)

Notes

Circled portions indicate the only clues the teacher will find *she* needs to give. If she gives these she should try to give them only once so the learners feel responsibility from the beginning to take in and make use of what assistance is given.

As before, the arrows marked with a letter (*s, r, a, i*) indicate the four transformations—two of them always reversible as the arrow shows.

Where – – – – → is found it indicates some other transformation or combination of transformations which are allowed in Visual Dictation 1 but not in the Game of Transformations.

Numbers in circles indicate the group of sentences which relate to this point in the word study.

Description of Alternative Directions

Alternative directions for the very first lessons of Visual Dictation 1 are provided since feedback from a particular group of learners may indicate lack of readiness for one direction at a given moment yet readiness for another. A teacher must have all the alternative sequences well enough in mind so that, when some difficulty occurs in one direction and is not resolvable immediately, she can take her pupils in another direction *so as not to bore them*. This makes them feel equally confident of their powers and strong enough to return to the point of difficulty from another angle and to conquer it easily.

[1]See page 57.

For example: Some pupils may have difficulty blending syllables to form a word like *pop* or *pat* on first encounter, yet be equal to a long sentence like *is it as it is*.

The teacher does *not* supply the answer if pupils have some difficulty. Telling them does not help.

Alternative 1: Essentially the progression outlined in this chapter. It is the order of introduction to be followed first, since it is the most direct and works well with most pupils.

Alternative 2: If difficulty is encountered in blending *po-op* into *pop*, this alternative may offer sufficient help by suggesting how the blending of syllables *pa* and *at* form *pat;* work with two different consonants and the very familiar white *a* may be easier for certain groups of learners. In *pat,* it also generates immediately a name useful in sentences. *pitt* can follow easily to give another name, if needed. Since these pupils may have shown a slower pace in working out reversals of syllables, it may be easier for them not to take the reverse of *at* now, but to take instead the syllable *sa* which requires only substitution from *pa,* and makes *sat* immediately. Since they have *it* also, *sit* is readily obtained. Moving in this way opens up a number of more interesting sentences as indicated on the diagram, so that more headway is made in relating all of this to spoken speech, even though the vocabulary is very restricted.

After this it seems easy indeed for the learners to return and find *pip,* from *pit;* or *pop* from *pot,* and so *pep, pap* and *pup.* This last word may come by addition from *up.* From *sit, sip* can easily be deduced; from this *tip, tap* and *top;* or from *sat, sap* is found and from this *tap,* then *tip* and *top.*

Alternative 3: This is for students finding difficulty even with blending *pa* and *at* into *pat* when first encountered. Since they have *at, it* is easily found. *is* may be given by the teacher to introduce the lilac-coloured *s,* and *as* is found.

is can be used immediately with *it* and *up* in four sentences made only with words with one syllable with the vowel in the initial position. ①

Once *as* has been found two more sentences ② are possible.

If blending is still a problem, *us* might be given and it is easily understood since it is only a slight change from *up.* This yields two more sentences. ③

At this point enough of the game would be understood to make it easy to blend *pa* and *at* into *pat,* or *pi* and *it* into *pit.* From these *pap, pip, pop, pup* and *pep* can follow. Now a reservoir of sentences is available. *pa* can lead to *sa* and *sat* as in Alternative 2 and the study can continue in the same fashion from there.

II. Words Linked by Meanings and by Structures into Sentences

The symbol (r) indicates that reversing the order of the words will create another English sentence. A name given in italics indicates that this name could be placed at the beginning or the end of the sentence to produce two sentences with slightly different meanings. Thus

step it up

may yield

step it up pat

or

pat step it up

Parentheses ( ) around a word means this word could be substituted for the word before to form a new sentence.

Wherever one name is used, one or more names (or nouns) that use some of the signs met already could be substituted, thus producing more sentences. Specifically:

pat, pop, pitt, sis, tess ⎫
and sometimes   ⎬ can all be substituted one for the other depending on the meaning
pup, spot, tip, pet ⎭ of the sentence.

Numbers in ◯ are for cross reference to the preceding diagram illustrating the introduction of words in Visual Dictation 1. By referring back to this diagram, one can estimate the appropriate time for introducing the sentences.

IV.

Oral Dictation, and Reading and Writing
Visual Dictation and Writing
Visual Dictation 3
Individual Work and Testing: The Worksheets

1. With the language restricted as it is at present it is possible to do little more than read isolated sentences such as those which

appear at the end of Primer 1. But writing can nevertheless be introduced, as well as two types of oral dictation.

2. Writing has two meanings. One is concerned with the activity of making the designs of words; this is a power resulting from the co-ordination of senses, muscles and imagery, and is primarily an activity of drawing. The other involves putting down a sequence of designs which are considered to be the equivalent of certain spoken statements, in such a manner that anyone can read it (turn it back into speech) and find the equivalent of the spoken statements originally in mind before writing. This requires a continuous control of a process of transcription of ideas.

A distinction is made here between these two meanings because the second, which involves a higher intellectual activity, is the one that makes the writer while the first makes the scribe.

Exercises of co-ordination can be separated in actuality from those concerned with the second meaning of writing if the teacher never comments on legibility so long as it can be guessed that the words put down are what has been intended by the writer.[1] Either co-ordination cannot improve and therefore reading should not suffer from this, or it *can* and, like all skills, improvement will come with practice. It does pay not to stress bad writing in the first sense when the learner is engaged in the activity of the second type, which requires all the energies available for its correct performance—especially since practice, and not stress on errors, is the only way legibility can be helped if it can be helped at all. It is the author's experience that legibility *does* improve in due time through the practice that comes as a by-product of involvement in numerous intellectual challenges requiring writing for their execution—as in the present programme.

3. Since with writing there is physical activity adding requirements to those of reading, it may be wise to start oral dictation in a way that necessitates only the purely intellectual activity of reading words in order to know which should be associated with the sounds uttered by the person dictating.

Word Chart 2 being already on the wall, the teacher may say one of the sentences met earlier through Visual Dictation 2: for

[1]See Appendix 1 for examples of six-year-old pupils' writing.

instance, *is pat up*. Then the pointer is offered to whoever thinks he can come up and touch these three words on the chart in the right sequence.

If one volunteer attempts it, it should be left to the class to agree or disagree and to produce corrections if any are needed. Sometimes questions such as 'Is it the one?' or 'Do you agree with him?' will assist the pupils in checking the reality of what was shown against what is suggested by their own criteria and those of their colleagues; they might then offer another solution if needed, and analyse the volunteer's or their own difficulties. The teacher should not show approval or disapproval but proceed to another sentence if all goes well, or assist pupils in analysing difficulties if any arise. For example in the latter case:

The teacher could ask for the sounds when she points to *pat is up;* or for each of the words separately; and then ask for the solution to the original problem of *is pat up*. In this way she takes the pupils back to a simpler challenge already met so that in their own minds they can bridge the gap to the new insight.

Once it is clear that any sentence dictated by the teacher from words on the chart can be shown on the chart by the pupils, the teacher can increase the intellectual challenge by dictating sentences whose words are not all there but can be formed by the transforming gesture of the pointer.[1] For example:

pat sits up

which requires adding *s* to *sit* as the pointer touches the words; or the more difficult:

is pat as apt as tess

which requires inserting *p* in *at* and indicating the reverse of *set* while pointing.

The third challenge can then be for pupils to suggest their own sentences within the restriction of signs met, and to ask the rest of the class to find these sentences on the chart, making any transformations that are necessary.

4. At any point in this sequence of challenges the activity of writing may be undertaken at the level of the challenge mastered (i.e. words on chart, words transformed from these, sentences dictated by

---

[1]See technique outlined on pages 47–49.

pupils). It may be well to start on the chalkboard where one person at first, later perhaps part or all of the class, can work since the results of the written forms are then before everyone and near the word chart which may be needed for comparison. The class again is the judge of correctness. The teacher accepts what is offered; only if the writer, or any other student, cannot on his own put right a slip or error or omission in writing does the teacher ask for what has been written to be compared with the words on the chart. But, even when this assistance has to be offered, the pupils correct themselves.

5. After some time is spent on this, the ordinary oral dictation can be undertaken with the whole class now writing on paper. The teacher says each statement only *once,* but clearly, at the speed of speech, starting with such simple examples as

is it us   or   *as pat is*

and progressing to

pitt spat at spots   or   *pat stops at steps*

Pupils will need time to write, and it should be given freely. Experience will show how long a time is required for writing by different pupils. The need for time may be due to the level of co-ordination and not at all to the existence or non-existence of an image in the mind for what needs to be put down. Since teachers cannot really know at first which is the cause of the delay, the wisest course is to allow sufficient time for all the pupils, and learn about their difficulties by observing them during this period.

Correction of work written on individual papers should be done by the pupils themselves. Different procedures may be used as the work progresses. All, however, will cause each pupil to compare what he has written with something suggested as the correct solution by another, and also to discover whether he agrees or disagrees with what his colleague has written. If he finds he disagrees, he must then sort out whether he still agrees with what he himself wrote, or whether on reconsidering the situation he can now agree with the other solution proposed. Fruitful discussions may result in this way, showing the learners more and more what it is to rely on their *own* criteria and encouraging them to sharpen these rather than depend on the teacher for any judgment or approval. Here are some procedures:

—After each sentence is written under dictation, a volunteer can offer a solution through Visual Dictation 2 on the word chart (with whatever transformations that may be required).

—Or after each sentence a volunteer can write his solution on the board.

—Or at the end of the oral dictation lesson, one or more volunteers can write on the board one solution for each sentence and all can check their own papers against this record.

—Or pupils may work in pairs and compare papers, raising for class discussion disagreements they are unable to solve between themselves.

6. In this beginning stage it may also be valuable to do some oral dictation of words and simple sentences, asking pupils to volunteer to dictate the solutions visually by moving the pointer over the arrangement of signs on the chalkboard—that is, to produce them by Visual Dictation 1. Such words and sentences could also be written, and these checked by Visual Dictation 1. This type of oral dictation leading to solution by Visual Dictation 1, once it has proved an additional challenge in this early stage, could be then dropped for a time, to be resumed usually at the level of the restricted language of Table 11 in the Word Building Book.[1]

7. Visual dictation by the teacher (or later on by pupils who create their own sentences for their classmates) can also lead to writing. In fact the challenge is even greater to the writer than oral dictation because he must do a *double* transformation within his mind instead of a single one:

—he must first rapidly, in his head, transform into speech (i.e. read) the sequences of signs he sees dictated visually;

—then he must hold both the meanings of what he has read and the exact words used long enough for him to turn them back into signs and transcribe the result on his own paper through writing. The writing takes longer than the reading since it involves additional physical activity, which must also be co-ordinated with the mental activity.

Therefore the outcome in terms of the increased power of the pupils is also greater.

[1]See pages 87, 88.

Visual Dictation 2 is the most valuable at this time and can include transforming some words on the chart with gestures with the pointer if one wishes to increase the challenge further. Visual Dictation 1 using the chalkboard arrangement of signs is useful at this stage, but, as with the oral dictation leading to solution through Visual Dictation 1, it should then be dropped until the restrictions of the language met in Table 11 of the Word Building Book are met.

Visual dictation should be checked by the pupils by reading aloud to others the solutions written on their papers. This (1) ensures comprehension of what has been put down, and (2) uses again one medium (speech) to check another (signs)—thus assisting in catching errors—rather than have the same medium to check itself.

8. After becoming confident of their own power to write from oral and visual dictation and on forming their own sentences for oral dictation or visual dictation, pupils—either on their own initiative or in eager response to a suggestion—will write down on paper many sentences of their own and will even illustrate them in unusual ways. Parents and teachers, the parents sometimes before the teachers, report on the occurrence of this spontaneous activity. In this the true beginning of independent writing can be seen, and the true test that writing has now become an integrated aspect of the linguistic power of the learners.

9. The ground has been prepared by this stage for a new form of visual dictation to be introduced, although it will not be possible to extend it far with so restricted a language. As the programme progresses this new technique will become easier to use and more interesting.[1]

On Word Chart 2 the teacher may point to a sequence of statements such as:

sit up pat
pat is up
pat steps up   All these sentences use the words as
pat sips pop   they are printed on the chart
tip it up pat
pat stops

[1]See page 117 and 155.

or she may point to:

> it is *pat's* pup
> *tess pets* it
> *pitt pats* it
> pop *tests it*
> it *sits* up
> it *steps* up
> it stops
> it sips (*pepsi*)
> it *sups*
> *pat's* pup is *tops*
> it is as *apt* as *pitt's*

Some of these sentences require the transformation of words by means of gestures with the pointer (see words in italics)

Because these sentences concern one or more persons undergoing a succession of states or performing a sequence of actions, they are as near as it is possible to come to writing a story in this restricted language of nine sounds. This technique is given the name Visual Dictation 3, because it involves using the pointer to make a sequence of sentences whose joint meaning produces a story.[1]

What is of interest here is that the use of this exercise can be contemplated at all with such a restricted language. The result is the preparation of the pupil for more complex sentences and stories as the language becomes less restricted, without requiring that new principles and insights be acquired. Pupils soon become skilled enough to take in a number of short sentences or a few quite long ones all at one time, reading back the whole story as naturally as it might have been told. The relation of all of this to comprehension in reading books is obvious. A variation sometimes can be to ask them to tell the whole story in another way.

All of this prepares the way for giving oral dictations and visual dictations where more than one sentence is to be written. It is obvious also that the beginning of spontaneous and creative story writing by the pupils is stimulated naturally by these extensions based on Visual Dictation 3.

10. It may be felt, while working in this way, that a very slight addition to the range of words available would make a great

---

[1]Similarly Visual Dictation 2 is the use of the pointer to make a sequence of words whose joint meanings produce a sentence, and Visual Dictation 1 the use of the pointer to make a sequence of signs whose sounds produce a word.

difference. Indeed if the indefinite article (*a*) were present the quality of sentences would be greatly improved and more could be written. This feeling is good preparation for the next stages and such a step might be taken without loss if felt necessary.

But as author of an approach in which *restrictions are proposed as a stimulus for creativity,* we do not see the need to do today what will become possible tomorrow, and prefer to explore the full possibilities of the present circumstances. The possibilities so far are:

—that the signs of the restricted language can be used for reading and for writing
—that reading can be fluent and natural where most of what is said, written or read is understood
—that sentences can be taken under various forms of dictation, spellings being observed, and graphemes and phonemes related in a controlled way with mental images

11. *Worksheet 1* which forms part of the material of this programme can now be considered. The preceding activities have created a background of experience that can lead the learner through the worksheets to (1) enriched and extended intellectual activity; (2) individual ingenuity and creativity; and (3) a test of what has been learned about the written language.

Since the basis for doing the games proposed in the worksheets has been given, they should not pose any special problem coming at the last. But even so, learners need to be introduced to each different type of game in the worksheet the first time it is played so that they are clear about the rules—especially since beginning readers are not yet expected to read the printed instructions. The first seven worksheets present, by intention, the same games—and these in the same order. Consequently, once a game is understood in Worksheet 1 and the pupil can recognise it from the format of the page, there should be no need for its special introduction in each succeeding worksheet.

Each worksheet is meant to be worked on within the limits of the restricted language indicated by the table[1] of the Word Building Book given in the instructions to the first exercise, although at a later time pupils may return to any worksheet and work without restriction

[1]What is referred to in this text as a 'table' of the Word Building Book is in some editions of the worksheets called a 'chart'.

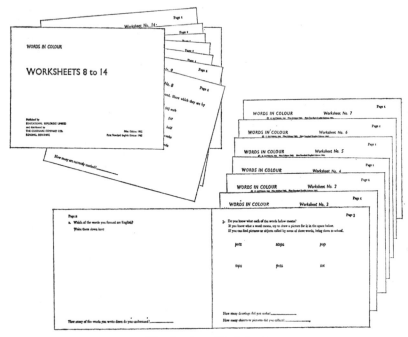

The fourteen Worksheets

(other than the limits of their own understanding) and see what additional examples or answers can be found for the challenges—recording an improved 'score' at the bottom of the page.

Exercise 1 of Worksheet 1 is concerned with what the pupil understands of how to form words as combinations of signs, on the basis of Table 2 in the Word Building Book. He is allowed simply to combine signs and to put down his suggestions. It gives him practice in putting down the signs in sequences—noting with the restricted set of signs the permutations, reverses, etc. It also invites him to become familiar with a number of concepts that cannot be regulated; here he may prove his awareness since he feels free to put down whatever he sees as an answer to the instruction.

The teacher has nothing to correct: she need only note for herself whether the pupil

—uses the script of the word charts and Primers, and the signs of the table in the Word Building Book in front of him;

—inserts signs beyond those asked for;

WORDS IN COLOUR   *Worksheet No. 1*

© C. GATTEGNO, 1962   Pilot Edition 1962.   First Standard English Edition 1965.

1. Use the Word Building Book Chart No. 2.   Form words that are different from those on the wallcharts and those in book 2 and write them in the space below.

How many words did you find?..

Page 1 of Worksheet 1

—writes horizontally or otherwise;
—separates signs and words or not;
—needs time to shape signs and words;
—can keep his score.

The teacher need *only* note for herself the pupil's performance on the worksheets. She should comment directly to the learner only if she is sure the comment will not hamper him in his future work by making him aware of what he interprets as the teacher's disapproval and by increasing his dependence on the judgment of others.

Exercise 2 of Worksheet 1 is based on the previous work. Can the pupil recognise

—which of the written designs can be sounded?
—which of those that look like English, sound like English?
—which of them he understands?

His own score will reveal his insights through the eye and the ear into even those words he uses, those he may recognise he has heard

65

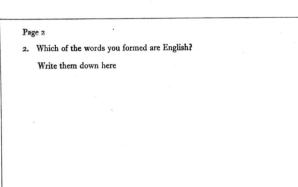

2. Which of the words you formed are English?

Write them down here

How many of the words you wrote down do you understand?..

Page 2 of Worksheet 1

but never uses, or those he may not recall hearing and so never uses. For example, he may have formed *opt* and *apt,* words which are simply permutations of the signs in *top* and *pot, pat* and *tap* respectively.

Exercise 3 proposes, in contrast to the intuition used to guide on the previous page, a method of inquiring that can be developed to ensure deeper understanding of words. The pupil must look closely enough at the words to distinguish between them and so utter them correctly in order to yield their meaning (such as *pots* and *tops, steps* and *pets*). At the same time he must illustrate the ideas they represent. Of the six words offered, only one (*tot*) may pose a problem, and it is interesting to let learners solve it in their own way.

What matters here is *not* that the task suggested be performed and finished but that the learners acquire ways of working that will develop into research and inquiry tools. The results of work on Exercise 3 may well be an exhibition of children's contributions that display treasures of imagination, inventiveness, observation. All

3. Do you know what each of the words below means?

If you know what **a word** means, try to draw a picture for it in the space **below.**

If you can find pictures **or** objects called by **some** of these words, bring them **to school.**

pots   *steps*   *pup*

tops   *pets*   tot

How many drawings did you make?..

How **many** objects or pictures did you collect?...

Page 3 of Worksheet 1

this could be lost if the exercise is a pure stimulus-response situation. Teachers' sensitivity towards the value for the individual of a rich experience as against a good mark for answering the question will serve their charges well.

Exercise 4 tests recognition both of signs that have been seen already and of those that have not. It also tests previous experience which may well include, in particular cases, an unsuspected knowledge of signs. The experience thus demonstrated will guide the teacher in what to expect from the learner concerned as the programme develops.

Exercise 5 on pages 5–10 leads to the awareness that

—images of words are flexible enough to suggest a variety of answers to an incomplete word pattern

—signs can be removed from any place in a word, leaving pupils still able to evoke the completed words

—one can take stock of one's knowledge within a restricted

In the words just below, make a circle around the signs that are not on Chart 2 of the Word Building Book.

s*i*ps	*p*u*ff*s	*si*ts
sets	stem	sent
toss	plus	t*i*ps

How many of the above words use only signs of Chart No. 2?.....................................

How many of the above words use other signs?.....................................

Now, in the space below, add as many words as you can write. Look at them to see whether or not the signs you have learned are in them. In the words you have written, make a circle around any signs that are *not* on Chart No. 2.

Page 4 of Worksheet 1

language and find that the same word can on occasions provide a solution to two or more differently formulated questions
—not all questions have the same number of answers

Additional classroom games or techniques may be used to introduce these 'gap' or 'completion' games. For instance: *pat* could be written on the chalkboard and the middle sign erased; the pupils might then be asked if anyone could put in a sign that would make another word (*pit* or *pot* could be generated). The middle sign could then be erased again and again in a quest for alternative solutions—and then the last sign also.

Thus   *s ...... t*

could be put up and the students asked to find all the different signs that might be introduced to produce various English words.

Then   *s a* ......   and next   ...... *a t*

could be substituted with the same object each time.

68

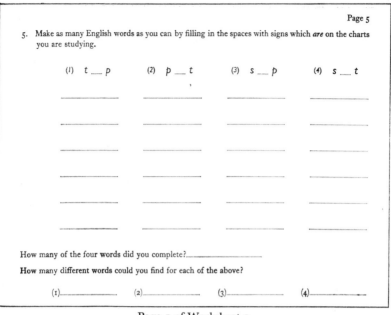

5. Make as many English words as you can by filling in the spaces with signs which *are* on the charts you are studying.

(1) *t* ...... *p*   (2) *p* ...... *t*   (3) *s* ...... *p*   (4) *s* ...... *t*

How many of the four words did you complete?...

How many different words could you find for each of the above?

(1)................................. (2)................................. (3)................................. (4).................................

Page 5 of Worksheet 1

This game can be also played with two sounds missing:

s .... *t*,   *s* .... *s*, ... *a* ......,   *s* ...... *t* ......,

An exercise in Worksheet 1 is *not* completed while pupils are still on Table 2 of the Word Building Book. They can go back to it whenever they feel their new experience is relevant to the questions it contains. Hence teachers must *not* mark corrections on these pages but allow students to add to their solutions and correct them on the basis of their further experience. Teachers can take down in one of their own books the details and the answers and date them— doing so from time to time to measure for themselves the progress of the pupils.

Exercise 6 on pages 11 to 13 gives examples of the *Game of Transformations*. What matters here is:

—that pupils are led gently into a difficult and challenging game through questions of gradually increasing complexity

—that pupils be encouraged not to think of a question as answered once and for all, but attempt to find alternative answers

Game of Transformation

6.

(1) from   *pat*

      to   *pits*

(2) from   *top*

      to   *stops*

Page 11 of Worksheet 1

and compare their relative merits in terms of length, inventiveness, and elegance

The function of this game is to bring together within the dynamics of the mind the products of the activities so far encountered. Through this game the power of *imaging* is maintained at the centre of the activity while the forming of a network of linkages between words generally unrelated by either sound, shape or meaning is stimulated.

The psychological significance of the exercise lies in its being based on the analytic and synthetic powers of the mind, calling on these to work simultaneously.

The mysterious way words are recalled, recognised either by shape or by sound as having something in common with other words, is at the centre of the mental operation. But as words may also be altered physically, permitting a willed relationship to other words of which one is yet unconscious, worlds are opened to the imagination. It is not excluded that playing such games may have a lasting effect on the flexibility of the mind, the imagination, the intelligence of verbal communication, one's sense of mystery, and lead everyone to a better acquaintance with the working of his own mind.

It should be clear that the basis for learners' finding individual solutions to the Game of Transformations has been implicit in all the work done by the teacher with the pupils through Visual Dictation 1, and on the word charts in which the links-by-transformation between words have been studied. In addition the learners have been encouraged continuously to apply their full imaginative powers in order to evoke in their minds, and use, an imagery far more extensive than the limits of the word chart or even Primer 1.

Even so, introducing the game itself is necessary so that its rules now become explicit and thus usable by the pupils, rather than serving mainly to guide the teacher in choosing alternative directions for the visual dictations. A way of beginning work with this game using Word Chart 2 has already been described.[1]

As presented in the worksheets this game is still one of considering various pairs of words. The object is to pass from the first member of each pair to the second by making only *one* of the allowed transformations at a time (*s*ubstitution, *r*eversal, *a*ddition, *i*nsertion but *excluding* subtraction) and with each transformation generating a new, and proper English word. (Note that *toss* $\xrightarrow{\text{ s }}$ *top* is *not* a subtraction, but a substitution of one sign for another, as has been seen above.[2])

Before introducing the full game, teachers may find it helpful to do some work with *each* of the four transformations allowed so that pupils are completely clear about them. Once this is done they may want to move gradually into using all transformations in the full game. The following indicates one possible approach.

(i) The work on *substitutions* done by erasing signs to introduce the 'gap' or 'completion' games may be developed by the teacher, writing on the chalkboard, for instance:

$$pat \xrightarrow{\text{ s }}$$

and asking 'What is this?'; then, 'Who can change it into another word by substituting a different sound in the middle (or at the beginning, or at the end)?'; and then saying, 'Write it here', indicating the space after the arrow.

[1]See page 45 et seq.
[2]For a discussion of this game in its full complexity see page 126 et seq.

As many examples can be used as the feedback from the pupils indicates are needed. For example, from

how to go from *at* to *is* or from *it* to *as* can be asked.

(ii) The teacher can now (or in the next lesson) work on *reversals*. She can write one word on the board followed by an arrow

pat $\xrightarrow{\text{r}}$

and ask, 'What is this? Who can write its reverse?' repeating examples as often as needed.

Other examples might start with:

set ($\xrightarrow{\text{r}}$ tess)   pets ($\xrightarrow{\text{r}}$ step)

r is written under the *s* in the corner of the chalkboard.

(iii) Similarly *addition* could be developed by writing on the board

top

and asking, 'What is this? Who can make it into a new word by adding a sound at the beginning or at the end?' Someone comes to add to the word an *s* and makes either

stop

or   tops

'What did he make? Who can add a sound at the other end and make a new word?' Someone comes and adds to the work on the board in the appropriate way to make it into

stops

Now this could be put on the board:

pot $\xrightarrow{\text{a}}$

'What is this? Who can write a new word after the arrow that is this word with one sound added to it?' Someone writes

spot *or* pots

'What did he make?' Then the teacher puts another arrow on the board with an $_a$ over it, so that the following is now available:

$$\text{pot} \xrightarrow{\text{a}} \text{spot} \xrightarrow{\text{a}}$$
$$\textit{or} \quad \text{pot} \xrightarrow{\text{a}} \text{pots} \xrightarrow{\text{a}}$$

She asks, 'Who can put another word after the arrow that is this word with one more sound added to it?' Someone comes and writes with this overall result:

$$\text{pot} \xrightarrow{\text{a}} \text{spot} \xrightarrow{\text{a}} \text{spots}$$
$$\textit{or} \quad \text{pot} \xrightarrow{\text{a}} \text{pots} \xrightarrow{\text{a}} \text{spots}$$

Other examples to work on if needed are the following:

$$\text{up} \xrightarrow{\text{a}} \text{pup} \xrightarrow{\text{a}} \text{pups}$$
$$\text{pit} \xrightarrow{\text{a}} \text{spit} \xrightarrow{\text{a}} \text{spits}$$
$$\text{pit} \xrightarrow{\text{a}} \text{pits} \xrightarrow{\text{a}} \text{spits}$$

Now a can be written under the r in the corner of the chalkboard.

(iv) In the same manner *insertion* could be worked on, the teacher first writing, for example:

$$\text{a} \quad \text{t}$$

and asking, 'What is this? What will it be if I insert the 'brown' between its two signs?' actually doing this as she says it to make

$$\text{apt}$$

Then she may write, for example,

$$\text{pet} \xrightarrow{\text{i}}$$

and ask, 'What is this? Who can write another word after the arrow that is this word with the "curly green" inserted between two of its signs?' If there is understanding on the part of the pupils, this should result in

$$\text{pet} \xrightarrow{\text{i}} \text{pest}$$

Other examples if needed could include the following:

$$\text{sop} \xrightarrow{\text{i}} \text{stop}$$
$$\text{sat} \xrightarrow{\text{i}} \text{spat}$$
$$\text{sis} \xrightarrow{\text{i}} \text{sits (or sips)}$$

Now i is written under the a in the separate list on the board.

(v) Now looking at the separate vertical listing the teacher may put a few questions to the pupils to summarise the understanding of which letter stands for which transformation, asking for instance:

'Which of these letters did we put over the arrow to show we have used substitution (or addition or insertion or reversal)?'

That subtraction is not allowed may then be brought out since it is not on the list.

(vi) Sequences of operations may now be tried, first perhaps two different, then two the same and one different, then all three different, and so on.

The teacher starts by writing a word on the board, followed by an arrow marked to indicate the type of transformation desired. When a solution is found she writes it down with a second arrow after it. On being offered the next solution, she writes it down followed by a third arrow, etc. Unlike the next game to be described, this preparatory game is not concerned with what the final word in a sequence should be. Consequently at any point a new sequence of operations may be initiated.

(vii) Now the full game can be played.

The teacher asks pupils to look at the pair of words she has written on the board

tap

stop

and think how they could transform the first into the second making only one transformation at a time and each step producing an English word.[1]

She may rewrite the problem thus

tap $\longrightarrow$ $\longrightarrow$ stop

so that the learners will see that they have one or more intervening steps. Here they should quickly see that they can make *tap* into *top*, and then make *top* into *stop*. Someone can write the solution in its place, and he or someone else can mark the arrows to show which operations of transformation have been used.

If there is any difficulty in marking the arrows the teacher may ask, 'What did we do to change *tap* into *top*?' and point to the vertical list on the board which is there to serve as a ready reference:

---

[1]In a special case where children are very young or very limited the restriction of having to form an *English* word at each step may be lifted for a few lessons and imposed later on.

s

r

a

i

Students are usually able to analyse quickly which letter is needed. They can then ask, 'What did we do to change *top* into *stop*?' and mark the arrow accordingly.

(viii) A few more simple examples should serve to bring most learners to the point where they can work on their own in these games and analyse the type of transformation to be used. For instance:

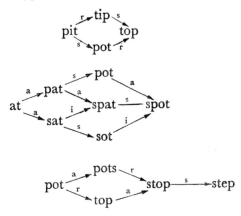

The teacher can ask, once one 'route' is completed, if there is another way, and then for another and another, and so on.

The Game of Transformation on Worksheet 1 should by this time not pose too difficult a challenge. For this first worksheet several possible solutions are given below to assist the teacher in seeing that there may be many alternatives and that there is rarely one answer only.

(1) from *pat* to *pits*

(2) from *top* to *stops*

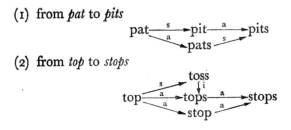

(3) from *pet* to *sat*

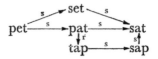

(4) from *pit* to *step*

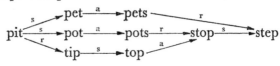

(5) from *pot* to *tip*

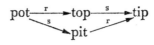

(6) from *ass* to *pit*

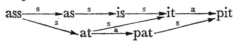

It is suggested that when pupils first work by themselves on their worksheets they all work at the same time, and that the teacher circulate among them and give individual help where needed. Collecting answers on the board after each example has been done can be very interesting for the discovery that there are several possible correct solutions among them. The challenge from now on can be to see how many different solutions can be devised for each game, rather than to concentrate on supplying one solution quickly or on finding the shortest one only. Teachers may find themselves often surprised at the solutions, beyond what have been shown here and even beyond what they had themselves thought out, that are produced by their pupils.

Additional solutions may be added after a day, a week, or a month has passed, or much later, when the insight into these games is deeper. The improved score may be shown at the bottom of the page.

Page 14 of Worksheet 1 continues Exercise 6 and opens the door to pupils' own proposals for this game. Here their autonomy is tested as well as their aptitude at choosing pairs of words that are close to those studied, or those that are more challenging or even

6. Write down any two words. Try to transform the first word into the second. Do this with as many pairs of words as you can.

How many pairs of words have you written down?...

How many transformations did you work out for each pair?...

Page 14 of Worksheet 1

impossible according to the rules of the game. Teachers may again find themselves surprised at the inventiveness shown in meeting this challenge, including the many additional pairs of words pupils may suggest to challenge their classmates beyond what can be put on this page.

Exercise 7 on pages 15 and 16 encourages the composition of sentences and tacitly of stories, and thus comprehends all the ground covered in the education from spoken speech to its written form within the restricted language of Primer 1 and Table 2 in the Word Building Book. The visual and oral dictations have prepared the way for this beginning on creative writing within the restrictions of what has been mastered. Most children soon fill more pages with their spontaneous efforts than are provided in the worksheets.

12. This first worksheet can clearly be used for testing purposes, but the contribution it can make is far greater than providing the means to arrive at a score. Teachers are reminded that what matters is to

7. Make sentences with words that can be made with signs that belong to Chart No. 2 then write the sentences in the space below.

How many sentences have you written?...................................

Page 16

7. Write down more sentences using words you now know.

How many sentences have you written?...................................

Now add up all your scores. This is your total score for Worksheet No. 1.

Date

Published by Educational Explorers Limited, Reading, England.
Printed in Great Britain by Lamport Gilbert & Co. Ltd., Gun St., Reading, Berks.

Pages 15 and 16 of Worksheet 1

see children or other learners grow in awareness of their powers, and hence of themselves, rather than to score here and now at a particularly high level.

Learners have been considered here, involved in the process of acquiring a code for their speech through a number of activities designed to mobilise their senses, their intuition, their intelligence and hence to stimulate observation of words and their behaviour within the whole dynamics of the self.

The materials, including the worksheets, have an inbuilt power to assist the teacher in keeping in contact with what goes on in the learning process. Through this she can gain a degree of control of the teaching situation rarely possible in the case of other approaches.

It is for this reason that it is possible to talk of *subordinating teaching to learning* in connection with this approach even though prepared materials are offered to educators.

We wish to test at every moment by the achievement of our pupils whether *we* are doing a good job; this will be the case if, as a result of joyful and powerful activities, we find pupils reading fluently, naturally, and with understanding and proper intonation, materials produced from the very restricted language considered in this section.

If they do so, we award them their *first reading certificate*.

13. One last remark about this section must be added. To retell what is seen in one second from a window, or what has been experienced in a momentous minute, may take hours or months. Here an attempt has been made to describe at length what has over and over again only taken hours in many classrooms. The implementing of the programme leading to the first reading certificate could require not more that the *first few hours* at school for ordinary first year pupils. This should be kept in mind in spite of the elaborate discussion needed to complete this chapter.

Chapter Two

MEETING THE SOUNDS OF ENGLISH

1. In this programme the stages of progress now lead to meeting the full range of sounds used in English together with some of their spellings, the remaining spellings being left until the next chapter.

2. English in the analysis proposed here presents some forty-eight[1] well-distinguished sounds, though in terms of the most refined linguistics many more sound components could be isolated. But for the purpose of teaching reading this list will prove adequate. With each sound a different colour is associated. While this rule was also applied throughout the last chapter it was not evident as such except in the case where the *s* signs were introduced. To distinguish the different sounds that these two similarly-shaped signs have, a lime green colouring was adopted for the *s* in *us* and lilac for the *s* in *is*. Then to indicate that the same sound—the one given the lime green colour—may be spelled in three or more different ways—(as in *sit*, *toss* and *pat's*) *s*, *ss*, *'s* were placed in a single column on the chalkboard all in this one shade of green.

These principles for applying colours will be observed up to a point. Blending three primary colours in varying strengths and combinations can produce a range of colours that are secondary, tertiary, and so on. The object is to obtain shades that are readily distinguishable, but fifty is a large number to select and control for consistent matching and contrasting within single charts and between different charts. This question of colour control was a major commercial and technical problem in producing a set of twenty-nine separate coloured wall charts that were both relatively low in cost and sufficiently consistent in colouring for easy use.[2]

---

[1]Mute r edition—fifty-two.
[2]The printing process adopted for the Fidel in the Standard English Edition entails in certain instances slight differences in colours from those used on the word charts. But this does not hinder the learners because the Fidel tableau appears only late in the programme after clues other than colour have come into extensive use.

3. A number of considerations related to the use of colour as an additional dimension indicating sounds in words can be of use to readers:

(i) The principle of sound-colour correspondence can be restated: like sounds are identified by like colours whatever their spellings and unlike sounds are distinguished by the use of unlike colours even if the same sign is used. The following two sentences illustrate each of these aspects respectively:

*a*ll w*a*s d*a*rk *a*s m*a*ny vill*a*ge h*a*res r*a*ced *a*round

which gives nine distinct sounds for the letter *a* used in isolation,[1] and

he s*ays* m*e*n s*ai*d m*a*ny fri*e*ndly l*eo*pards b*u*ry h*ei*fers d*ea*d from h*ae*morrhage

in which one sound is represented by ten different signs.

(ii) Related sounds can be represented by related colours. This principle is not possible to follow far in view of the number of colours involved. But, for example, the sign *th* as in *that* is given a colour close to that of *s* in *is* since this second sound becomes identical to the first if sounded with the tongue between the teeth. Similarly and for the same reason *th* in *thin* has a colour close to that of *s* in *sat*.

(iii) Colouring should not create new problems while solving some others:

    a. Colour-blindness is taken care of by the shapes and shades and other clues that colour-blind people develop spontaneously with their existing sensitivity to colour. Colour-blindness has never been reported as an obstacle to learning with Words in Colour.

    b. Many teachers report that children confuse the signs *d* and *b*. It would have been valueless to have given these two signs, so close geometrically, colours that were very distinct, since the power of retention might then have been focused on the colour

---

[1] A sentence conforming to the Mute r analysis would be: p*a*rents w*a*shing *a*ny b*a*by spl*a*sh b*a*th w*a*ter *a*bout—giving eight distinct sounds for the letter *a* used in isolation.

clue, leaving the shapes still to be confused. So the colours for these two signs are intentionally very close, attention being better drawn to shape by other means. One such means is by the mastering of one of these signs before introducing the other. This is the path followed in this programme: *d* occurs for the first time on Word Chart 4 while *b* appears first on Word Chart 7. Words such as *burden* which use both signs challenge the learners soon after.[1]

(iv) Where, as in the case of diphthongs, the sounds associated with some signs involve a merging of two otherwise distinct sounds, this phenomenon is reflected by including the tint selected for each of the sounds concerned in the representation of the sign in colour, the colour of the first sound uttered being applied to the top half of the sign and that of the second to the lower. Examples:

in *hour*, the sign formed of the first three letters of the word contains both purple and pale aqua, using in the uppermost portion the same colour as used to denote the sound of *a* in *father*, and below the colour used to indicate the sound of the sign *w* in *with*.

in *quick*, *qu* is in two colours, the top being that of the *ck* in *truck* and the bottom again that of the *w* in *with*. (Later on, in *quay* and *liquor*, *qu* is met with only one colour since here the sign has only one sound, that of the gold-coloured *k*.)

in *next*, *exist* and *anxious*, the signs *x* employ in each case different pairs of colours—found, separately, in signs already met— making each *x* different in appearance from the others while at the same time reflecting faithfully the particular sounds each indicates. Later on, in *anxiety*, *x* has only a single colour and one sound, that of the lilac-coloured *z*.

(v) Of all the materials associated with this project only the twenty-nine wallcharts are in colour. Words appear in colour on twenty-one of these charts. The remaining eight form the tableau previously referred to, and called the Fidel.[2]

[1]See also in this connection page 114.
[2]Miniature reproductions of the Standard English Fidel and the Mute r Fidel are inserted in the back of this book, together with miniatures of the Word Charts. Three charts (22–24) have been added that show some less frequently used words.

On this tableau no whole word appears but only those parts of words, or signs, which indicate separate sound components, the various spellings for each particular sound being arranged in a single column. There being forty-eight sounds in this classification of English, forty-eight columns are used on the tableau and these include in all over two hundred and eighty signs.[1] On the twenty-one word charts more than six hundred words provide the phonetic clues for reading English. All materials other than the charts are printed in black like ordinary reading material.

This chapter is mainly concerned with meeting some of the sounds of English not previously introduced in the very restricted language discussed so far. In the first chapter the central techniques of the approach were presented in detail so that teachers could see that

—as the language becomes progressively less restricted

—and as Word Charts 3–21 and Primers 2 and 3 are met

the approach maintains the *same* characteristics which are only extended and developed to meet the needs of the continually expanding reading vocabulary. These extensions of the techniques are now discussed, based on the understanding of what has been offered in the previous chapter.

I.

WORD CHARTS 2 TO 12

VISUAL DICTATION 2 AND 3

ORAL DICTATION

1. The next ten word-charts are introduced progressively and remain on display as a gradually expanding group. They are hung up on a vertical surface in the classroom following one arrangement or

---

[1]On the Mute r Fidel there are fifty-two differently coloured columns comprising over three hundred and seventy signs.

another. The frames below in black on white correspond to the
first four charts.

a a aa aaa	pat pit pet	mat tim met tom	fan fun fist fit
u u uu uuu	pot at it up	mum must mumps	if of fat puff fuss
au ua uau aua	tap tip top	miss mist mess	spend spent dad I
i i ii iii	pep pup pop tot	map am stamps	sad mad fed and
aiu uia uiu iau	as us is	a mops pump sum	send mend sand
e e ee eee	sat sit set	sam pam not nut	mud fund stand end
aei eua eaiu	stop step toss	net ten men man	dust did that this
o o oo ooo	stops steps spat	an sun in on	them then than the
aaeeoo ieoii	sap sips test pest	tent upon sent	thin yes yet fifty
oaa aoie oou			

2. On looking at the actual charts in colour, one soon recognises
that each has an atmosphere of its own.[1] This is due to the impact of
new colours successively making their appearance on each new
chart in words in which new sounds occur. The atmosphere each
chart has introduces a new feeling which is readily associated with
the words encountered on each, enhancing their retention. Pupils
rapidly learn what words are to be found on what chart and can
locate any particular word in a very short time—much shorter than
would ever be possible through memorisation. Visual Dictations
2 and 3 and their complementary oral dictations maintain this
knowledge at a level of immediate availability.

3. The set of word charts is so designed that most of the consonants
are met in conjunction with simply the five vowels introduced on
Word Chart 1. Two exceptions are: first, the 'schwa' or unstressed
vowel found so commonly in English; and second, the sign and word
'I' which permits so many sentences referring to the readers themselves to be made. The schwa sound is introduced very early (Word
Chart 3) as it is involved in the ordinary usage of the indefinite
article a. In this scheme it is always identified by the colour bright
yellow. This colour was chosen since the pale yellow of u as in up
must register a change when left unstressed, as in the word upon
(Word Chart 3). This shade of yellow is maintained for all spellings of
the schwa, which, in English, can include practically any sign or
combination of signs.

[1]See miniature reproductions in Appendix 6.

4. In this programme reference is not made to long and short vowels as such. Twenty-one[1] vowel sounds are isolated and the principle is followed of introducing new sounds when the material already presented has been thoroughly assimilated and sufficient practice given. If it is true that a great deal can be achieved with only seven vowel sounds, then this should be attempted before the others are introduced. And if it is possible to overcome more readily the obstacles raised by the demand of learning to read by keeping the number of ambiguous situations to a minimum through a restriction on vowel sounds available, then proceeding as far as possible with these few vowels only will be well worth while. Later the remaining vowels will be able to be introduced several at a time because of the increased insights into the reading process acquired by the pupils, which further illustrates the concept of the cumulative effect of learning.

Once the sound for *I* has been met (Word Chart 4) a number of its useful spellings, as occur in the words *my* and *line*, can be brought in without mention being made of the 'long *i*'. The colour used will indicate that in the words *mind, wild,* and so on, this new sound for the shape *i* is required rather than that found in *till* and *with*. Indeed in the programme the question 'Why this sound?' is answered by 'Because this colour is there'. If the sign is lemon coloured, you make the sound as for *I*; if it is pink, you make the sound for the *i* as in *it*. Such consistency as there is in the behaviour of sounds and spellings in English will be discovered by the learner through observation of colour similarities and differences between words such as *my, mile* and *mill*.

Up to and including Word Chart 7, then, only seven vowels are met.[2] But on Word Chart 8 five more are introduced together:

[1]Mute r Edition—twenty-two.

[2]In the Mute r Edition, only these seven vowels are met up to and including Word Chart 5. Then one more sound spelt in three different ways with salmon-coloured signs appears:

ur as in *fur* (Chart 6) and *er* as in *her* and *or* as in *word* (Chart 7). With the coming of Word Chart 8, five vowel sounds are introduced at once, together with a fourth salmon-coloured sign:

red	*e*	as in he	pale green	*u*	as in use
sea green	*a*	as in hate	brown	*ore*	as in more
ochre	*o*	as in home	salmon	*ir*	as in girl

red	*e*	as in he
sea green	*a*	as in hate
ochre	*o*	as in home
pale green	*u*	as in use
brown	*o*	as in more

The colours indicate that these signs differ in sound from the same sign shapes previously met; the sound attributed to each sign by the learners is ascertained from the sound of a word in which it occurs as uttered by the teacher. (Some learners may deduce the new sound for the sign *a*, for example, by comparing *hat*, which they learned on Word Chart 7, with *hate* as pronounced for them on the newly introduced Word Chart 8.)

5. When Word Chart 3 is introduced and displayed alongside Word Charts 1 and 2, it can be used without reference to Visual

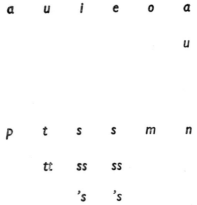

The signs on the chalkboard at this stage

Dictation 1. But it is possible also to use Visual Dictation 1. That is, once the new signs *m* and *n* have been placed on the chalkboard in their respective colours, they can be introduced by the teacher pronouncing aloud such words as *am* or *an* at the same time as she touches the appropriate signs on the chalkboard with the pointer. Then by linking signs with the movement of the pointer she can elicit from the class all the words found on Word Chart 3 and many others besides, such as *tam, tan, pan, pin, pen* and so forth, just as was suggested in the last chapter for the introduction of Word Chart 2.

As this procedure was explained thoroughly in Chapter 1 the opportunity will be taken here to consider an alternative means, where the second stage of the teaching is begun by displaying Word Chart 3 and using Visual Dictation 2 and 3 as the technique for mastering its content and its possibilities. The awareness of a growing systematic organisation of new sounds and signs begun on the chalk-board is kept, through work on the Word Building Book as it is used in conjunction with the worksheets.[1]

This alternative is the procedure suggested for most groups when they are ready for Word Chart 3; it involves dropping Visual Dictation 1 at this point as the means of introducing new sounds. However, in *two cases* the use of Visual Dictation 1 for the introduction of sounds is still advised:

(i) In remedial cases, where several small words are known by sight, it is suggested that Visual Dictation 1 be continued for the introduction of the new sounds found on Word Chart 3 (*m, n* and the schwa) with no word charts in view until this has been completed. This forces the pupils in question to think of sounds rather than rely on superficial visual clues. When Word Charts 2 and 3 are subsequently displayed following this extension in Visual Dictation 1, enough will have been achieved for the reading to be effected— which cannot be done by reacting to superficial clues alone since reading *pat* and *pet, sat* and *set, stop, step* and *stamps, set* and *sent, is, it* and *in,* and *in* and *on* requires more than superficial recognition.

(ii) With the few five or six year olds who are much slower than most in the beginning stage of the programme it is suggested that, after Word Chart 2 has been introduced, teachers continue with Visual Dictation 1 for the introduction of sounds on Word Chart 3 (and if necessary on Word Chart 4). For meeting the next word chart (Chart 4 or 5 as applicable) the alternative procedure with Visual Dictation 2 is to be used—which is now described.

[1]See page 65.

6. For the word charts already met, as for all those yet to appear, entries into the set of words each presents can always be effected at a variety of points through the technique of associating one or other of the new words with related and known words on previous charts. Each new chart can thus be viewed as new territory through which different routes are possible according to the starting point selected. On examining a new chart, teachers soon spot 'landmarks' in words that are similar to those on the previous charts; these provide the starting points for exploration. Many teachers find that the colouring of sounds offers the most consistent and striking clue to the landmarks they are looking for.

Teachers can also look at the chart (here Chart 3) to see what landmarks might be recognised by their pupils, who are as yet unable to read many words, but who, from their work on the previous chart, do understand how colour is used to isolate sounds and how a written word can be turned into speech. The assessment made by the teachers will indicate to them where to point first to introduce new words and then what sequence of movements to make so that the bare minimum only need be told to the pupils. When the teacher takes all this into account, what she says and does might follow a pattern like this:

—What is this?	*at*	She selects a word already familiar and points to it;
—If I tell you this one is 'am' ...	*am*	She selects on the new chart a word containing only one new sound and gives it aloud as an example.
—then what will this one be?	*sam*	She selects a different word containing the new sound and others already known;
—and this?	*pam*	She points to a new word in which all the sounds are now known. To read this, pupils use only what

they already know about transforming one word into another by the substitution, reversal, addition or insertion of sounds.

—and now this?

map She points to yet another word requiring only one transformation—here reversal.

She proceeds in this way until all the words of the new chart have been explored.

With the above study of words linked by the sounds they have in common the teacher may alternate a study of words linked by meanings, or by their use in sentence structures. If, from Word Chart 2, the following sentences are easily read:

> *sit up pat*
> *is pat up*
> *it is pat*
> *pat sat up top*

then, after the new words on Chart 3 have been decoded, pupils will clearly be able to read sentences like these made from Visual Dictation 2:

> *sit up sam*
> *is pam up*
> *is it tom*
> *tim sat on a map*

The second set of sentences is generated by transforming the first set in one or more ways:

—substituting one word for another;

—reversing the order of the words in some way;

—adding a new word;

—inserting a new word;

—and in some cases subtracting a word.

89

Here it is the related meanings of words and their relation to the structure of one sentence, and to that of another, that guides the teacher in choosing how to make new sentences. These relations form the basis for the teacher's expanding use of Visual Dictation 2.

Each new chart stimulates consideration of its words in terms of

—their equivalent sounds[1]

—their equivalent meaning and structure

But more assistance is given the teacher in this guide with the first type of study—the word study—and more initiative left her for developing fully the second—the study of sentences.

Below are reproduced Word Charts 2 and 3.

pat	pit	pet	
pot	at	it	up
tap	tip	top	
pep	pup	pop	tot
as	us	is	
sat	sit	set	
stop	step	toss	
stops	steps	spat	
sap	sips	test	pest

mat	tim	met	tom
mum	must	mumps	
miss	mist	mess	
map	am	stamps	
a	mops	pump	sum
sam	pam	not	nut
net	ten	men	man
an	sun	in	on
tent	upon	sent	

(i) Here are some examples of how the study of Word Chart 3 can be developed:

—from *am*, *sam* and *pam* can be formed by the operation of addition;

—reversing *pam* gives *map*;

—substitution then gives *mat*, then *met*, *mess*, *miss*—then *mist* by addition;[2]

—another substitution would yield *mop*—then *mops* by addition;

[1] See Appendix 3.

[2] In this game it is both permissible and correct to pass from *miss* to *mist* by addition since *ss* and *s* are both single signs standing for the same sound. As such they may be used interchangeably in accordance with the conventional spelling of this sound as it occurs in different words. See also page 45.

—by substitution from *sam, sum* and then *sun* or *mum* can be obtained.

When these words are used in conjunction with those on Word Chart 2, several sentences become possible by Visual Dictation 2. Among them are the following:

> *pam is up*
> *sam met pat*
> *pat mops a mat*
> *sum it up*
> *is it a map*

(ii) From words on Word Chart 2, *tip* could lead to *tim, top* to *tom*, *at* to *mat, pup* to *pump*, and so on, where the second word in each pair is derived by substitution, addition or insertion respectively. From *top, mop* can be derived, leading to *mops*; *mop* also gives *map* which can then become *pam* by reversal, and then *sam* by substitution —to link up with the sequence developed in (i) above.

A number of suggestions for comparisons between Word Charts 2 and 3 could be tried in turn:

pet and *set*	leading to	*met* and *net*
at and *as*	leading to	*am* and *an*
it and *is*	leading to	*in*

These open up alternative routes for the conquest of words on Word Chart 3. Teachers should refrain from giving more than one example word to introduce *m* and *n*. Discovering how the other words are read should be left to the inquiring minds of the learners.

(iii) From *mat, met* can be found and in turn *mess* and *miss* by substitutions.

From *miss, mist* can be derived by addition of the sign *t* (the sign *ss* being simultaneously exchanged for the equivalent single *s* form which has the same sound).

From *mist, must* follows by substitution.

mum can lead to *mump* by addition (seen in the word *mumps* with the last sign covered with the hand).

mumps as a whole is then revealed, representing an addition of a sign.

From *stops, stomps* can be formed by insertion, and then *stamps* by substitution.

The following sentences are only a few of those that could be given for practice:

> *tom must pump it up*
> *pam stops as it is mumps*
> *mum mops up a mess*
> *tom met sam in a mist*

(iv) *pot* could lead to *not* as the first word, then naturally to *nut*, *net* and by reversal to *ten*. *met* to *net* would also yield *not* and *nut*. More sentences are possible including:

> *tim stamps on a nut*

(v) *man* could be arrived at by addition from *an* or by substitution from either *mat* or *map*. From *man*, *men* follows, then *ten*, *tent*, *sent*, or *ten* and *net*—to link with the sequence in (iv) above. But *men* could also be obtained from *met*, and so on.

In choosing alternative routes between words, teachers should attempt to find those which require only one transformation (substitution, reversal, addition, insertion) between words. For instance, it is preferable to approach *must* from *mist*, requiring one substitution, than from *miss* which requires one addition and an equivalence as well as a substitution:[1]

> mist___^{s}___$\rightarrow$must
> *or* miss___^{a}___$\rightarrow$mist___^{s}___$\rightarrow$must

But sometimes, as seen above, unless one or more mental transformations are made by a gesture with the pointer, it is impossible to shift from one to another of the words printed on the chart without more than one transformation. For example:

> *stops*___$\rightarrow$*stamps* requires an insertion and a substitution;
> *mum*___$\rightarrow$*mumps* requires two additions.

The following sentences are only a few of those that can be found by knowing all the words on Word Charts 2 and 3 (and excluding other words in Primer 2). In the arrangement here they tell a simple story:

---

[1]See page 126 *et seq* for further discussion on equivalences.

tim sent sam on a test in a mist
a map is a must in a mist
as a mist is not on a map, must tom miss sam
sam is in a mess
tip is a pup
must a pet pup sit on a map
a pup is a pest on it
tom must spot sam
in ten steps, tom met sam at a pump
on it is a tap
sam sips at it
tim spat on a step as a pump in a mist is on a map
tim is upset
sam stops as tom steps up
it is sam, it is us
tom sent sam in
at sunset in a tip top tent sam sips pop
tim stamps as sam is not in a mess
must a mist not mess up a test[1]

All of this shows how flexible the materials can be and how much richer the word charts are when worked on in this way rather than if they were read from left to right and top to bottom as a page of unrelated words. Teachers using these charts will gain a great deal if they recognise this flexibility and make use of it wherever an opportunity presents itself. This flexibility even allows that not every word on a new chart need be done immediately. A few might be left until some on the next charts have been found.

In Appendix 3 a diagram summarises the links by sounds among the words on Word Chart 3, and between the words on this chart and the preceding one. Some teachers considering the introduction of the new chart will find the diagram helpful in sorting out routes through the words alternative to those indicated above. They may also find it assists in working out different solutions for the games of transformations as played in the worksheets. Others may regard it as too complicated even to consider at this time (hence its placing in an appendix) but may find it very helpful a month or two after beginning to implement this programme — or even a year later.

[1]Contributed by J.M.S.

7. Though attention has so far been concentrated mainly on words, the few examples of sentences given hint at the extensions of Visual Dictations 2 and 3 that become possible as new charts are added. As soon as a new word has been uttered by the class it thus becomes usable in conjunction with previously mastered words; then sentences and stories can be dictated visually with the pointer. Teachers should attempt not to dictate sentences that allow boredom to develop owing to the ease of the challenge in the new words; at the same time they should not hinder progress by using in rapid visual dictation words not yet fully decoded.

In the pupils' primers the pages follow this same alternation of word study with sentence study but the challenge is increased by the absence of colour clues, and the inclusion of additional words.
(i) Primer 2, pages 2 and 4 offer for study not only words on Word Chart 3 but additional words also which can be made from the new signs introduced there (such as stump, maps, nap, nest, ant, etc.)[1]
(ii) Primer 2, pages 3 and 5 give many more sentences than those suggested in this text or by the new chart since they include words not on the new chart even though within its restrictions.[1]

It is essential that the teacher be sensitive at every moment as to how the lesson is moving. Feedback is available to her in the way the pupils respond to the silent movement of the pointer. From this she is able to assess how to alternate the activities to avoid boredom on the one hand and challenges that are still too difficult on the other. This alternation involves not only the word and sentence study on the charts which has been outlined, but the reading in Primer 2, the games in the worksheets, and oral dictation. The oral dictation suggested earlier can now be expanded as Visual Dictations 2 and 3 are developed. These are the natural stimuli for the generation by the pupils of their own sentences which are either made on the chart with the pointer or produced on paper, or written in the worksheets.

8. These remarks on the techniques associated with the introduction of the study of Word Chart 3 apply equally to subsequent charts and the approach outlined should be maintained through the series. The content of particular charts may occasionally require detailed description of the treatment of specific new challenges

[1]See pages 105–106 for illustrations of these pages of Primer 2.

encountered. Each chart, too, is different in character from the last and can be tackled in many ways; a variety of different entries are possible in each case, yielding a variety of routes through the words and a plurality of sentences beyond what it is convenient or possible to record. However, the process sketched above offers teachers adequate guidelines to the general approach to be adopted and will not in this text be repeated on the introduction of each new word chart. The type of detailed diagram for the study of the words on Word Chart 3 mentioned above is also provided in the appendix for Word Charts 4 to 6 inclusive, but the analysis is left to the teacher after this. Sentences for visual dictations are now also left entirely to the ingenuity of teachers and pupils since the possibilities are almost unlimited.

9. In the top two lines of Word Chart 4 the signs *f* and *ff* are introduced, both mauve-coloured, and sounding as in *fan* and *puff* respectively. At the same time *f* in *of* appears, distinguished by the new colour khaki to indicate the difference in its sound This colour is later found in *seven* where it is used to denote the sound given to the sign *v*.

Word Chart 4 introduces a further three consonants.[1] These are:

> green-coloured *d* as in *and*
> pale purple-coloured *th* as in *that*
> pale green *th* as in *thin*

fan	fun	fist	fit
if	of	fat	puff	fuss
spend	spent	dad	I
sad	mad	fed	and
send	mend	sand	
mud	fund	stand	end
dust	did	that	this
them	then	than	the
thin	yes	yet	fifty

Word Chart 4

In the word *fifty* the sign *y* occurs with the same pink shade as met earlier in the *i* in *pit*. It might be thought on first looking at this word that the value attributed to the sign *y* is incorrect. But if, for example, 'fifty-four' or 'fifty-seven' is said aloud, the short sound is what is heard. On more than one occasion in selecting colours for signs it was necessary to make a choice between the sound a word has when pronounced in isolation and when it is uttered naturally in a sentence. In some cases the first principle was adopted, in others the second, with the object of providing points for discussion to increase

[1]Mute r Edition—four; *y* as in *yes* and *yet* appears coloured pale pink.

the pupils' awareness of sounds and of their spoken language. Teachers are invited to exploit these opportunities in their own classrooms.[1]

10. Should any pupils be lagging behind in word recognition, exercises such as the following can be given, asking them:

(i) to indicate with the pointer all words on these three charts containing the sound *a*, represented by the sign coloured white, and likewise for other of the vowels studied;

(ii) to point out all words containing, for example, the combination *at*, or *it*, or *et*, or *an*, or *en*, and so on;

(iii) to show all words containing, for example, *and*, or *end*, or *if*, where these are words in themselves (as are *it* and *an* and *at*) but which have not yet been practised for finding on the word charts.

In this programme, word transformation has been used to generate bonds between words as well as to introduce new words. On these charts it can be seen that such examples as *fan* and *fun* are intentionally placed near each other, and *fund* appears soon after the sign *d* has been introduced. *sad* and *mad* and *mud* provide other examples of links, while *and*, *sand* and *stand* illustrate one unfolding sequence of words; *end*, *men*, *send* and *spend* illustrate another, and so on. The 'confluence' of routes on some words is obvious and can serve as another exercise. For example: *spent* can be obtained from *sent*, or from *end* via *send* and *spend*.

The schemata below illustrate this more clearly:

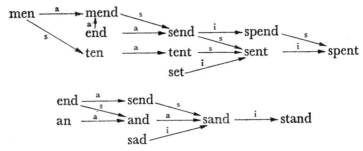

Further study of coloured Word Chart 4 will make clear to the teacher alternative ways of introducing the new sounds or spellings.

[1]See in particular *from* (Word Chart 7) and *to* (Word Chart 12) discussed on page 100.

For instance, as *an* is known from a previous chart, *fan* could be given to introduce *f*; *and* would similarly introduce *d*; and *than* could introduce the light purple-coloured *th*. Since *in* is known, *thin* could be given to introduce the sound for the pale lime *th*.[1]

The game of transforming one word into another on the same chart, sometimes calling in a word from an earlier chart, can be followed easily up to Word Chart 12. The links discovered will help whole groups of words to be called to mind every time any single one is seen or thought about, producing out of verbal material a network of connections in the mind. The game will at the same time prepare pupils for later games of substitution where synonyms are demanded.

11. By maintaining some aspects of the work and changing others, it is possible to keep flexibility at the centre of the programme. To play the Game of Transformations to excess or to concentrate on it for too long will generate fatigue and boredom. But to spend some time examining each new word chart when it appears in order to see what sort of problems it presents and what discoveries can be made from it is important and serves to enliven the class and keep the game attractive. Teachers may find it worth while to play the Game of Transformations for a time once pupils have taken note of some specific words on the charts; these can then serve as landmarks and a starting point from which to try to deduce the sound of other words through the operations of transformation.

For example, on Chart 5 the sound of the newly appearing royal blue sign could be understood if the teacher gives *lad* (since *sad*, *mad* and *dad* have already been met). Then *let* can be decoded by analogy with *pet*, *met*, *set* or *net*. From *let*, *less* can be obtained by substitution (as it can from *mess* and *yes*). *tell* can be found from *let* by reversal. This last transformation is another example of what happens to some spellings in English when sounds are reversed.

On Word Chart 6 a still more interesting observation can be made when transforming one word into the other in the mutually reversible pair *kiss* and *sick*, which involve the gold, pink, and lime-coloured signs. Here written English demands exchanges for

[1]Some teachers might find it helpful to refer at this point to the diagram in Appendix 3 which summarises the links by sound among the words on Chart 4, and between these words and some of those on preceding charts.

equivalents in the case of the gold-coloured and lime-coloured signs. For, in passing to *kiss*, the lime green *s* (in *sick*) must receive a mute letter *s* of the same colour to make *ss*; and in passing to *sick*, a mute gold-coloured *c* must be inserted after the vowel to form the gold-coloured sign *ck* (equivalent to the simple *k* of *kiss*). These are examples of two general rules for spelling which, however, need not be pointed out to the pupils as they will be discovered after a few weeks with this programme, and will remain much clearer in the mind as a result.

let	lad	sell	tell
lots	smell	spell	slap
list	slit	doll	dull
mill	ill	until	till
lend	lent	land	less
unless	filthy	funny	
wet	wit	with	
swim	was	will	
sunset	slept		

pant	wins	thus	rat
ran	red	fur	strip
my	sister	wild	mind
rest	kid	kit	kill
neck	milk	skill	silk
kiss	pile	mile	
skip	sick	line	fine
truck	track	struck	
run	rust	strike	

Word Charts 5 and 6

Word Chart 5 shows that if *un* (met already as part of *sun* and *fun*) precedes *less*, no alteration to *less* is required; but that if it precedes *till*, one member of the final double sign *ll* is dropped. Examples of this could be studied at this point as an alternative to work with the Game of Transformations.

Sentences made from these and the preceding charts by the teacher using the pointer in Visual Dictation 2 will maintain the interest of the class. Now a sufficient variety of words is available for the sentences to have an element of humour:

> *I am a dull nut*
> and *did the mad man land in the sand*

Others could stir the imagination:

> *I will swim at sunset*

Others might make one stop and reflect, like:

> *I am sad as dad is fed up with this man*

Reading from Primer 2 and answering questions from the work-sheets will provide on their own all the variety one could wish for.

12. The game of transforming the printed words in the imagination by a gesture with the pointer, and then using these transformed words in sentences[1] can greatly increase the scope of Visual Dictations 2 and 3. For example:

—in the case of *will*, what would have resulted had the blue *e* been used instead of the pink *i*?

—with *wet*, what would have resulted had the lilac *n* been inserted between the blue *e* and the magenta *t*?
or alternatively with *sent* had the aqua-coloured *w* replaced the actual lime-coloured *s*?

—*slap* can easily become *slip*; *ill* can become *pill*; *spell* can become *spill*; and *filthy* can become *filth*.

Such transformations which have not actually taken place on the charts are carried out in the mind and retained in readiness for use. By using these in Visual Dictations 2 and 3 teachers bring the capacity of the learners to use their imagery rather than their vision to bear on the extension of sentences that can be produced from charts. Now sentences like the following may be elicited from the pupils:

sam fell in a dam, not a well

while showing

sam tell in a mad, not a will

and perhaps

did ted slip on the sill and spill the pills

while showing

did fed slap on the sell and spell the ill

13. The six word charts met up to this point have introduced the pattern of work through the medium of this display material in colour. The treatment of subsequent charts is similar to what has preceded, though the interval between the appearance of one chart and the next is likely to diminish throughout the programme. With the first six charts already available and the next six introduced in subsequent lessons, practically all the sounds used in spoken English are met and most of the regular part of written English is

[1]See pages 48–49.

covered—though a significant section of the irregular part is included as well.[1]

When the first twelve charts have appeared it can be seen that each individually offers certain opportunities and challenges different from those presented by the rest.[2] Some aspects on particular charts which may be singled out for special mention here are as follows:

(i) In the word *from* (Word Chart 7) the colouring adopted for the sign *o* is not that customarily found when the word is pronounced in isolation; in using yellow rather than orange for this sign, the word is given the indication for its sound when it occurs in sentences as in the examples below:

> *tim must go from his home*
> *he ran far from the hungry tiger*[3]

(ii) On the other hand *to* (Word Chart 12) is coloured to sound the same as *too* or *two* though it is pronounced like this only when used in isolation or stressed. Ordinarily, as in the infinitive form of verbs (e.g. to sit, to run, to go, etc.) it has simply the indeterminate sound of the schwa. This point has already been discussed but it is nevertheless useful to consider examples that are met when the sounds of English are studied.

(iii) Wherever appropriate, words such as *till* and *until* (Word Chart 5), *egg* and *leg* (Word Chart 8), *big* and *bigger* (Word Chart 9), have been placed near each other to draw attention to irregularities of spelling. In Word Chart 10, for example, the three sounds of *ch* can be viewed not only as introducing a new sound—the dark magenta sound spelt *ch* in cherry—but also as offering the same spelling for two other sounds: the sound of the sky-blue-coloured *sh* in *shop*, spelt *ch* in *michigan*; and the sound of the gold-coloured *k* in *kid*,

shop	she	ship	china
church	chin	shall	
shred	michigan	chicken	
wish	cherry	for	or
nor	chorus	child	
children	hotel	far	
shut	channel	charm	
shell	shot	done	does
chips	goes	chill	have

Word Chart 10

---

[1]See above page 84 and Appendix 6 for illustrations of the word charts referred to here.
[2]Should it be helpful now or later to some teachers, Appendix 3 contains diagrams that summarise for the words on Word Charts 5 and 6 the links by sound with one another and with words met previously.
[3]In the Mute r Edition the orange colouring was adopted.

spelt *ch* in *chorus*. These words, *michigan, cherry* and *chorus*, three examples among a number of others provided, appear the one above the other on the chart. Word Chart 11 gives two new spellings for the dark magenta *ch* of cherry—*tch* as in *match*, and *t* as in *question*.

(iv) *qu* and *x* (Word Chart 11) each appear as double-coloured signs.[1]

(v) *n* in *thanks, hungry* and *bankrupt* (Word Chart 9) is found to have the olive colour which will later be used for the *ng* in *young* and *sing* (Word Chart 13) indicating its equivalence in sound to this sign and at the same time distinguishing it from the sound it has when coloured lavender as first given in *man* and *sun* on Word Chart 3.

(vi) *child* and *children* (Word Chart 10) show a unique relationship by the difference in colour; on Word Chart 11 *crime* and *criminal* are related in a similar fashion.

(vii) Long words appear sufficiently early to permit an attack to be made on them in a variety of ways.

14. Let us consider in particular the point about long words. From the start the learners have been involved in solving the problem of sounding new written words through using the techniques of substitution, reversal, addition and insertion of signs. In the first week of reading they attacked *sat* or *pat* from their knowledge of *at*; likewise *pest* from their knowledge of *pet*. In the second or following week they met and solved by themselves the reading of:

stamps, mumps and *upon* (Word Chart 3)
stand and *fifty* (Word Chart 4)
filthy, until and *unless* (Word Chart 5)
struck and *strike* (Word Chart 6)
brick, promise, impossible, suddenly and *burden* (Word Chart 7)
fatal, unite and *fuse* (Word Chart 8)
usable and *bankrupt* (Word Chart 9)

The next three charts offer:

michigan, hotel and *chorus* (Word Chart 10)
tomorrow, family, soldier, education, generation and *judge* (Word Chart 11)

[1]See page 82.

clutch, orchestra, character, phrase, question, fantastic and *criminal* (Word Chart 12)

While the challenge presented by short words should not be underestimated, neither should that offered by long ones be exaggerated.

What may be involved here is the stubborn pursuance by some pupils of false trails suggested by elements that may or may not be related to what they are looking at. If anyone really *looked* at a word in colour on the charts, all the clues for its pronunciation would be there and only the right sound could be uttered. But some people after a time can no longer keep themselves at the task, so follow any clue they seem to find in a word. For such pupils what is needed is a re-education of looking and listening. For beginners it is rather an education that requires them to offer a solution only after they have processed all the clues and are sure that they are right. To help them all it is advisable for teachers to relate the problem on hand to problems already solved, but never to tell them the answer. In this connection some of the examples above may be considered.

chorus can be found through linking *or* and *us* and seeing that the first sign has the same colour as the *ck* in *chicken*

orchestra in colour can be easily solved: *or* has already been sorted out, *ches* has the same colour pattern as *kiss* and 'or-kiss' carries the *tra* to give the right sound

hotel; nose from *no*, and *hose* from *nose*, yields the first syllable; *tell* yields the second

michigan, which a number of older boys read as 'machine-gun', can be divided into mich-igan, and *miss* yields *mich* once it is seen that the *ch* here is the same colour as the last sign in *wish*

soldier may be obtained by relating *sold* to 'sold', in which the *d* has the colour of the *g* in *gem;* the addition of the ending of *sister* for the sound of *ier* completes the word

education and *generation* are usually decoded with equal ease—*gem* serves as an entry to *gen* *ed* is taken from *red* or *fed*, though the *d* has the sound and colour of this sign in 'soldier' The ending *ation* is recognised because of the colours, the *t* having the colour of *sh* in *shut*

Naturally not all pupils follow the same path. Often it is very difficult to know how they have succeeded since success is the least revealing of events. Errors on the other hand help by revealing the problems encountered and are made the more valuable since we cannot force our pupils to be right or wrong to please us.

15. In the remaining sections of this chapter, while reference will be made to the Word Charts considered here, the emphasis will be on the other materials.

II.
PRIMER 2—WORDS, SENTENCES, STORIES

1. The sections of Primer 2 are arranged as far as possible to show in the conventionally printed form (that is, signs and words ordered from left to right) the two visual dictations. The first page of each section shows the result of signs linked into words (as in Visual Dictation 1); the page opposite shows words similarly linked to form sentences (as in Visual Dictation 2). By this stage it is more convenient to make sentences with Visual Dictation 2; for while it is possible with Visual Dictation 1, this is more time consuming.

This does not mean that on a number of occasions teachers will not resort to the well-practised exercise described in detail in Chapter 1. It simply means that since the forming of words has through practice been established, Visual Dictation 1 may for the most part be omitted and the yield increased at the same time. This game can then be reserved mainly for work with the signs in the Word Building Book when it may be necessary. This can happen, for exanple, during group work when there is need to generate words wanted for producing sentences by Visual Dictation 2 on the word charts.

In the various sections of Primers 2 and 3 words are introduced first, those actually appearing being simply examples. Some can be seen again in colour on the charts, or may be generated from these; others are new and could be studied as soon as the group disperses for individual work on the relevant page. More words still can be generated by the pupils from the signs on the corresponding table in the Word Building Book.[1] This study of words leads not only to

[1] At the top of each page of separate words in Primer 2 are presented the *new* signs being considered, which makes it easy to choose the particular table in the Word Building Book that includes these.

their careful decoding, but to awareness of their spelling since it focuses attention on their structure, and to greater understanding of the set of meanings which goes with each.

The sentences which follow in each section of the primers for the most part contain words newly introduced on the preceding page and those met in the classroom sessions. Occasionally words are used that can be decoded by analogy.

2. It is clear from a perusal of the word pages of Primer 2 that the rule of restriction is observed throughout. No sign is used whose sound has not already been introduced in the preceding pages or at the head of the section concerned. In this way ambiguities are avoided and practice in sounds is given to the exclusion of sounds and signs still to come.

3. The first four pages of Primer 2 refer to Word Chart 3. This has been described in detail in the preceding Section. If the order of presentation is first the word chart and second the Word Building Book and Primer 2, it is easy for the teacher to ask the group, to whom she has just introduced the chart, to work at their seats with the words on page 2 of the Primer 2. While they are doing this, she may go around and visit those whom she knows take longer to recognise words already met and to look at new words. If the first group is still having difficulties, reference to the words in colour on the charts should suffice to eliminate them. Teachers should *never* tell pupils what to sound for any of the printed words.

The pupils who can read page 2 are asked to read page 3 of Primer 2 in conjunction with Table 3 of their Word Building Book and proceed with individual work in Worksheet 2.

4. It seems reasonable to ask teachers to devote more time to the pupils who are struggling with some point not yet fully clear and to let those able to engage in their own education by individual creative work to proceed with it. The result of this subdivision of a group, however small, into still smaller groups is to reduce the gap between pupils since the difficulties being encountered at this stage are only of an understanding of how signs reflect sounds. Insight into this relation, achieved after a few minutes of intensive individual or small-group work, often permits those who have met difficulty to

a	*m*	*'s*			
	mm				
am	ma	im	mi	um	mu
	om	mo	em	me	
pam		sam		tom	
tim's		mat		met	
map		mum		mumps	
must		miss		mist	
sum		mops		maps	
stamps		stump		pump	

— sam sat up

— sit up sam

— pam met pat

— pam's map

— sam mops a mat

— tim sits

— sam must mend it

— tom's stamps

2   3

Pages 2 and 3 of Primer 2

proceed successfully from then on. That some pupils will devise as many as thirty new words while others produce as few as five may have no bearing on future work, since it is possible for principles to be understood equally well on any number of examples. Quantity can be valued by teachers, but here it may be simply a sign of the use of time available and of the easiness of the work, rather than of a deeper insight that would set one ahead of others at all times. While teachers should note who does what, they should refrain from drawing immediate conclusions, waiting for other events to suggest whether this productivity really reflects power and insight, or simply the use of time in generating words forming part of a plentiful supply of examples of one relation of sign to sound.

5. Page 4 is interchangeable with page 2 and can for some be taken in the same assignment, or even before page 2. These two pages

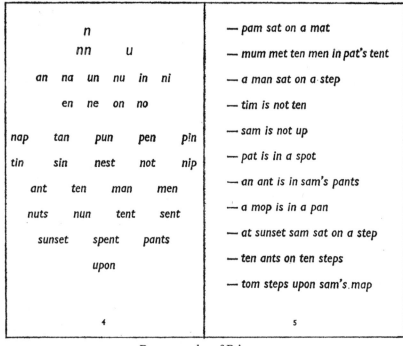

n					
nn		u			
an	na	un	nu	in	ni
	en	ne	on	no	
nap	tan	pun	pen	pin
tin	sin	nest	not	nip
ant	ten	man	men
nuts	nun	tent	sent
sunset	spent	pants
upon

— pam sat on a mat

— mum met ten men in pat's tent

— a man sat on a step

— tim is not ten

— sam is not up

— pat is in a spot

— an ant is in sam's pants

— a mop is in a pan

— at sunset sam sat on a step

— ten ants on ten steps

— tom steps upon sam's map

4   5

Pages 4 and 5 of Primer 2

with their accompanying sentences are to be regarded as a first step towards a 'second reading certificate'.

This should be understood to mean that the pupils beginning Primer 2 are those who have graduated from Primer 1. They are no longer the beginners they were a week earlier. They know that signs are used to suggest sounds, they know that some games generate noises sounding like speech, and they have transferred from the one activity to the other a number of times.

All this knowledge of rules and procedures makes the learners incomparably more effective than they were when they first began. To meet this new competence teachers show their awareness of it in the way they work with their class at this stage.

The author was not able in pages 2 to 5 to reflect the increase in competence of the pupils, but if teachers look at Primer 2 as a whole they will see that though spacing and type size used are the same as adopted in Primer 1, the ground covered in the twenty-four pages is much greater than a direct proportion law would give as compared with Primer 1. The awarding of a second reading certificate, in perhaps two weeks from the start of Primer 2, should be justified by the ground covered. This can be achieved if teachers do not inhibit their pupils' progress by allocating equal amounts of time to each sign or new page but instead allot time for the different sections of Primer 2 with progress in mind based realistically on the increased power of the learners.

The cumulative effect of learning will be evident when

(i) less time and effort are taken to resolve the problem of reading each new page

(ii) pupils increasingly visualise more new words and sentences than are actually shown

(iii) the number and variety of words used by pupils increases when writing or using the worksheets.

Naturally, pupils needing more time should not only be given more time but also greater variety.

6. It is already clear that while there are on page 2 of Primer 2 many of the words from Word Chart 3, page 4 presents a number of new words. Stress could be put on this difference and pupils made to look for more and more new words. Thus still more new sentences will follow, as required in one section of the worksheets.[1]

Pages 6, 7 and 8 are devoted to signs appearing on Word Chart 4. This separation of letters is an artificial device, as will be seen by what follows in the book, but it can already be useful if only to prove to the learners that it is possible to work on each new extension of the restricted language to find some interesting expansion of vocabulary.

It must again be noted that many more words exist than are given and therefore that many more sentences could be proposed by taking them into account. The pages of the book, and the word charts, offer proposals intended only to indicate examples of what is possible, leaving pupils free to do more. If teachers see this at work from the start when the task is still manageable they will agree to let pupils forge ahead on their own with more confidence since

[1]See page 138.

f   f
ff

of

off   fan   fin   fun

fuss   fit   fist   fat

oft   if   puff   stiff

— pat is fun

— sam is as fat as a man

— if pam stops tom must step up

— tom is stiff

d
dd   I

did   don   dam   den   fed

dim   damp   dad   sad   mad

dust   and   sand   stand   add

end   send   spend   mend   mud

— don is sad and tom is mad

— sam is fed up

— mud is damp dust

— pam is soft and I am not

— pat mends a tent

— ten and ten is a sum

y   th   th   e

that   this   then   them

thus   than   the

thin   sunny   penny   tenth

tommy   fifty   daddy

yes   yet

— yes tommy is thin and daddy is fat

— miss patten must spend them

— the sand is at the dam

— yet sam stands in the mud

Pages 6, 7 and 8
of Primer 2

the restricted language is wider and the possibilities vastly more plentiful than the scope presented in the primers and word charts alone.

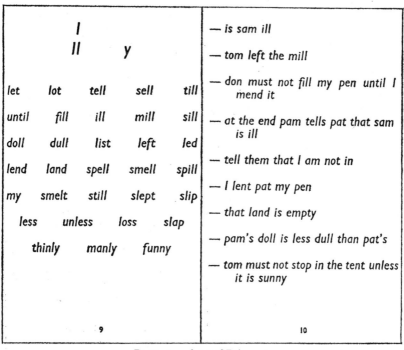

let	lot	tell	sell	till
until	fill	ill	mill	sill
doll	dull	list	left	led
lend	land	spell	smell	spill
my	smelt	still	slept	slip
	less	unless	loss	slap
	thinly	manly	funny	

I
II *y*

— is sam ill

— tom left the mill

— don must not fill my pen until I mend it

— at the end pam tells pat that sam is ill

— tell them that I am not in

— I lent pat my pen

— that land is empty

— pam's doll is less dull than pat's

— tom must not stop in the tent unless it is sunny

9   10

Pages 9 and 10 of Primer 2

7. Pages 9 and 10 go together. They do not face each other. This opportunity is offered to the teachers as a new test of the ability of pupils to work mentally rather than in the presence of the selected words, and also of their aptitude at forming sentences with these words. Earlier, when Visual Dictation 1 was being practised, the skill of composing sentences mentally from lean material was developed. Now a similar application of the mind is presented, for here a set of words that have been met, but which can no longer be seen, must be used to form sentences. How often pupils will need to turn the page provides an indication both of the level of their dependence on the visual sign and of how well the imagination is working.

As many more words and sentences than actually offered do exist and could be made, the compiling of additional examples can form part of the use of these pages. In this connection, a log book could be started where new words as they are thought of are entered.

8. It must be stressed that through comparing words on the charts with those in the pupils' primers, teachers will find the complementarity of these materials evident; at the same time they will become better users of both. Advantage has been taken of each medium to broaden the learner's insight. Though space on the coloured charts is limited, sufficient examples of words have been given to help establish phonetic clues and relationships. While space is not so restricted in a book, nevertheless only a small number of additional signs and words are provided, the worksheets and classroom opportunities being the means intended for extending the field of experience.

Let it be noted that *dd* appears on page 7 but no example of this sign in a sentence is given before page 8; *pp* is indicated on page 11[1] but no such sign appears on the word charts before Word Chart 15. It was considered that to become strict and uniform in such matters would create boredom; uniformity is in any case unnecessary since pupils very quickly learn to work well with the flexibility of the materials and have the feeling that no restriction is imposed on them.

9. With page 12 the practice of reserving two pages for each set of new signs is resumed. On the left are the words chosen as examples, on the right a

<table>
<tr><td>w</td><td>pp</td><td>le</td><td></td><td></td></tr>
<tr><td>with</td><td>wet</td><td>win</td><td>went</td><td>will</td></tr>
<tr><td>wit</td><td>well</td><td>dwell</td><td>swell</td><td>wind</td><td>west</td></tr>
<tr><td>simple</td><td>apple</td><td>little</td><td>settle</td><td></td></tr>
<tr><td>swim</td><td>swam</td><td></td><td></td><td></td></tr>
</table>

— tim spells well

— I went west with pat

— pam dwells in the mill

— I slept well in the wind

— will sam win the lot

— sam swam and swam

11

Page 11 of Primer 2

[1]Mute r Edition—page 12.

110

selection of sentences. At the top in heavier type the new signs are set out. There is no fixed rule for the presentation of these signs nor for the placing of the words in a particular line, only the acceptance that signs in one column are related to each other by the one sound associated with them. Note that much more ambitious sentences are now attempted on page 13. The way is

i	r	k	ne	a	— my sister is kind
	rr	ck			— I met a rat on the ramp
	re	ke			— kiss my doll, mum
file	pile	mile	wild	kind	— my pan is rusty
	rest	run	ran	rat	— my sulky pet rests at sunset
		fur	purr		— this sock is still wet
line	fine	wine	mine	wire	— sam was sick with a stiff neck
was	sister	swamp		swan	— I felt fine as I smelt the wild smells of the forest
kid	kit	kept	kill	skill	
strike	track	struck		truck	— the truck struck a wire ten miles from the ramp
neck	sack	rack	sick		
		12			13

Pages 12 and 13 of Primer 2

open for teachers and pupils alike to take flights of imagination in the creation of their own sentences with the signs available. Naturally it is not easy to regulate the imagination and some classes will be more at ease than others with this opportunity.[1]

[1]In *Creative Writing*, a volume in the series *Words in Colour in the Classroom*, by Sister Mary Leonore Murphy R.S.C. of Sydney, Australia, ample examples of pupils' work within a restricted language show what can be achieved when the teacher is sensitive and free.

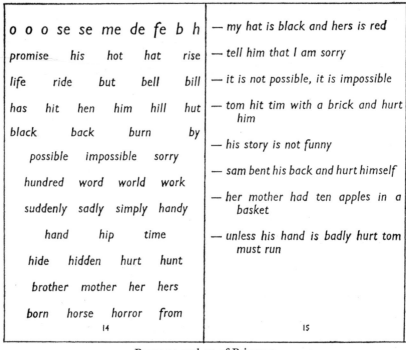

o o o se se me de fe b h	— my hat is black and hers is red

The table structure:

o o o se se me de fe b h
promise   his   hot   hat   rise
life   ride   but   bell   bill
has   hit   hen   him   hill   hut
black   back   burn   by
possible   impossible   sorry
hundred   word   world   work
suddenly   sadly   simply   handy
hand   hip   time
hide   hidden   hurt   hunt
brother   mother   her   hers
born   horse   horror   from

14

— my hat is black and hers is red

— tell him that I am sorry

— it is not possible, it is impossible

— tom hit tim with a brick and hurt him

— his story is not funny

— sam bent his back and hurt himself

— her mother had ten apples in a basket

— unless his hand is badly hurt tom must run

15

Pages 14 and 15 of Primer 2

10. Page 14 reflects the cumulative effect of learning in presenting a considerable number of signs to be studied at almost the same time. The author's confidence that pupils can learn as fast as this and retain it all should be tested thoroughly by every user of the method. If this is seen to be realistic, teachers will find they are able to speed up progress by removing prejudice with respect to the amount of material learners can absorb.

11. Though the so-called 'long I' sound was first introduced on page 7 (and Word Chart 4) in the shape it takes when it forms a word on its own, and more thoroughly as y and i on pages 9 and 12 respectively[1], all the other 'long vowels' are introduced together on a single word chart and on one page in Primer 2. It has been shown in practice that learners are able to take a development of this order

[1]Mute r Edition—pages 11 and 12.

a	u	e	o	pe	te	be
						bb
	late	male	pale	tale		
use	unite	fury	futile	usable		
	he	me	we	be		
bone	hope	rose	broke	rope		
date	mate	rate	wake	april		
fire	tire	nine	ninety	like		
told	sold	so	home	robe		
lame	rode	nose	brake	broken		
	fatal	durable	duty			
		bubble				

— the date of the sale is the tenth of april

— he broke his promise

— nine hundred and thirty pins

— the old man is bankrupt

— the sun burnt his nose red

— pat went home so suddenly

— he sold his old hat for a penny

— sam rode a horse home

16   17

Pages 16 and 17 of Primer 2

in their stride, that it is unnecessary to consider the contrast between letters—which is in effect a complication—and that it is helpful to present a block of signs and words all at once. The book is now a mine revealing its wealth in the quality, length and number of sentences possible. On page 19 in particular the example

my elder brother uses logarithms in his sums, I don't

is given both to indicate that in the author's experience this level of reading *is* the child's, and to offer one example of what could be done by teachers.

12. It is not necessary to describe in detail what each pair of pages offers. A quick glance at the illustrations included here provides this information. It may be useful to stress once more that when the sign *b* is introduced no confusion must be left between *d* and *b*.

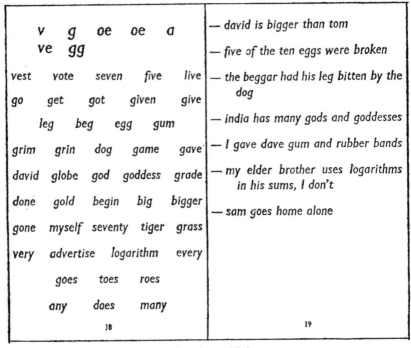

Pages 18 and 19 of Primer 2

The care taken here consists in first presenting a list of words with *d*'s only in them, then a second with *b*'s only, and then one including both *b*'s and *d*'s at random, and in particular together, in such words as *bad, bed, bud, band, dabble, blind, burden, bored, subdue, abdomen,* and so on.

13. An interesting feature seen to be developing is the triplet of spellings for each consonantal sound: the single sign, the double letter, and the sign with the 'silent *e*'. The corresponding types of signs for each consonant, whenever possible, are arranged to appear in one horizontal line in the Fidel or Word Building Book, making three horizontal lines of each type.[1]

In a later section on the Game of Transformations[2] it will be seen

[1]See also page 141, § viii.
[2]See subsection 8, page 126.

114

how consonants that are given a double-letter sign can be treated to generate greater insight into spellings. Here their systematic appearance is seen. Teachers are thus provided with opportunities to observe how images are formed and how these help spelling.

sh ch ch ch qu a ch	— I shall get it quickly for my sister
shell short shock shot shop	— we swam in the lake and got a bad chill
church china chin chill chip	— she had a shock as the children in her shop broke some bottles
she shy ash shall	
chef michigan chorus chrome	— roses have thorns and cherries have stones
quick quickly quest quaker	— she does several chores at home
quite quiet eskimo have hotel	— my brother and my sister are very shy
chore shore sore wish shut ship	
father far farther further	
orchestra cherry child children	
arm are loch charm	
20	21

Pages 20 and 21 of Primer 2

On pages 18 and 19, *oe* as in *goes* and *oe* as in *does* are introduced. On page 20 several sounds for the sign *ch* are introduced. Two of these offer no difficulty but *ch* as in *chrome* presents a problem. Reference to *ch* in *chorus* on Word Chart 10 may be necessary.[1] All of this is met on the charts and in Primer 2 before *orchestra* and *character* are met on Word Chart 11, both of which also occur later in the book.

The book concludes with another set of new signs.

[1]See page 102.

o	c	tch	x	a	— he is an able conductor of the orchestra
oo	che		xe	e	

						— there the criminal shot himself
to	do	too	pool	fool	stool	— I set a trap to catch the rat
cock	cork	cat	cry	crest	crime	— the children go to school by bus
capable	criminal	cab	close	core		— do not cry if I go
fetch	match	batch	catch	clutch		— the fool sat on a stool in the pool
box	ox	oxen	axe	taxi		— I have to go home too
cool	school	character	car	ache		— the cock's crest is very red in the sun
next	pretext	text	context			— we broke the box with an axe
there	care	dare	fare			

22   23

Pages 22 and 23 of Primer 2

14. All the sounds of English, with the exception of the few listed below, have in this small volume been met under one or more guises.

Vowels
ow as in cow
oo as in book
ea as in nearest
oy as in boy
oi as in reservoir
o as in one

Consonants
j as in jug
ng as in song
s as in leisure
x as in exist
x as in obnoxious

The sounds and all their spellings met up to this stage are reproduced here from Table 9 of the Word Building Book.

This greatly expanded restricted language—compared to the first table in the Word Building Book—can be used at this point to compose sentences and stories whose length is limited only by the

a	u	i	e	o	a	I	a	o	a	u	e	o	a	o
o	y	a	a	u	y						oe	e		oo
oe			e	i										
			o											

p	t	s	s	m	n	f	f	d	l	th	th	w	k	r	b	h	g	sh	ch	qu	x
pp	tt	ss	ss	mm	nn	ff	v	dd	ll				ck	rr	bb		gg	ch	tch		xe
pe	te	's	's	me	ne	fe	ve	de	le				ke	re	be						
		se	se										ch								
													c								
													che								

Table 9 of the Word Building Book

imagination. Both the Book of Stories and Visual Dictation 3, with its complementary oral dictation, assist learners in writing stories, in the same way that Primer 2 and Visual Dictation 2 with its complementary oral dictation assisted them in making sentences.

15. The earliest stories in the Book of Stories are interesting in a special respect. The *first story* is as follows:

- at sunset pat and pam went in with sam

- tim and tom were still on the sand

- sam sat on a step and pam on a mat

- pat was upset as she had lost ten stamps

- the sand was full of wet lumps but tim and tom sat on them

- mum and dad told them to run in as it was dinner time

On comparing this passage with one of the pages of sentences in Primer 2 it hardly seems a story at all. But it provides a transition between sets of sentences that seem unrelated and another set that tell a story.

While the *second story* opens with a single descriptive statement, the sentences that follow reveal a principal characteristic of stories: each adds its meaning to the previous ones.

2

- in the family there are mum and dad and five of us, sam, pam, tom, pat, and tim

- sam is up first, tim last

- sam has a bed and tim and tom a bunk

- pam and pat have a room on the first floor

- pat is tall and tim is small

- tom is as tall as pam but pam is older

- sam is nine and tim is five, tom is seven

- sam is the oldest and his sisters and brothers love him very much

---

The *third story* is now expected to be a continuous narrative since the re-reading of the first after the second gives the feeling that the first story is meant to be the beginning of a longer narrative. The third passage, still more than the second, is what one would call a story.

> **3**
>
> *- pat has a pet, it is fat and sits on mum's lap*
>
> *- sam has a thin and dull cat found on the rocks, pat's cat is not his friend*
>
> *- sam's cat wants to go out, pat's cat wants to stay in*
>
> *- when sam's cat is out, pat's cat starts to play around the house and to drink and eat*
>
> *- when sam's cat is back, pat's cat hides in mum's lap*
>
> *- pam, tom, and tim have no pets*

From now on the Book of Stories unfolds as a continuous narrative as its title suggests. But for the present this set of stories is not the principal concern it will be later on, when it can be used for exploring meaning and for the beginning of a study of composition and style.[1] The pupils, having manipulated the restricted language of Primers 1 and 2, will, like the author, have ideas of their own that are story-like and can be written down.

16. Every teacher will receive the spontaneous gifts of her class if she makes it a natural thing for her pupils to write as freely as they can within the limits imposed by each successive restricted language as may be defined by the tables of the Word Building Book. Since the learning moves at a swift pace, pupils find themselves less restricted every day in the language. As writing freely is not simply a question of vocabulary, teachers will need to find a means of letting their classes use Visual Dictation 3 (and its complementary

[1] See Chapter Three.

oral dictation) as early as possible, allowing the pupils to judge the results as a story rather than as a set of sentences.[1]

Initially, two sentences can be put together by one pupil or several pupils working in teams. Then the class could be invited to join in and suggest additional lines, developing a theme which unfolds further as each new sentence is added. After such group work the pupils could return to their desks to write down on their own whatever should come to them. Reading aloud to the class what they have written could take place in the following session should time not permit an immediate sharing of experience.

There are many variations on this procedure, any of which might be preferred by teachers. Each teacher may wish to develop her own way of stimulating the pupils' enthusiasm so that each pupil develops *his* own personal approach to writing within the restricted but developing languages that form the sequence of the programme. Eventually a class—or even an individual—'book of stories' might be added to the classroom bookshelf. Such books could prove to be among the most creative ever written.

III.
WORKSHEETS—CONTROL OF PROGRESS

1. Of all the materials included in this programme the booklets of worksheets are potentially the most valuable to the learners since so much latitude is allowed in the research to answer questions and so much opportunity given to be inventive.

2. The worksheets were conceived as a tool which changes with the learners' advance. Worksheet 1 has been described in the previous chapter.[2] For the study of sounds and of the words used in Primer 2, Worksheets 2–7 include a number of proposals which steadily increase in difficulty and complexity and therefore in the demands they make upon the powers of the learner.

As Worksheets 1–7 all follow the same pattern, pupils soon become efficient in handling the tasks; they can use the worksheets as a steady record of their own progress. The worksheets can also be used as a battery of tests of linguistic power not only for the pupils themselves but for the teachers and for researchers, once a sufficient

---

[1]See page 61 for examples of Visual Dictation 3.
[2]See page 63 et seq.

number of them become available for examination. From such an investigation by researchers the possibility may emerge of studying in a complex way the complex act of learning to read as well as learning to speak one's mother tongue.

3. In Exercise 1 on the first page of each of Worksheets 1–7, learners are asked to make up 'words', using signs from the tables in the Word Building Book, that are different from those on the word charts and those found in the relevant sections of Primer 2.[1] They are therefore required to make combinations of the various signs whose sounds have been studied in class. With the knowledge that the words to be produced here must be different from those met in class and in the primers, pupils are thrown back on their use of the wider tool of combination and permutation of signs in order to obtain the words asked for. There should be no end to the production of answers for Exercise 1. The freer, more imaginative, minds will produce the most creative responses without special encouragement. The teacher need only leave pupils alone and observe what they do with the challenge, noting what they offer.

A question at the foot of the page asks for the number of words found. This is the only question that can legitimately be asked of all learners engaged in such a task. It will measure the interest in the game, the degree of understanding of it, and how well time has been used.

Exercise 2 of the worksheets goes deeper into the material produced on page 1 and asks for the recognition that some of the words produced through the combining of sounds are proper words in the English language.[2] The result will test:

(i) whether the words produced can be sounded by the learner;

(ii) whether, once the learner has sounded the words, there are criteria within him that enable him to recognise whether a word is either one known to him or one that could be part of the language as he views it;

(iii) whether the learner accepts random words as English or is guided by random criteria.

[1]See page 65 for an illustration of the presentation of this exercise.
[2]See page 66 for an illustration of the presentation of this exercise.

4. The insight into the difference between groups of signs on the one hand and words one knows on the other will grow as the first pages of the successive booklets are considered. This insight is much more important than the objective product formed using the signs on the paper. It is this that should be cultivated in each learner. Teachers will see that they should refrain from correcting what is proposed by the pupil and instead study it in order to increase their own understanding of their pupils. To correct is to reduce the value of the efforts and to interfere with the data.

In order that pupils be able to recognise their progress, they should be allowed to go back and take a deeper look at what they have done on previous occasions. Could anyone exaggerate the importance of the recognition by a learner that he himself now possesses criteria which permit him to make up his mind about the accuracy or otherwise of what he believed to be right not long ago? He will be master of the criteria that teachers apply to *know* what is right or wrong in a certain situation. To test this is important and should not be interfered with.

5. The question of recognition of words has two meanings: one is concerned with insight into their shape as it relates to the sounds of speech; the other relates to the ability to evoke experiences, images, and other materials in response to the sounds found hidden in the signs of the written word.

Exercise 3 on the third page of the worksheets shifts from the first meaning, partly covered in Exercise 2, to the second, by asking for drawings or for newspaper cuttings or actual objects to be found and brought to school that illustrate what meanings are evoked in the learners' mind by the sound of a word.[1] When a word is abstract —as, for example, *empty* (Worksheet 3)—it may really challenge the imagination of learners, producing whatever is in their mind as an answer.[2] This precious aptitude of the imagination should not be interfered with. The results should all be accepted by the teacher, errors being handled by the class in full session.

It may be possible in some classrooms to display on a board the

[1]See page 66 for an illustration of the presentation of this exercise.
[2]Sister Leonore, in *Creative Writing* (pp. 27, 36–37), gives a record of the interesting ideas children brought to this game.

various solutions found by the class members. Such a display would be like an objectification of a section in a dictionary where several different meanings are given for one word. These displays may occasionally be of such a standard for teachers to want their colleagues to share in their delight; photographs of the displays could be taken and sent to language journals, through the medium of which the work of a single child could serve to enrich all.

6. Exercise 4 tests recognition of signs within words.[1] Because words here are printed wholly in black, compound signs (digraphs, trigraphs, etc, such as *oa* in *boat*) could appear to some learners not as one sign but as two letters whose two different sounds have been met. Through such exercises it can be ascertained whether pupils who are learning with this programme no longer consider letters as objects but rather consider signs, made up of a group of letters, as the units of sound in words.

If the association of graphemes with phonemes has been successfully established, it is reasonable to expect that some pupils will recognise graphemes in words rather than letters of the alphabet, which have been ignored altogether as such in this approach. The fourth page of the worksheets therefore provides a double test. On the one hand it will measure the success of an idea in the programme and on the other it will reveal whether pupils at this stage can keep the sign concept in mind, not seeing only the letters in words. The Word Building Book if well used could help establish this idea, assisting in the perceiving of signs as related to sounds rather than letters to sounds (or to their alphabetical names).

The second section of this exercise on the lower half of page 4, asking the pupil simply to write down any words he can and then to make a circle around any signs not to be found on the Word Building Book table being studied, provides a further opportunity to learn about the pupil's experience outside school. But it also gives the learner a chance of knowing that this experience is acceptable to his teacher.

For the teacher the answers to such questions can provide clues about what every pupil brings to his work, and show where this

[1]See page 67 for an illustration of the presentation of this exercise.

might prove a help or a hindrance. The exercise also makes it easier to insist on the importance of looking at each word again, considered as a combination of the units referred to as 'signs'. This will have greatest impact on the retention of shape, which is equivalent to saying that it will turn spelling into a game.

7. This insight into word formation will be enhanced by Exercise 5, extending over pages 5–10 of the worksheets. This is a game which is to be considered as a whole; that is, the six pages of the first booklet should not be separated from corresponding sets of pages in later booklets, nor the twenty-four columns in one worksheet from one another. This exercise, known as the 'completion' game, presents various combinations of signs with spaces to be filled in, using other signs to be chosen by the pupil; the object is to complete in one column as many proper English words as possible for each particular combination offered.[1]

As each attempt at the worksheets bears a date, pupils and teacher will know

—what has come to mind on each of the various occasions concerned, and
—how the passage of time affects the results by allowing for extension and self correction.

Since words may be truncated in various ways, pupils can be asked to reconstruct, or complete, for a given truncated example the one or more words whose form contains the shape presented. Mere examination of this exercise in the pages of successive worksheets reveals how pupils are made aware of what words so treated would look like. This exercise has a tremendous potential, particularly since every pupil can return to any of the questions as his experience develops.

What is requested of teachers is that they understand that any dynamic vision of a word can only add strength to the retention, and that the exercises presented here show each word in a number of aspects. There is at least one example on the word charts or in the primer books for each proposal, so that by simply referring to such an example pupils will be led to understand—if they do not already—that images of shapes change if parts of the shapes are covered.

[1]See page 67 for a detailed description of how this game may be introduced, and for an illustration of its presentation in the worksheets.

Here again the unit is the *sign*, not the letter, though it often will be found that the sign required is a letter. With practice at imagining completed answers, and seeing them as fully printed words in place of the partial combinations, pupils will come to appreciate how it is possible for one particular word to be a solution in more than one column.

Among the exercises some are immediate while others are more demanding for people coming newly to the game. But for those whose imagination is of the kind required here, relating a partial signal to particular words from a set stored in the mind as sounds and shapes will be as little demanding however the challenge is presented. What is meant here is that there are some who, while completing

......et

at once as *pet, met, set, net* or *let* and so on, will find

f..... ....y

much more of a challenge, requiring the scanning of word charts or pages in Primer 2 before *filthy* is found as one possible solution. If *funny*, where *nn* is a single sign having a single colour only, were offered it would not be acceptable since it is a solution for

f..... ......y and not f..... ....y

Sometimes for a long period only one example may be found to satisfy a request for a word, as in the case of

....l.....s s

which can be answered by reference to *unless* on a word chart; eventually *useless* or *airless*[1] might be found among alternative solutions.

When teachers undertake to present such games seriously to their classes, refraining from making suggestions themselves, they have at their disposal a means for testing, and at the same time a teaching tool leading to continuous development, of which it is in turn a test.

Scoring here is so simple that it can be done by the pupil, being only checked by the teacher.

[1]Mute r Edition—*hairless*.

8. In the previous chapter[1] the function of the *Game of Transformations* found on pages 11–14 of each booklet was discussed thoroughly, and a detailed description was given of how the game may be introduced. Here some additional assistance needed for playing the game with ease in its more complicated form is offered to the teacher.

A deeper understanding of the four operations of transformation used—*substitution, reversal, addition, insertion*—and of the operation not allowed (subtraction) may be helpful. Two general rules may be stated.

> *a.* Each new stage of a transformation must be effected by operating on a *single sign* only (except in the case of reversal where the word as a whole is involved), signs being recognised as the units that appear in the columns of the Word Building Book or Fidel.[2]

An understanding of this rule is important for, although most signs represent only one sound, a certain number denote a combination of sounds and as such are indicated by the use of a double-colouring on the Fidel; and the majority of signs, even those representing single sounds only, are composed of two or more letters.

> *b.* Subtraction of signs is an operation that is never permitted in this game.

However, there are many transformations that are actually allowed which teachers, who are accustomed to spelling words in terms of letters rather than signs, might at first sight consider infringements of either of these two general rules.

One such set of transformations concerns the apparent subtractions. In this game, where the number of letters used in words is reduced in successive stages of a transformation, no subtraction is considered to take place unless the number of signs involved is also reduced. For example, the transformation:

$$\text{sigh} \xrightarrow{\ s\ } \text{so}$$

is no more than a straightforward substitution of the sign *igh* by the sign *o*; the number of signs remains unchanged although the number

---

[1]See page 6o et seq.
[2]See 'allowable exception' on page 128.

of letters in the words is cut from four to two. No operation of subtraction has taken place.

A further type of transformation which increases the possibilities for changing one word into another involves an apparent infringement of the first rule, against simultaneous multiple transformations. In such cases, while the operation of transformation is being carried out, two types of equivalence (closely related to the operation of substitution) may be introduced, affecting some or all the signs in the word concerned. It should be noted that the operation of *substitution* requires the changing of both the spelling and the sound of a sign in a word; *equivalence* with respect to signs on the other hand involves a single change, either to the spelling or to the sound but not to both, during an operation on another part of the word—or on the word as a whole in the case of reversal. The two types of equivalence may be described as follows:

1. Horizontal equivalence

This expresses a *visual* equivalence of one sign to another as shapes, even though the sounds for them are different. Thus if the sound should change for any sign not directly concerned in an operation of transformation, this is not considered as a second operation provided the shape of the sign is maintained. Since colour may be used to represent sounds, the hidden change would be apparent visually only if the transformation were carried out in colour. The signs are said to be 'horizontally' equivalent, since although they represent different sounds they bear the same shape, and can be located by a horizontal scanning of the different columns of the Word Building Book or Fidel. Examples of horizontal equivalence during an operation of transformation are given below:

to $\xrightarrow{\ s\ }$ go (the sign *g* is substituted for *t*)	Horizontal equivalence of *o* The shape *o* is maintained although the sound for it changes
if $\xrightarrow{\ s\ }$ of (the sign *o* is substituted for *i*)	Horizontal equivalence of *f* The shape *f* is maintained although the sound for it changes

2. Vertical equivalence

This expresses a *phonic* equivalence between signs whose shape alters during the course of an operation of transformation on another part of the word (or on the word as a whole in the case of reversal). Such signs, having the same sound, belong to the same column in the Word Building Book or Fidel, and can be located by a vertical scanning of the column. They can replace each other without this being counted as an operation of transformation.

For example:

kit $\xrightarrow{\text{s}}$ cat　　　　　　Vertical equivalence of *k* and *c*
(the sign *a* is substituted for *i*)　which represent the same sound

day $\xrightarrow{\text{s}}$ weigh　　　　　Vertical equivalence of *eigh* and *ay*
(the sign *w* is substituted for *d*)　which represent the same sound

There is one *allowable exception* to the rule of carrying out transformations with single signs (and in some cases also to the rule of no subtraction of signs). But only if there is *no* alternative route can one make the following types of transformations via sound which do not conform to the rule. Some teachers may rightly object to them because they do not find them fun and their pupils do not find them easy; others may delight in the additional challenge they contribute to finding solutions to difficult transformation problems.

    a. Two signs condensed to a single sign, double-coloured on the Fidel.

    won $\xrightarrow{\text{a}}$ once　　　　　　*w* and *o* are replaced by *o*
    (the sign *ce* is added)

    packs $\xrightarrow{\text{s}}$ tax　　　　　　*ck* and *s* are replaced by *x*
    (*t* is substituted for p)

    b. One sign, double-coloured on the Fidel, split up into two separate signs.

    ox $\xrightarrow{\text{a}}$ rocks　　　　　　*x* is replaced by *ck* and *s*
    (the sign *r* is added)

Through the use of these phonic equivalences far more is done in one step than when the operations are taken more strictly according to the definition. They make the game possible when otherwise not, and more challenging and exciting.

Given below is a full analysis of the operations of the Game of Transformations

(i) *Substitution* of one sign for another:
When an operation produces a change in both the sound and the shape of a sign, it is counted as a transformation by substitution.

Examples:

$$\text{pat} \xrightarrow{\quad s \quad} \text{sat}$$
$$\text{high} \xrightarrow{\quad s \quad} \text{hay}$$

In the following examples besides substitution there have been used:

a. struck $\xrightarrow{\quad s \quad}$ strike   Vertical equivalence
   (*i* is substituted for *u*)   —of *ck* and *ke*

  whose $\xrightarrow{\quad s \quad}$ shoes   —of *o* and *oe*
   (*sh* is substituted for *wh*)   —and of *se* and *s*

b. gone $\xrightarrow{\quad s \quad}$ lone   Horizontal equivalence
   (*l* is substituted for *g*)   —of *o*, having two different
                             sounds

  thin $\xrightarrow{\quad s \quad}$ then   —of *th*, having two different
   (*e* is substituted for *i*)   sounds

c. doubt $\xrightarrow{\quad s \quad}$ route   Vertical (v) and horizontal
   (*r* is substituted for *d*)   (h) equivalence
                            —of *bt* and *te* (v)
                            —of *ou* (h)

  him $\xrightarrow{\quad s \quad}$ time   —of *m* and *me* (v)
   (*t* is substituted for *h*)   —of *i* (h)

But the following are not allowed since they are not substitution of one sign for another but of two signs for one:

ship $\longrightarrow\!\!\!/\!\!\!\rightarrow$ slip   —*sh* is replaced by two signs,
                        s and *l*

tames $\longrightarrow\!\!\!/\!\!\!\rightarrow$ taxes   —*me* is replaced by two signs,
                        x and *e*

(ii) *Addition* of a sign at either end of a word:

$$\text{top} \underset{a \searrow \text{tops} \nearrow a}{\overset{a \nearrow \text{stop} \searrow a}{}} \text{stops}$$

In the following examples besides addition there have been used:

a. go $\xrightarrow{\text{a}}$ goes
(the sign *s* is added)

Vertical equivalence
—of *o* and *oe*

b. go $\xrightarrow{\text{a}}$ got
(the sign *t* is added)

Horizontal equivalence
—of *o*, having two different sounds

c. at $\xrightarrow{\text{a}}$ hate
(the sign *h* is added)

Vertical and horizontal equivalence
—of *t* and *te* (v)
—of *a* (h)

quay $\xrightarrow{\text{a}}$ queen
(the sign *n* is added)

—of *ay* and *ee* (v)
—of *qu* (h)

Note also that while

rate $\xrightarrow{\text{a}}$ rates
(the sign *s* is added)

is correct

race $\longrightarrow\!\!\!/\!\!\!\to$ races
(the sign *s* is added)

is *not* allowed since the sign *ce* is replaced by two signs *c* and *e* representing separate sounds

(iii) *Insertion* of a sign between other signs:
at $\xrightarrow{\text{i}}$ apt
pet $\xrightarrow{\text{i}}$ pest
sap $\xrightarrow{\text{i}}$ slap
stuck $\xrightarrow{\text{i}}$ struck
sooner $\xrightarrow{\text{i}}$ schooner

In the following examples besides insertion there have been used:

a. base $\xrightarrow{\text{i}}$ brace
(the sign *r* is inserted)

Vertical equivalence
—of *se* and *ce*

sigh $\xrightarrow{\text{i}}$ sly
(the sign *l* is inserted)

—of *igh* and *y*

b. hat $\xrightarrow{\text{i}}$ halt
(the sign *l* is inserted)

Horizontal equivalence
—of *a*, having two different sounds

pot $\xrightarrow{\text{i}}$ post   —of *o*, having two different
(the sign *s* is inserted)   sounds

c. pack $\xrightarrow{\text{i}}$ plaque   Vertical and horizontal
(the sign *l* is inserted)   equivalence
                            of *ck* and *que* (v)
                            —of *a* (h)

though $\xrightarrow{\text{i}}$ throw   —of *ough* and *ow* (v)
(the sign *r* is inserted)   —of *th* (h)

(iv) *Reversal* of the order of signs:

pat $\xrightarrow{\text{r}}$ tap
spots $\xrightarrow{\text{r}}$ stops

In the following examples besides reversal there have been used:

a. kiss $\xrightarrow{\text{r}}$ sick   Vertical equivalence
                            —of *k* and *ck*
                                 and of *ss* and *s*

time $\xrightarrow{\text{r}}$ might   —of *i* and *igh*
                                and of *me* and *m*

b. on $\xrightarrow{\text{r}}$ no   Horizontal equivalence
                            —of *o*, having two different
                                sounds

not $\xrightarrow{\text{r}}$ ton   —of *o*, having two different
                                sounds

c. pass $\xrightarrow{\text{r}}$ sap   Vertical and horizontal
                                equivalence
                            —of *ss* and *s* (v)
                            —of *a* (h)

note $\xrightarrow{\text{r}}$ ton   —of *te* and *t* (v)
                            —of *o* (h)

The following examples are not allowed. They are not reversals of
the signs since the words in each pair have only one sign in common.
In each case the first word has two signs and the second has three.

saw ——╱——► was

ought ——╱——► tough

Reversal of words involving double-coloured signs may be considered in either of two ways.

a. With simple reversal of the order of the signs from left to right:

towns ——ʳ——► snout   Vertical and horizontal
                               equivalence
                               —of *ow* and *ou* (v)
                               —of *s* (h)

ow and *ou* are coloured purple over light aqua on the Fidel.

b. With both reversal of the order of the signs from left to right, and from top to bottom in the case of double coloured signs:

fox ——ʳ——► scoff   where *x* is gold over lime, and *s*
                               and *c* lime and gold-coloured
                               respectively

The inverting of the sign *x* also introduces the facility of the 'allowable exception' described on page 128 above, together with the vertical equivalence of *f* and *ff*.

(v) *Subtraction* of signs is not allowed:

A word proposed in a sequence of transformations must not contain fewer signs than the word immediately preceding it. Hence additions and insertions are never reversible operations (since the number of signs in the word they produce is greater than in the word they operate on) while substitutions and reversals are (where the number of signs remains unchanged).

mist ——╱——► miss   Vertical equivalence
(the sign *t* is subtracted)   —of *s* and *ss*

sworn ——╱——► sword   —of *s* and *sw*
(the sign *w* is subtracted)

This cannot be considered as a case of horizontal equivalence of '*sw*' since *sw* is a single sign in the second word and two separate signs *s* and *w* in the first.

slip ——/—→ship   —the sign *sh* is also substi-
(the sign *l* is subtracted)   tuted for the sign *s*, pro-
    ducing a multiple trans-
    formation as well as a
    subtraction.

Unlike the examples above the following are not subtractions since
the number of signs in the first and second members of each pair is
the same.

high ———^{s}——→ hay
(*ay* is substituted for *igh*)

knit ———^{s}——→ kit
(*k* is substituted for *kn*)

sew ———^{s}——→ go   Vertical equivalence
(*g* is substituted for *s*)   —of *ew* and *o*

sing ———^{s}——→ sin
(*n* is substituted for *ng*)

9. Below are offered a few of the many solutions that are possible
for each of the games of transformation set in Worksheets 2 and 3.[1]
    For Worksheets 4–7, specimen solutions are still provided. While
in most cases these have been restricted to a single example only,
the number of different solutions possible remains undiminished.

WORKSHEET 2

    from *pat* to *not*

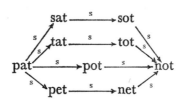

    from *net* to *nuts*

[1]See page 75 for specimen solutions for the games of transformation set in Worksheet 1.

from *tin* to *mints*

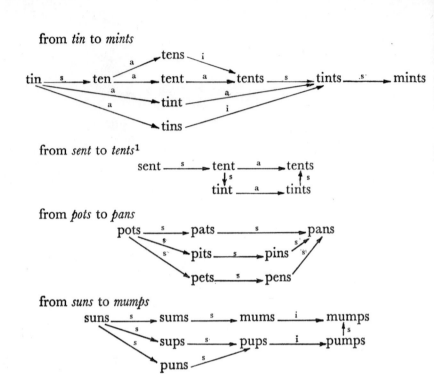

from *sent* to *tents*[1]

from *pots* to *pans*

from *suns* to *mumps*

WORKSHEET 3

from *fed* to *funny*

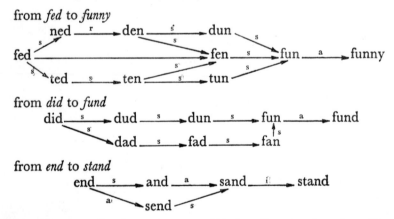

from *did* to *fund*

from *end* to *stand*

[1]The worksheet actually gives *sent* to *sense* which is a direct transformation without intermediate stages.

from *fat* to *thin*

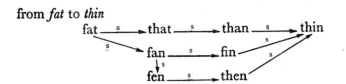

from *off* to *left*

off ──s──▶ if ──s──▶ it ──a──▶ lit ──s──▶ let ──i──▶ left

from *lot* to *well*

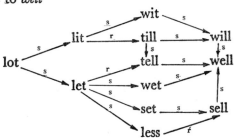

WORKSHEET 4

from *red* to *don*

red ──s──▶ rod ──s──▶ nod ──r──▶ don

from *kit* to *silk*

kit ──i──▶ kilt ──s──▶ silt ──s──▶ silk

from *fur* to *work*

fur ──a──▶ firm ──s──▶ form ──s──▶ fork ──s──▶ work

from *wild* to *skill*[1]

wild ──s──▶ mild ──s──▶ mills ──s──▶ pills ──s──▶ picks ──s──▶ licks ──r──▶ skill
                                                    ╲r   ╱s
                                                     ▶ skip ──

[1]For the Mute r Edition, one solution would be:

wild ──s──▶ mild ──s──▶ milk ──s──▶ mills ──s──▶ pills ──s──▶ picks ──s──▶ licks ──r──▶ skill
                                                            ╲r   ╱s
                                                             ▶skip ──

The difference is simply in the introduced word 'milk'. In this analysis the bright yellow over blue *l* used in 'mild' is not equivalent to the all blue *ll* in 'mills' since it involves both a different spelling and a different colouring. This distinction in the treatment of the sign *l* is not found in the Standard English Edition (*cf.* the reproductions of the Fidels in colour on the card supplied with this text).

from *hot* to *brick*

hot $\xrightarrow{s}$ hat $\xrightarrow{s}$ pat $\xrightarrow{r}$ tap $\xrightarrow{s}$ tip $\xrightarrow{s}$ tick $\xrightarrow{i}$ trick $\xrightarrow{s}$ brick

from *word* to *sorry*[1]

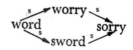

WORKSHEET 5

from *bone* to *stone*

bone $\xrightarrow{\quad s \quad}$ tone $\xrightarrow{\quad a \quad}$ stone

from *go* to *globe*

go $\xrightarrow{\quad a \quad}$ gone $\xrightarrow{\quad s \quad}$ lone $\xrightarrow{\quad s \quad}$ lobe $\xrightarrow{\quad a \quad}$ globe

from *home* to *nine*

home $\xrightarrow{\quad s \quad}$ hose $\xrightarrow{\quad s \quad}$ nose $\xrightarrow{\quad s \quad}$ none $\xrightarrow{\quad s \quad}$ nine

from *ship* to *child*[2]

ship $\xrightarrow{\quad s \quad}$ chip $\xrightarrow{\quad s \quad}$ chill $\xrightarrow{\quad s \quad}$ mill $\xrightarrow{\quad a \quad}$ mild $\xrightarrow{\quad s \quad}$ child

$\xrightarrow{\quad s \quad}$ shape $\xrightarrow{\quad s \quad}$ shale $\xrightarrow{\quad s \quad}$ male $\xrightarrow{\quad s \quad}$ mile $\xuparrow{a}$

from *make* to *bank*

make $\xrightarrow{\quad s \quad}$ bake $\xrightarrow{\quad i \quad}$ bank

from *dog* to *misty*

dog $\xrightarrow{s}$ log $\xrightarrow{s}$ loss $\xrightarrow{a}$ lost $\xrightarrow{s}$ most $\xrightarrow{s}$ mist $\xrightarrow{a}$ misty

WORKSHEET 6

from *chin* to *tell*

chin $\xrightarrow{\quad s \quad}$ tin $\xrightarrow{\quad s \quad}$ till $\xrightarrow{\quad s \quad}$ tell

from *ate* to *cable*

ate $\xrightarrow{\quad s \quad}$ ale $\xrightarrow{\quad i \quad}$ able $\xrightarrow{\quad a \quad}$ cable

from *or* to *worthy*

or $\xrightarrow{\quad a \quad}$ for $\xrightarrow{\quad a \quad}$ forth $\xrightarrow{\quad s \quad}$ worth $\xrightarrow{\quad a \quad}$ worthy

[1]One Mute r Edition solution would be:

word $\xrightarrow{s}$ wed $\xrightarrow{s}$ led $\xrightarrow{s}$ lad $\xrightarrow{s}$ sad $\xrightarrow{s}$ sap $\xrightarrow{s}$ sop $\xrightarrow{a}$ soppy $\xrightarrow{s}$ sorry

[2]A solution in accordance with the Mute r Edition analysis would be:

ship $\xrightarrow{s}$ chip $\xrightarrow{s}$ chill $\xrightarrow{s}$ mill $\xrightarrow{s}$ mile $\xrightarrow{a}$ mild $\xrightarrow{s}$ child

$\xrightarrow{s}$ shape $\xrightarrow{s}$ shale $\xrightarrow{s}$ male

from *does* to *robes*

does ——s→ toes ——s→ rose ——i→ robes

from *home* to *camel*

home ——s→ hot ——s→ cot ——s→ cat ——i→ cant ——i→ cannot ——s→
carrot ——s→ carol ——s→ camel

from *are* to *host*[1]

are ——s→ ate ——a→ hate ——i→ haste ——s→ host

WORKSHEET 7

from *might* to *salt*[2]

might ——s→ mate ——i→ malt ——s→ salt

from *hall* to *front*

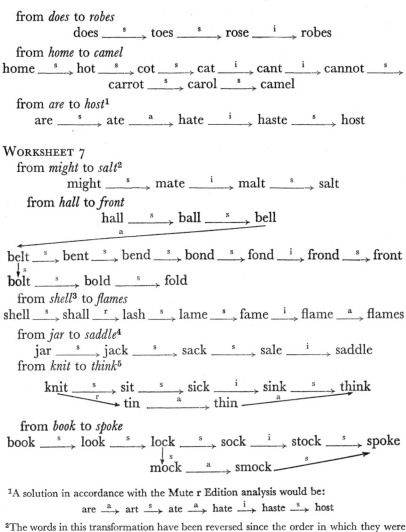

hall ——s→ ball ——s→ bell

belt ——s→ bent ——s→ bend ——s→ bond ——s→ fond ——i→ frond ——s→ front

bolt ——s→ bold ——s→ fold

from *shell*[3] to *flames*

shell ——s→ shall ——r→ lash ——s→ lame ——s→ fame ——i→ flame ——a→ flames

from *jar* to *saddle*[4]

jar ——s→ jack ——s→ sack ——s→ sale ——i→ saddle

from *knit* to *think*[5]

knit ——s→ sit ——s→ sick ——i→ sink ——s→ think
tin ——a→ thin

from *book* to *spoke*

book ——s→ look ——s→ lock ——s→ sock ——i→ stock ——s→ spoke
mock ——a→ smock

[1]A solution in accordance with the Mute r Edition analysis would be:

are ——a→ art ——s→ ate ——a→ hate ——i→ haste ——s→ host

[2]The words in this transformation have been reversed since the order in which they were printed in Worksheet 7 up to and including the 1965 edition required the subtraction of a sound.

[3]This replaces the transformation found in Worksheet 7 up to and including the 1965 edition.

[4]A solution in accordance with the Mute r Edition analysis would be:

jar ——s→ car ——a→ card ——s→ cad ——s→ sad ——a→ saddle

[5]*Quit*, found in Worksheet 7 for this transformation up to and including the 1965 edition, is replaced since it required the subtraction of a sound.

10. The test of progress in the Game of Transformations is to be found in

   a. the speed developed in the game;

   b. the variety of alternative routes proposed;

   c. the aptitude in relating one word to a large number of others through a succession of proper English words by utilising the four operations of transformation discussed fully above.

Ample space is allowed in the worksheets for recording a variety of different routes from one word to the other. No criteria are imposed for judging any particular route to be preferable to any other, and scoring for the game is based simply on the number of different ways found for making each of the transformations asked for. Pupils (and even teachers) will find themselves able to go back to them weeks, months and even a year or so later and discover additional routes—especially once the language is no longer restricted and the whole content of the Fidel is available.

The exercise on page 14 of the worksheets is provided as a further elaboration of point *c* above. In this exercise the learners are requested to choose pairs of words themselves and to try to link them, through a succession of words derived from them, using the four operations of the game.

11. An overall test of progress and experience in general is presented in Exercise 7 on pages 15 and 16, the last two pages of the worksheet, which are left virtually blank, the space being intended for use in the most comprehensive exercise of all: free writing.[1] Pupils are asked on page 15 to make up sentences with words using only those sounds and spellings included in the particular table they have reached in the Word Building Book, selecting the correct spellings from the restricted range available. Then, on page 16, they are asked to compose other sentences, on this occasion availing themselves of whatever words they happen to know, regardless of the signs or sounds involved.

The author believes that in addition to testing what has been learned through the programme, it is useful to establish what else the pupils may have acquired through either their wits, or their enhanced awareness of words, or their own linguistic behaviours.

Thus these two blank pages are an essential part of the tests presented in the worksheets.

12. While the various exercises in the first seven worksheets follow a similar pattern from one booklet to the next, each has been carefully compiled for use in conjunction with a particular stage reached with the accompanying materials. It is the author's view that these sheets present the outlet for individual work and growth, permitting the pupil to contemplate on his own what he has done and is doing, and what is at work in himself. By being asked questions the learner is led to a succession of deeper awareness; these ultimately represent the full extent of the education he will gain through this programme, reading and writing resulting as a by-product of the activities as a whole.

In each worksheet there is an inner development taking one from a contact with the unknown through the broadest and widest net of algebraic character to flights of free imagination through a succession of analyses and syntheses that mobilise the whole self. The structuration of each worksheet by the stages of learning—*contact, analysis,* and *mastery*—will show how much more useful this material is than other ways of recording or other forms of individual work.

There is further an inner development of the seven booklets as a whole. Together they aim at using increasing powers that become instruments of the mind for meeting the ever-growing challenges as wider and wider areas of the language are taken in. To become aware of oneself involved in a certain task requires that the whole of the self is not fully taken up by the task. This is made possible by maintaining the format of exercises in successive booklets as closely invariant as possible and allowing the learner to go back as often as he wishes to his earlier attempts to modify them and revise them. But it is also achieved by moving stage by stage from challenges of one order that evoke responses as an immediate intuition to those of another that would tax anyone. Learners and masters of a particular task differ only insofar as the ones have not yet gone through it while the others have. While going through the task they come to know it, to know about it and about their own mental struggle with it.

By the time they have completed their work on the first seven bookets the pupils as individuals will have been involved in sufficient experiences for them to be expected to function much better linguistically in the use of their mother tongue—written as well as spoken.

The remainder of the programme will take care of other attributes of their minds.

IV.
Word Building Book—
Phonemes and Some of Their Graphemes

1. In this section the first nine tables of the Word Building Book will be considered, together with some of its uses.

The Word Building Book reflects more than does any other of the materials the novelty of this approach to the English language and towards learning to read. The reader will find no words in this book. These have to be supplied by himself, after the manner of chemists who, with a table of atoms and isotopes in hand, must seek particular combinations to produce the substances that make up the world. Here, there are algebraic rules permitting words or groups of words to be obtained through the combination, permutation and repetition of signs.

There are conventional rules of the English language that on the one hand associate one sound with the set of signs in each column—and different sounds with the sets of signs in different columns—and on the other hand make it understood that consonants sound only in conjunction with one of the vowels already introduced. These two sets of rules produce particular groupings of signs and sounds which shall be called 'words'. Since some of these combinations when sounded trigger *meaning*, these will be retained as 'words' of the English language (or some language).

The linking of signs to form words is not done by physically cutting up signs and pasting them side by side (or writing them together) but by generating subsets on the set—represented by any particular table in the Word Building Book—through touching signs with a pointer to form sequences which correspond to the temporal order of sounds which reflect the spoken word.[1] The forming of an image of a word structured in time in this way will

[1]This is the continuation of Visual Dictation 1 and can be done by the pupil using his pencil as a pointer on his Word Building Book.

permit both transcription into the conventional spatial sequence of signs, and its utterance. Graphemes can easily be associated with phonemes through these images-structured-in-time. These images are therefore of prime importance if reading and writing is the aim.

2. In this next chapter particular attention is devoted to spelling: here it can be noted simply that the Word Building Book is a tool with a number of useful characteristics:

(i) It indicates a sequence of restricted languages, growing through successive steps towards the whole of English.

(ii) It makes it possible to introduce, in the course of the move towards the inclusion of all the sounds of English, a number of different signs that correspond to the same sound and a number of signs each corresponding to a number of different sounds.

(iii) It shows that with the seven sounds of the so-called vowels—the 'short vowels', the schwa and the sound of the first person singular (I)—almost all the consonants can be introduced and words and sentences formed that are English.

(iv) As the pupils advance, the increase in the number of new signs introduced from one table to the next is much greater—a fact justified by, and justifying further, the concept of the cumulative effect of learning.

(v) By Table 9[1] the complete content of Primer 2 is covered as well as that of eleven of the word charts.

(vi) It shows that from signs in each restricted language many *more* words can be obtained and recorded in the worksheets than have been suggested anywhere by this programme or by the teacher in class through the visual dictations. Words of extremely recent origin or recently in common usage can therefore be generated and used; (for example, pepsi, jet set . . .)

(vii) The signs met up to and including Table 9 do not display the wide range of spellings that are left for the last five tables associated with Primer 3 and the last ten word charts—but they do prepare for the shift by developing an organisation of the sounds and spellings met so far which need only be added to.

(viii) Certain types of spellings for consonants are placed on the same horizontal line on the tables to indicate that similar alterations

[1]See page 117 for an illustration of Table 9 of the Word Building Book.

apply to a number of consonants—for instance, the double-letter signs and those with the 'silent' *e*.

(ix) It reveals that in English almost any letter can be a *silent* one.

3. Although in the study that follows in the next chapter the content of the tables will have to be considerably extended to include all the graphemes of English, the feeling has nevertheless already been well established that in English a large number of signs are used to represent a large number of words. A certain respect for words is shown in meeting them for what they are and as they have developed through time under varied historical influences which cannot be fully known or understood. The feeling is imparted to learners that their language has a unique set of representations, and that by selecting the accepted signs for making particular words they are analysing and synthesising procedures in a way that leads to a better and deeper acquaintance with a living language.

4. Let us now look at the state of mind of learners who have met a number of graphemes for the phonemes introduced up to Table 9, which include practically all those used in English. Since words have always been organised into sentences in this programme, the learners know how their spoken speech can be codified, and have grown familiar with the outline of words through the particular character of each. They have experienced that to read is:

a. to look at signs aligned,

b. to receive from these the signal implicit in each of them,

c. which in turn leads one to produce sounds with a certain melody that when heard resembles speech and delivers a meaning—*its* meaning.

They have found that to write spontaneously what one thinks is:

a. to know and understand a meaning,

b. and let *it* select the words (of speech) for its expression—

c. words whose images appear in the mind as signs arranged in particular orders.

d. This in turn orders the muscles of the hand to transcribe them onto paper, chalkboard, or other surface.

In what has been experienced by the learners, *images* closely knit together, actions (of the organs of phonation, or the muscles of the hand and arm) and *meanings* have been combined to form as strong an association as possible; together they relieve memory and assist in the co-ordination of automatic appearances of words in the two media of uttered and written speech.

Memory having been relieved, the problems of spelling encountered by so many learners are eliminated. Words have 'character'; this lies in their form, and that it has been taken into account is reflected in the respect given to them in recognising the singularity of each word design, as when entering the realm of spoken speech a baby has to recognise that sounds have a character of *their* own, and through this retains them.

The energies of the learners have been used to the best advantage. The pupils have shown at every stage that they can accomplish proportionately more in each analogy they have been left free to do. No repetition has been necessary. No mistakes due to lack of attention have been made, only slips which are recognisable immediately by the mind kept alert by the variety of the exercises and their intrinsic interests. Each stage of progress has increased the already heightened awareness of oneself at work, to the extent that now each learner is ready to forge ahead and complete the task in hand.

The learners are now entitled to receive their Second Certificate of Reading, which indicates that practically all the sounds of English have been encountered, and all the exercises of the language have been met time and again in the successive restricted languages, each broader than the last.

Chapter Three

MEETING OF SPELLINGS

This chapter covers the study of the remainder of the word charts and completes the survey of graphemes used in English as presented in the Word Building Book and Primer 3.

What has been attempted so far, described in the previous chapters, involves what seems to the author to be the deeper aspects of reading and analysis of the spoken language insofar as sounds are concerned. What remains to be treated is simpler and will be covered more easily although the area is much greater than that examined so far. A path of controlled teaching and extensive learning has been closely followed, yet contact with the linguistic aspect of the language has been maintained throughout. In this chapter the field is extended to involve the learner in the language as a means of extending experience as a whole. This is achieved through the Book of Stories.

Following on from what has been learned in working up to this point, linguistic dimensions will develop naturally while oral dictation is considered, and progress will be tested as the new study advances. The freedom given by greater powers and greater means will permit much more of the written language to be covered in less time than hitherto.

The next and final chapter will consider further widening the awareness of what language means and does, both in its details and as it behaves as a whole.

I.
Word Charts 13–21
Visual Dictations 2 and 3

1. A glance at the words on the remaining charts gives an idea of the extent of the ground covered as far as spellings are concerned. Few of the spellings of English are not included. Leaving out

geographical and personal names has made the task manageable. The few words omitted are for the most part to be found in Primer 3, and these and the remainder can be constituted in colour from the signs on the Fidel phonic table. Teachers, whenever the need arises, may put such words on the board (even using coloured chalk in the appropriate colours for the sounds if thought necessary). In so doing they will avoid any delay while the value and flexibility of the materials will in no way be lessened.

2. In Word Charts 13–21 as the occasion arises, each new chart presents different sounds for a single spelling, as well as several different spellings for a number of sounds previously met. Through this type of contrast learners become aware of sets of sounds for one spelling or sets of spellings for one sound. This expands the network of relationships between words which already exists in the pupils' minds—the development of which has been the concern of this programme throughout.

On Word Chart 13 there are several interesting studies:

—five words contain a red *ee*
sounding as *e* in *be*
—three words contain a light aqua
wh as in *when* or *while*, and
three with *wh* coloured pale
blue as in *who* or *whole*[1]
—six words appear involving five
colourings for *ou* indicating five
of its different sounds
—*ng* in *sing* appears olive-coloured as
the *n* in *thanks* and *hungry* on Chart 9

elephant	*physics*	
photograph	*foot*	*be*
see sleep	*feet*	*been*
why where	*when*	
who whom	*whose*	
these between	*you*	
youth our	*your*	*soup*
hour young	*sing*	
house courageous		

Word Chart 13

Other words are included to assist in making sentences with these words and with those already available. Teachers will at once be able to make through Visual Dictation 2 a number of sentences incorporating these new words in association with those of previous charts. Pupils could likewise be given the opportunity to use this chart for their own sentence formation and also to alter some of

[1]In the Mute r Edition *wh* is pale blue over light aqua in *when* or *while*; it is pale blue in *who* or *whole*.

the words on it or on previous charts in order to assist in forming whatever sentences should come to mind. They might derive 'sang' or 'sings' from *sing*, 'yours' from *your*, 'seed' from *see*, and so on.

Here is one of several sentences that could be produced from the words on the charts available up to this point, if mental transformations are included:

> *this youth thinks that he sings well but he sends me to sleep with his songs*

In it 'thinks' comes from *thanks* (Chart 9), 'sings' and 'song' from *sing* (Chart 13) and 'sends' from *send* (Chart 4).

3. Word Chart 14 always proves very useful whatever the group of pupils. Even very slow learners in remedial classes attack the words offered promptly and with enthusiasm.

It is recommended that pupils be led back to the lemon-coloured *I* on Chart 4 in order to re-establish this sound before opening the new chart through *eyes* or *night* which involve the same colour (and therefore the same sound) but with very different spellings. *thigh* may prove difficult to sound but reference back to *thanks* on Word Chart 9 may assist with the first sound. It can also be related to the part of the body.

saturday with the pink ending as in (*fifty*) rather than the sea-green colouring for the ending *ay* (as in *day*) is very often

eyes	day	may
high	thigh	night
they	saturday	
gray	greyhound	
money	honey	prey
prayers	wood	would
should	cool	field
aged	finished	
conceived	conceit	

Word Chart 14

questioned by teachers but it is the sound they themselves make when not stressing the ending (as in 'saturday night')[1].

A number of interesting links can be found in words with *ey* and *ay* endings on this chart.

[1]In the Mute r Edition on the other hand *saturday* appears with the ending sea green as the *ay* in 'day' rather than with the pink colouring of the terminal *y* in 'fifty'. As this represents the sound given to this part of the word by a considerable proportion of the speakers of English sharing the 'Mute r' speech characteristic, it was selected for this edition.

conceived and *conceit* test learners' capacity to attack unusual words. The teacher in some cases may decide to assist in opening these by going back and touching *see*.

To contrast *wood* and *would*, the teacher can dictate a sentence orally to the class making use of these two words, letting one pupil point out the sentence on the charts and show which shape of the word goes with which meaning. The class can be the judge and the teacher the witness. *would*, *should* and *field* may also be contrasted since *l* is mute in the first two of these words.

Of further interest is the ending *ed* which, when this chart is considered in conjunction with the next, can be seen to be treated in a number of different ways. In English, the sign *ed* has sounds that link it with magenta-coloured *t* (as in *finished*) and green *d* (as in *rolled*) and it is coloured accordingly on the word charts. But the *e* can also be associated in sound and colour with the preceding consonant. This occurs in cases where the infinitive form of the verb already ends with a mute *e*, as in the case of *conceived* on this chart, where only *d* is in green; or, similarly, as in a word such as *priced*, but where the *d* alone would be given the magenta colour. *aged* on the chart with the blue[1] *e* is a challenge which can benefit the learners by forcing them to look more carefully. Here this is obviously not the single syllable word (which would have involved three colours only, divided a-ge-d) but a different word where *e* and *d* form a separate syllable together, and where *e* has a separate colour to denote its sounding on its own. For this sign either the blue colour or the bright yellow of the schwa found in unstressed syllables could have been used, the particular colour actually chosen simply reflecting the degree of stress applied to the sign in pronouncing the word.

Interesting examples of all of these ways of sounding *ed* could be collected, since in each category many examples can be found. For instance:

green ed
stabbed, hugged, banned, hummed;
green d
robed, dodged, timed, stored—the *e* being associated with the preceding consonant;

[1]Mute r Edition: bright yellow.

magenta ed
sniffed, hopped, picked, hissed;
magenta d
knifed, hoped, liked, faced;
separate colouring for the sign e
learned (as in 'a learned man'), posted, started, mended.

4. Word Chart 15, likewise rich in signs and links between words, deserves careful study and many examples included in it would repay remembering photographically for their spelling.

The word offering the greatest challenge is, in the experience of the author, *heir*. Learners are mesmerised by the *h*, even though this is not isolated by the use of a separate colour. Several ways of working are possible here, all valid and all useful.

(i) The teacher, saying nothing, may indicate the word with the pointer and keep looking at it while the class repeats the sound for *hair*, until the sheer passage of time suggests a revision of the proposal.

(ii) The teacher may preface the pointing by asking how many colours are used for the word. Receiving the answer 'two' (for the turquoise-coloured *hei* and the dark orange *r*)[1] she may then ask for the number of sounds that can be expected to be heard when the word is read correctly. When 'two' is again offered she asks the pupils to read the word and listen carefully to their own voices to ascertain how many sounds they actually do hear. When all pupils read it as it should be sounded a new task can be begun. But if some do not, the teacher has only to bring their attention back to the need for a two-sound word, which can then be achieved by contrast with the three-sound word they are producing.

stopped	*rolled*	*told*
talk	*walk*	*sigh* *lie*
listen	*lesson*	*push*
fast	*fasten*	*door*
sugar	*sure*	*busy*
business	*heir*	*one*
once	*england*	*lamb*
ocean	*dumb*	*put*

Word Chart 15

(iii) The teacher can touch *there* (Chart 7) asking students to utter the word without the first sound (*th*). Then if *heir* is studied, its two colours indicate almost immediately that the two sounds represented are the same as those just uttered.

[1]In the Mute r Edition the whole word is turquoise-coloured.

(iv) This word may be put into circulation in the class verbally. For instance, the teacher might ask someone, 'Are you your father's heir?' thus stimulating recognition of meaning, or provoking discussion of the word before she asks someone to find it on the chart.

Other features on this chart are:

—the three spellings for the sound of the sky-blue signs in pu*sh*, in *s*ugar and *s*ure, and in o*ce*an

—the two examples of lime-coloured *st* sounding as *s*, in *listen* and *fasten*

—the mute *l* in *talk* and *walk*

—the similar colour sequence in r*olled* and t*old*

—the mute *i* in *business* forming part of the lilac sign *si*; also the pink *u* in both *business* and *busy*

—the mute *b* in *lamb* and *dumb*

—the sound of *o* in *one* and *once*, where it has a combination sound forming a syllable (light aqua over pale yellow).

This chart also provides many new possibilities for sentence formation.

5. Word Chart 16 presents a number of new insights into spellings in a very compact way;

—seven sounds for *ea*, each used in one or more words

—a new dark orange coloured sign *wr* in *write*, contrasted with *r* in *right*

—a new lavender sign *kn* in *knew*, contrasted with *n* in *new*

—a lime *sw* in *sword*, contrasted with the lime *s* and light aqua *w* used in *sworn* to reflect two separate sounds in the beginning of this second word.

write	*right*	*written*
wrong	*sword*	*sworn*
know	*new*	*knew*
knowledge	*knee*	*tea*
news	*great*	*pear*
tear	*pearl*	*tear*
lead	*break*	*lead*
people	*hear*	*here* *their*
ear	*weird*	*heart* *buy*

Word Chart 16

—a rich concentration of signs for comparison and contrast for colour, spelling, and sound, provided in the confined area of this chart by:

lead and *lead*   *lead* and *people*

hear and *here*   *their* and *weird*

tear and *tear*   *know* and *knowledge*

tea and *tear*

There is, as usual, more than one way of effecting an entry into this chart. In fact there are at least four proposals, any of which may be taken first.

—Are spellings to be compared with sounds or sounds with spellings?

—Should written English be marvelled at for giving so many sounds to one spelling or one sound to such a diversity of spellings?

—Should a start be made with *tea* which is short? or with *know*, which has the same colours as the word *no* previously met (Word Chart 9)?

Wherever the start is made, this chart reveals a great deal about the written English language and paves the way for similar encounters in the next three charts where many new and related forms for sounds are introduced together. Making sentences using these words will develop a better acquaintance with each individually. One is:

I will buy new pearls for my earrings, said pam.

It can be seen that many other examples can be added to the sentences given on page 25 of Primer 3.

6. Word Chart 17 introduces one of the few sounds of English still to be met, the cobalt-blue *s* in *measure*. Three words on the chart include this sign. New spellings for sounds already met include:

—ochre-coloured *eau* in *plateau* contrasted with pale green *eau* in *beauty*

—blue *ai* in *said* contrasted with sea green *ai* in *paid*

—many spellings for the brown as shown in w*a*ter, p*au*l, t*augh*t,

measure	*leisure*	
either	*treasure*	
plateau	*beauty*	*paul*
lawn	*because*	*said*
mail	*maintain*	*paid*
doubt	*laugh*	*taught*
bury	*daughter*	*water*
paw	*poor*	*pour*	*pore*
raw	*therefore*	*quiet*

Word Chart 17

p*our*,[1] p*ore*,[1] p*oor*,[1] and p*aw*, among others.

It is interesting to note that there is a distinctive atmosphere of brown about this whole chart—as happened earlier with other colours—due to the concentration of spellings of the sound with which this colour is associated.

7. Word Chart 18, while mainly concerned with spellings, introduces a new double-coloured sign found in two spellings in *boy, buoy, moist* and *oil*. Coloured orange[2] over pink it represents a merging of the vowel sounds of *pot* and *pit* respectively, the colours in the sign being considered vertically and read from top to bottom.

Of special interest on this chart is the play made on signs and sounds in words within lines and between them.

—second line: *sew* and *sow* are both coloured lime-ochre, but *sow* and *sow* are differently coloured, the second being lime followed by purple over light aqua

—third line: *suit* and *suite* are seen to have such different sounds despite their very close spellings; and *suite* and *sweet* on the next line involve identical colour sequences, giving an example of the sign *u* with the sound of the light aqua *w*

flown	*flowers*	*boy*	
sew	*sow*	*sow*	*buoy*
fruit	*suit*	*suite*	
sweet	*moist*	*isle*	
zip	*zoo*	*zero*	*oil*
eight	*eighty*	*height*	
freight	*board*	*bored*	
boar	*soar*	*sore*	*saw*
cloak	*broke*		

Word Chart 18

—sixth line: *eigh* sea-green in *eight* and lemon-coloured in *height* illustrate the different values of this spelling in these example words

—seventh line: *board* and *bored* sound alike and are coloured alike, despite different spellings

—eighth line: *soar* and *sore* are another example of the same phenomenon

Vertically, the proximity of *soar* and *cloak*, *sore* and *broke* adds to the feeling of many that there is little point in formulating rules for

[1]Mute r Edition: p*our*, p*ore*, p*oor*.
[2]In the Mute r Edition this sign is coloured brown over pink, representing a merging of the vowel sounds in *all* and *pit* respectively.

pronunciation and that it is better to fix the images of these words indelibly in the mind when sounding them.

The lower section of this chart contains, like the last, many examples of the brown sign; and in particular the eighth lines on each, when the charts are placed side by side, present a continuous row of similar words for comparison:

paw, poor, pour, pore, boar, soar, sore, saw

8. From the top three lines of Word Chart 19 illustrated below it would seem that the problems presented by the sign *ough* are the principal concern of the chart. But in reality the most significant contribution it has to make is the further illustration of the concept of the cumulative effect of learning.

Here the whole set of sounds associated with one spelling are introduced all at once. Colour plays a decisive role in that its use clearly distinguishes the spellings from each other, showing how different sounds are associated with each. Note that it would be incorrect to classify the first two words as being equivalent in structure to the next five using the letter-group *ough*, because in these two words the group is composed of two signs *ou* and *gh* each with a separate sound and colour. These happen, when printed together in black, to have an appearance indistinguishable from the single-sign *ough* which is used, with various sound values, in the other words.

> tough cough though
>
> thought through bough
>
> examination thorough
>
> anxiety half mix exist
>
> thursday woman true
>
> women wednesday
>
> halves calves loaf
>
> hiccup taxi cramp
>
> loaves borrow swamp

Word Chart 19

—*tough* and *cough* also have different vowel sounds and colours (pale yellow and orange respectively) in the sign *ou* even though they share the same final consonant sound in the mauve-coloured sigh *gh*

—*tough* has three differently coloured signs *t-ou-gh*; but so has *thought*, as indicated by three differently coloured signs *th-ough-t*

The following pairs of words are related by transformation since horizontal equivalence applies in each case:

—*though* leads to *thought* by addition of the final consonant *t*, along with a change in the vowel (ochre to brown) and the change in the sound of sign *th*

—*though* becomes *bough* by simple substitution of the first sign, along with a change in the vowel (ochre to purple over light aqua)

—*though* leads to *through* with insertion of *r*, along with the change of the vowel (ochre to leaf green) and the change in the sound of the *th*

—*through* becomes *thorough* with insertion of *o*, along with a change in the vowel sound in *ough* (from leaf green to bright yellow)

This can be shown schematically as follows:

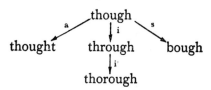

Other aspects of this chart are also of interest and can be noted:

—*hiccup*, which some people misspell 'hiccough' by analogy with 'cough', is included and presents the first example of the spelling *cc* for the sound of the gold

—Three colourings for the different sounds of *x* are given in close proximity to each other in *anxiety* (lilac), *mix* (gold over lime), and *exist* (grey over lilac); a fourth sound for the sign *x* as found in *obnoxious* and *anxious* (gold over sky blue) is not shown here but could be mentioned at this stage by the teacher or developed when these words are met in Primer 3. It does appear on the Fidel phonic table.

—Allocating colours to signs in *half* and *halves*, and *calves*, presented a problem and the ultimate choice could have been different without affecting the result. The colours actually appearing are purple *a*, mauve *lf* and khaki *lve*. Here the letter '*l*' has been associated with the consonants *f* and *ve*, but it could equally well have been combined with the vowel *a* to produce the sign *al* sounding as the *a* in 'raft'.

—*cramp* and *swamp* are placed one above the other to draw attention to their similarity in spelling and to their difference in colouring and pronunciation

—The pairs *half* and *halves, loaf* and *loaves* are included for comparison, *f* in each case being replaced by *ve* on forming the plural

—A striking change of colour is used when *woman*, with a beige-coloured *o*, becomes *women* where this sign is pink (and the same colour as the second vowel in this latter word)

9. Word Charts 20 and 21 can be taken together since these present a large number of words selected simply for the opportunities they provide for illustrating, studying and forming a photographic image in the mind of various spellings of particular sounds.

guard	calm	shoes	pneumatic	cage	scheme
guarantee	scissors		schist	rhythm	jewel
scythe	ghost	adieu	righteous	hallelujah	
service	diaphragm		tissue	amoeba	psalm
hymn	yacht	aisle	azure	bathe	vulture
science	indict	prosaic	trekked	pension	quay
sieve	friend	yield	blithe	clothes	awkward
debt	straight	seize	cube	queue	clique
siege	reservoir	receipt	vision	region	mayor

Word Charts 20 and 21

For example on Word Chart 20:
—The sound of the magenta is represented in four different spellings: ya*cht*, indi*ct*, de*bt* and recei*pt*
—The sound of the tangerine colour is represented in three spellings in ca*l*m, hy*mn*, and diaphra*gm*
—The sound of the lime-colour is given three times as *sc*
—The seventh line gives three sounds for *ie* to be contrasted with *receipt, science*, and *adieu* elsewhere on the chart—and with *lie* (Chart 15)
—The new diphthong of light aqua over purple makes its appearance in reserv*oir*
On Word Chart 21:
—The spelling *sch* is contrasted in *scheme* and *schist*; in the first

word it represents two distinct sounds and in the second a single and quite different sound. *schism* could be introduced here by the teacher as a word in which *sch* (found in the column of lime-coloured signs on the Fidel) again has a single sound only but one different from that found in *schist*.

—In *righteous* and *vulture* the sign *t* (dark magenta) has the same sound as in *question* (Chart 12) and as the *ch* in *chin* and *tch* in *watch*.

Since each word poses its own problems, these two charts provide a good test both of the growth in awareness of the pupils and of their speed of attack on unusual words. These charts also oblige the learners to look closely at the words and to attempt to retain them.

10. To conclude this section on Word Charts 13–21 it must be added that the purpose of the preceding analysis of content is not simply to suggest that the sole function of these charts is to help learners gain a mastery over spellings. If the value of Visual Dictations 2 and 3 is understood it will be clear that, as each new chart joins the rest on display, new sentences become possible using either the vocabulary on the charts or that obtained by the simple mental alterations discussed earlier. Incorporating the new vocabulary in sentence-making increases the range of reading and writing. Visual dictations should become routine uses of the charts even if far less time is taken up in exercises relative to that involved in looking at each of the newly introduced words for its own sake.

It can be stated again that reading is a process by which meaning is derived from a temporal sequence of words and that once the meaning is reached the words used may be forgotten; spelling, on the other hand, is the opposite process by which words are retained in the mind both as unified designs and as structures composed of signs related to sounds—since as structures they can be compared with other words similar or somewhat similar in signs or sounds. Hence there is great importance in having spatial arrangements like those adopted for the word charts, which neither make sentences nor produce any meaning but simply offer a static presentation of words demanding no more than that the eye should attempt to make a photographic image of them to be recalled later. Spelling cannot fail to be good with the problem tackled realistically and once it has been noted that it is not reading that is the process that helps with spelling (except in the case of those who examine each word separately when scanning a sentence to arrive at the meaning).

As each new chart is added, on which more varied words become available, the opportunities steadily increase for making more and more extended and interesting sentences with Visual Dictations 2 and 3.

A remarkable observation here is that so-called slow learners are able to operate with the large expanse of words displayed on the twenty word charts as the pointer darts here and there, touching one word after the other to form sentences that are involved and unexpected. Sentences so made are usually read back to the teacher with the fluency and understanding of ordinary speech immediately the movement of the pointer ceases. This reading is a true extension of the self and shows its value all the time.

II.

WORD BUILDING BOOK, FIDEL AND VISUAL DICTATION 1

1. Though the various instruments provided in Words in Colour are treated separately here, it is to be understood that each complements the rest and any one instrument may prove more useful than the others in overcoming particular difficulties in the case of different individuals.

The tables of the Word Building Book from 10–16 involve in the main additions to the signs in existing columns rather than new columns. Eleven new columns are however added to the thirty-seven[2] on Table 9, but as seven of these are double-coloured diphthongs this constitutes in reality only four completely new sounds.

2. Note that on Table 10 two new consonant columns displace the final *qu* and *x* columns to the right: these are not added on at the end as has happened previously. This change is only an inner convenience, the order of the columns adopted here being in part arbitrary but mostly following the sequence of introduction of new sounds in the word charts.

[2]Mute r Edition: forty columns, of which eight are double-coloured diphthongs.

3. The expansion of the tables of the Word Building Book now becomes more rapid as greater numbers of new signs are introduced at each stage. The effect of cumulative learning is such that large areas of the English language can now be taken in one lesson, where earlier in the programme movement forward was made only step by step. In fact the function of Primer 3 and the last tables of the Word Building Book is to bring learners to the contemplation of the full panorama of English as a language. With each new table of the Word Building Book the vista expands until, on Table 16, an almost complete view is obtained of the components of written English words.

4. The way in which each new table is tackled is not different from that already described in the previous chapter but now attention is concentrated on the increase in the number of spellings in each column.

Whenever a word with a new spelling for a sound appeared on one of the word charts or in Primer 3, the new sign concerned was added to the appropriate table in the Word Building Book. Now, starting from the Word Building Book, one can single out a sign and ask for words that include the sound it represents, using this particular spelling. For pupils to provide a full answer here involves their knowing, or deducing, the spelling of many words often not yet met in print.

For example, the reader might be asked to supply words including the sign *ie* sounding as the lemon-coloured *y* and *my*; or at a more advanced level sounding as the pink *y* in *hymn* (e.g. *die* and *sieve* respectively).

5. Hence there are a number of new exercises that can be played in the classroom.
—The teacher, or any of the pupils, may select one of the new signs added to the table;
    oa and *c* (which in colour would be ochre and gold respectively) can serve as examples here.
—The corresponding sound is then made for it, if it is a vowel:
    'What is the sound for the sign *oa*?'
    '*oa*' (as in *boat*)

a	u	i	e	o	a	I	a	o	a		u	e	o	a	o	oo
	o	y	a	a	u	y		a				oe	e	oo		
	oe			oh	e	i						oa				
	oo				o											

p	t	s	s	m	n	f	f	d	l	th	th	w	k	r	b	h	g	sh	ch	ch	ng	j	qu	x
pp	tt	ss	ss	mm	nn	ff	v	dd	ll				ck	rr	bb		gg	ch	tch		n	g		xe
pe	te	's	's	me	ne	fe	ve	de	le				ke	re	be							dge		
		se	se										ch									d		
													c									ge		
													che									dg		
													lk											

Table 10 of the Word Building Book[1]

—But if it is a consonant a word is chosen incorporating it, and only in this way is it sounded:

'Can you think of a word illustrating the sound of the sign *c*?'

'It sounds as in the word *cat*.'

—The pupils may then suggest other words they know which they suspect involve the signs spelt *oa* and *c* for the sounds under discussion:

goat   moan   load

can   become   act

If correct, these may be added to their log-book of words.

—Should their examples require, on the other hand, some other members of the same column in the Word Building table:

e.g. *note* and *goes* in the case of the sound for *oa*, or *sock* and *skip* in the case of the sound for *c*

it is a simple matter to point this out saying, 'This is the spelling you want', showing *o* and *oe*, *ck* and *k* respectively in these examples in place of the mistaken signs offered. These signs all occur on Table 10.

—But if a word suggested requires for its correct spelling one of the signs still to come:

e.g. *bowl* and *talk* in which *ow* and *lk* must be used

(a) the teacher may inform the pupil that while it will soon be possible to make the word suggested it cannot be done until the

[1]This table can be compared with Table 9, illustrated on page 117.

new sign it involves has been met. She could ask him to bear the word in mind until the sign is introduced.

(b) or the teacher may give the pupil the spelling of the word, showing the sign in question that will eventually make its formal appearance on a subsequent table.

It is now clear that the Word Building Book is concerned with spellings of English words.

6. When Table 16 has been reached the eight charts of the Fidel[1] phonic table can be displayed. This presents in full colour practically the same content as the final table of the Word Building Book. A few signs whose uses are either rare or very specialised are not included, as are not those in words recently derived from another language (e.g. pizza), or words from the speech of a restricted region, or proper nouns (e.g. Lincoln). Each column of signs appears in the particular colour already determined for the sound on the word charts. The various columns are separated by vertical white lines except in the case of the last two vowel sounds which are separated horizontally.[2]

The upper section of the Fidel tableau (Fidel charts 1, 2, 3, 4 in this order) lists the spellings of the vowels, the lower section (Fidel charts 5, 6, 7, 8 in this order) the consonants. The whole includes nearly 300 different signs.[3]

7. When the Fidel is hung up the array of signs is immediately much more challenging to the learner than the development provided by successive tables of the Word Building Book. For now in this first and only analysis of the signs in colour a summary of the entire content of the word charts is presented at once, while in the pro-

[1]The name of this tableau derives from a word used in Amharic, the official language of Ethophia, roughly equivalent in meaning to *syllabary*. It was the Amharic *Fidel* that inspired the grapheme-phoneme analysis of Words in Colour.

[2]In the Mute r Edition the last three vowel sounds and the last three combination consonant sounds of *x* are separated horizontally. Two other combination sound groups are also separated from the other columns by horizontal lines: the 'schwa—l' sign (bright yellow over royal blue) and the pale blue over light aqua *wh*; these are closely related to the 'all blue *l*' and 'all light aqua *w*' respectively and are placed in the lower part of the columns headed by these signs.

[3]Mute r Edition: 400. The Fidel as it appears in both the Standard English Edition and the Mute r Edition is illustrated in colour on a loose card supplied with this text.

gressive stages of the Word Building Book the impact of the full array of spellings was lessened since attention was inevitably drawn to the *new* signs only each time.

Generally teachers wait until reaching Table 16 in the Word Building Book and Word Chart 21 before putting up the Fidel, since a full understanding has then developed gradually for this summary of the phonetics of English. But frequently they find it is helpful with certain groups to bring out the tableau for reference, as soon as most of the sounds of English have been met—even though the remainder of the spellings have still to appear. This would be at a point when they were ready to introduce Word Chart 13[1] and Table 10 in the Word Building Book (for the study focused upon in this chapter).

The Fidel often helps to clarify the work in the Word Building Book since the difference between the two items is mainly in the length of columns, not—after Table 10—in the number of columns. And it can facilitate reference to the unusual spelling occasionally needed for words suggested by pupils but not yet met in the Word Building Book. But beyond this the Fidel serves to give pupils a general sense of what remains to be done before they have met the entirety of English—and it does this at a point when they could not possibly be overwhelmed since they will be, by this stage, confident with practically all the sounds, and will only lack full understanding with regard to certain spellings. Very occasionally a teacher will find that with a particular group she will want for some special reason to have visible from the beginning those charts of the Fidel that contain the colours of the new sounds being introduced.

But on the whole making this complete table available so early in the programme proves either confusing, or distracting from the

[1]When working with remedial cases who could read a little when the programme was initiated, teachers may find that they can introduce Chart 13 within the first two or three lessons. This is so since the main difficulties the pupils encounter, once the natural flow of spoken speech which carries meaning has been re-established through visual dictations from Word Charts 2–12, is with compound words and complex spellings.

If they continue to progress rapidly it is best to take Word Charts 13–21 as quickly as possible and then to return to study these in greater detail in conjunction with the Fidel and Primer 3.

But if they show they need to move at a slower pace in assimilating the new signs on Word Charts 13–21, it can be very helpful to produce the Fidel at this point and work with it and Primer 3 in conjunction with each new word chart introduced.

main work, and so slows progress since the same organisation of sounds met is found in Tables 1–9 in the Word Building Book in a simpler form.[1]

8. It is clear that the first form of visual dictation is the means for generating words and sentences on the Fidel; how the pointer is used in this connection has already been described at length. Visual Dictation 1 in the classroom, long since dropped owing to the increased difficulties of using the chalkboard and coloured chalks as the programme advanced beyond the stage described in Chapter 1,[2] can be taken up again at this point, but now so much more is involved in the exercise. The pointer is best moved first very slowly and only to produce short sentences of this kind:

—it is
—he is old
—is this girl ten

As the pupils grow accustomed to this new test, movement of the pointer should be accelerated in preference to generating longer sentences. This is because if one is slow enough, and the pupils manage to read each word in turn, retaining a great number of words is only a question of memory; acceleration on the other hand demands increases in alertness and concentration. However, becoming very swift in the use of the pointer over such an area is not a simple matter. Teachers will find it helpful to practise first with sentences without complications that lead to hesitations in pointing to the right signs with the right rhythm. When teachers are clumsy in this exercise they reduce the chances of learners successfully using the pointer on the Fidel to produce their own words and sentences, which is the ultimate test revealing mastery over spellings. Is is therefore a requirement of good teaching that teachers do not, in front of their classes, attempt to use the pointer on the Fidel until they are confident of their own reasonable efficiency, and confident that they are not asking too much of their pupils.

---

[1]With some groups, in order to have a reference that can be worked with by the whole class at one time, teachers may want to reproduce the current table in the Word Building Book in black, or in white on the chalkboard and large enough to be used from a distance. For this purpose colour would not be found necessary any more than it is in the Word Building Book.

[2]See page 20 *et seq.*

9. When teachers, with the Fidel before them, have thought of a sequence of sentences, they could produce each word by linking the component signs with the pointer, pausing slightly to symbolise the break after each word, lowering the pointer briefly at the end of each sentence, and finally stopping, facing the class to indicate the conclusion of the dictation and to invite the pupils to say out loud what they have followed with their eyes and read.

Then a pupil may be asked to change places with the teacher and make the same sentence while the class watches. If this is done without mistake another example may be considered in a similar manner. Where a mistake is noted by the class, other pupils can be given the chance to produce the sentence correctly until the right signing has been proposed and has been accepted by the class as a whole. But if no-one notes a mistake made, the teacher can ask the class to read each word aloud after it has been completed by the pupil taking his turn at the Fidel, making it clear that an error has been introduced somewhere. A correct showing by one of the pupils can then be asked for.

10. This can be followed by a session in which pupils make up sentences of their own and either ask one of their fellow students to point out the signs on the Fidel corresponding to those used in the words of their sentences, or go to the Fidel themselves and indicate the spellings they think are used in the words they have thought of.

It is idle to attempt to forecast what any class of pupils may propose. In the writer's experience the beginnings are timid but bold proposals are soon forthcoming.

Pointing at signs on the Fidel is a powerful tool in the dialogue leading to the mastery of spellings.

11. As pupils advance, teachers may become increasingly demanding, moving towards sentences involving what are usually considered difficult words. Pupils well familiar with Visual Dictation I using the pointer and the Fidel tend not to consider words difficult for their spelling but for the number of different signs they contain. In this respect *taught* may be simpler than *stops*: 'taught' requires only three pointings, twice at *t* and once at *augh*; 'stops' requires five, of which two are at the same sign *s*. Likewise *daughter* may

prove easier than *sister*, and *thorough* easier than *strike* or *children*, and so on.

12. Naturally such well-established games as the Game of Transformations played already can be included here as a further application of the Fidel, or it may serve in an exercise in which a form of verbal 'flash card' is used. The teacher or any pupil may say just one word and members of the class volunteer to point out its component signs from among the coloured columns. In this game it is advisable to allow time for pupils, with their eyes closed, to call to mind the shape of the word and its sound components before asking for it to be compounded from the Fidel. This reinforces the photographic use of the mind for spelling, as well as the scanning of words (which takes place in time) required for reading.

The transformations that change one word into another can be further highlighted by work on the Fidel. The teacher initiates, through oral dictation, sequences of words that require either a transformation in sound or in spelling from the one preceding. Each transformation is then effected by a student volunteer and accepted or corrected by the class.

If the spelling changes, but not the sound

so, sew and *sow*

then the teacher may need also to comment on the meaning of the word she is asking for in order to indicate to the pupil which spelling should be chosen.

All the beginning sequences that follow are examples of what can serve as entries into longer sequences:

so, sew, sow, sow, bow, bough, beau, bow . . .
tot, taught, taut, tote . . .

eight, rate, strait, straight . . .
weight, wait, hate, height, sight, site, mite,
might, fight, light, like, lake, bake, take, tale, tail,
sail, sale, male, mail, fail, pail, pale . . .

judge, fudge, budge, badge . . .
edge, ledge, pledge . . .
gem, gym, jim, jam, jamb, lamb, damp, dump . . .
in, sin, sing, sink, slink . . .

song, sung, sang, sad, sand, stand . . .[1]

These games further challenge the capacity of the pupils to evoke spellings; they also focus their attention on the structures of single words and the meanings of single words structurally related to them which are far beyond the scope of the word charts.

Since the goal is a retention as permanent and as early as possible, such games can be played seriously and with steadily increasing difficulty. But they should be abandoned at the point when the new challenges are not sufficient to avoid boredom.

13. If these word games are alternated with a game where the pupils are asked to use, in a sentence given by oral dictation, one, two or three of the words whose spellings have been compared, a new dimension is given to their power. When sentences such as the following can be completed by the class using the Fidel and the pointer, teachers will feel that these exercises are proving their worth, demonstrating the pupils' mastery over spelling in addition to other qualities they have acquired:

—the steamboat entered the straits straight after leaving the harbour

—the fisherman taught the stranger how to keep his line taut

—the cartwrights will write a letter right now about the tribal rites

14. The Fidel may usefully be left on display on the classroom wall after the word charts have been studied and taken down for storage for the following year's class. Its multivalence is obvious. Among other things, with its generous dimensions and unambiguous coding allowing cross references to be so readily made, it can serve far more simply as a phonetic analysis than the international phonetic alphabet does using diacritical markings. In addition, and once its

---

[1]With remedial classes having intensive courses and perhaps a certain fragmented understanding of spelling from their previous experience, such games initiated by the teacher are more welcomed and needed than in the first grade class where the pace is a little slower and a great deal of discovery of words, sentences and stories is done by the pupils on their own in their free time every day.

use is understood, students referring to it can do so even from a considerable distance, simply by lifting their eyes.[1]

15. A number of other exercises or games can now be played using the Fidel, of which the following are only examples:

(i) Looking at any one column, pupils can attempt to put down in a given time (say five minutes) at least one word exemplifying each of the spellings in that column.

(ii) In a given time (say ten minutes) the pupils can put down as many words as they can think of having a certain spelling for one sound.

(iii) In a given time pupils can supply as many examples as possible for all the spellings found in each column.

(iv) In a given time pupils can take one spelling and see how many words they can find in which this one spelling sounds differently each time.

(v) Without setting a time limit the teacher challenges the class to form sentences with words that contain as many spellings in one column as they can find examples for and use. A resulting sentence is considered more skilful the fewer words it uses that do not involve one of the signs in question, and the less it becomes stilted or meaning-less. In this respect

—he had s*ou*p, gl*u*cose and fr*ui*t for the rh*eu*matism he got thr*ough* l*o*sing the sh*oes* he thr*ew* in the t*wo* bl*ue* p*oo*ls

containing all the leaf green signs on Fidel Chart 4 may be considered less skilful than

—dr*ea*ming p*eo*ple bel*ie*ve s*ee*ing k*ey* pol*i*ceman rec*ei*ving qu*ay*side am*oe*bas s*e*cretly an*ae*sthetised

which in making a sentence with all the red signs on Fidel Chart 3 uses no extraneous words; but it is more skilful in that it is somewhat less contrived.

---

[1]Some schools are using their word charts—no longer needed in a first grade—for study of the language, or for providing remedial instruction in the upper grades where children did not have Words in Colour in the primary grades. In this situation, for each upper-grade classroom a Fidel needs be obtained—but only this—since the school's original copy of the Fidel is still necessary in the first-grade classroom for constant reference and deeper study of the language.

(vi) Without setting a time limit, the teacher can present the converse challenge to form sentences using examples of signs with one spelling having as many different sounds as possible. Two examples are:

> great mean overbearing earls fear heaven heartily

and

> this woman is one of the women who worked for only a month[1]

(vii) The class may try to see how many pairs or triplets of words they can find that

- *a.* sound alike but are spelled differently and have different meanings (homonyms: write, right; no, know, etc.)
- *b.* are spelled alike but sound differently (homographs: *wind* that blows, *wind* a clock; the metal *lead*, *lead* a dog, etc.)

16. In conclusion it may be stated that proper techniques for enhancing the facility to associate correct spellings with sounds have been developed and that if care is taken to employ these techniques from the start as part of the programme followed, most grades will acquire the desired expertise as one consequence of the many activities with words that are involved in *Words in Colour*. For older learners the result will be swifter, being obtained in a matter of hours.

III.
ORAL DICTATION

1. This short section will be concerned with one aspect of dictation, which can be called *oral dictation* to indicate that it depends on sound rather than on the use of the pointer in visual dictation, which is carried out silently and requires sight.

2. Anyone who has codified his own speech will recognise that the signs met so far correspond to sounds. Anyone who has succeeded in reading by visual dictation knows that every word has one

---

[1]Examples in accordance with the Mute r Edition analysis are:
> pouring soup out dangerously could encourage coughing

and
> mutton often worries women who once told wolf stories

aspect that is part of his spoken language and another that is part of his written language.

If anything has been achieved for the pupils, they will now be able to hear sounds as they always have done and at the same time evoke the correct images belonging to written speech. Testing this new skill is the purpose of oral dictation, and may also prove a useful training should the pupil later attempt to earn a living as a stenographer or secretary.

3. It has already been suggested that during the earliest exercise with oral dictation the word charts may be left in front of the pupils for reference. Later this support may be withdrawn, and later still any help the pupils may have derived from the Fidel can be eliminated by the removal of this item, since the real test of retention is that all this remains part of one's imagery and can be easily re-evoked when needed.

In oral dictation the teacher utters a sentence in a clear natural voice so that its meaning as a whole is conveyed with its clues of speed, pitch and intonation which are part of the synthetic experience of hearing speech. The learner then can use this meaning—registered in his mind—to provide the key enabling the flow of sound to be separated into words and put down in writing. But unless an image of a word is generated in the mind it will not be possible to reproduce it in a written form. Oral dictation, which calls upon the ability of pupils to evoke immediately, and in the correct spatial order, the signs for sounds uttered, is therefore the test of mastery over spelling via the understanding of words spoken by the teacher.

Teachers should say a thing once only but they must act responsibly in what they say and how they say it. This will stimulate responsibility on the part of the learners who will listen carefully, extract the meaning from the intonation and the words used and put down in a responsible way what they think they heard in the most appropriate transcription from sound to sign available to them.

It is not intended to count errors and award marks in this activity; indeed, if the programme is being correctly followed, oral dictation is the *last* stage of the apprenticeship in each restricted language. Since so many exercises have created imagery in the mind, few mistakes will be made; and those made will provide positive indications of what remains to be more fully mastered.

Looking at the final product will reveal to the teacher a great deal more than a mere total of errors made and the distance remaining to be covered on the way to perfection, which is usually all that is found out from marking. In particular, mistakes are now symptoms of a deliberate reflection on the part of the writer, not of haphazard responses. Bearing this in mind, teachers will treat errors as indicating what exercises remain to be gone through so that inner criteria may be induced to function properly to provide correct images.

Far fewer errors than may be expected will be produced by learners treated consciously in accordance with the proposals made so far. Whenever they do not know how to spell something, they are conscious of it; but they do know that certain probabilities exist favouring various signs as the correct version and that a choice has to be made between them. Certainty has not yet been reached allowing an automatic correct response to be forthcoming. Automatic and correct responses are equivalent to a proper functioning of inner criteria.

4. Oral dictation is used as an exercise for blending a number of mental activities together which produce, in a mysterious way, a better spelling ability. Blended in it are:

—The power to listen with understanding

—The power to visualise written forms corresponding to sounds heard

—The power to put down a sequence of marks on paper that can be deciphered by someone other than the writer, and that satisfy criteria that are not merely individual but which correspond to what was said while following the rules of the language.

5. Oral dictation is a mental transmutation of visual dictation. If visual dictation has been carried out carefully earlier, oral dictation will not present any difficulty. Should oral dictation present obstacles, these are best tackled not through more oral dictation but by strengthening the pupil's ability to cope with visual dictation and thereby creating a frame of reference for use with oral dictation. If an individual is able to visualise words or do an equivalent mental operation, then writing under dictation is not essentially

different from spontaneous writing. The difference may lie only in one's ability to write as rapidly as someone else speaks.

6. Because some of the usual obstacles to oral dictation have been overcome through *Words in Colour*, speed of writing increases following certain exercises that can be undertaken much earlier than is customary. Oral dictation can then become as rapid as that given in regular stenography courses.

The ability to write rapidly is not closely related to the ability to read rapidly since the first requires the use of muscles that customarily do not move as rapidly as the eyes when scanning the page. Oral dictation is one of the ways by which one can acquire speed of writing, so long as it is done deliberately and without tensions.

IV.
PRIMER 3 AND THE WORKSHEETS

1. While it has been assumed that the study of Word Charts 13–21 has been proceeding hand in hand with Primer 3, this third text in the reading scheme has not yet been considered nor the worksheets associated with it. A further text, the 'Book of Stories', will be reviewed briefly at the end of this section but more fully in the next when the two final worksheets accompanying the stories are studied.

2. The presentation of Primer 3 is as in the previous volumes, the only differences being:

(i) The use of a smaller type. As the technique of reading a text has by this stage been mastered, size is no longer an important factor since the learners understand what is required of them and their eyes are capable of readily discriminating between the now familiar letter shapes.

(ii) The restriction on sentence length, where these had been kept short for the ease of learners, is abandoned. Now sentences become as long as is necessary adequately to convey the thought concerned.

(iii) On the left hand page of every new section many or all of the several spellings for one sound, or the several sounds associated with one spelling, are given together, a feature hardly seen at all in the previous volumes.

(iv) When all the spellings of written English have been met and the complete Fidel phonic table has been displayed, two usual elements of printed matter are introduced: capitals and punctuation. This is done at the end of Primer 3 in the only piece of continuous writing contained in the book: a letter from a girl to her father.[1]

Roman type as found in conventionally printed texts is also introduced in this passage, as well as in Story 36 in the Book of Stories which is read after Primer 3 has been completed.

These conventions of reading are brought in at this stage to satisfy those who are more concerned that the letter rather than the spirit of the law with regard to reading teaching be properly observed. But the spirit is also observed in full in that the traditional use of the written word is ultimately reached.

In Primer 3 from page 2 to page 35 inclusive the new signs appear at the top of the left hand page in each section with a selection of examples of words incorporating these signs below; opposite, the use of these words is illustrated in sentences. All spellings sharing a single sound, with the exception of the signs on page 2[2], are arranged in one column. Conversely, where the same sign appears a number of times in different columns at the top of the left hand page it must be assumed that there are that many different sounds associated with this sign.

3. It becomes clear on leafing through the pages of this text that its study is only meaningful when each new section is introduced *after* the word chart or charts related to it have been met in class. Visual Dictation 2 will provide sentences similar to those appearing on the right hand pages. This aspect of the work has already been covered in relation to Primer 2 in Chapter Two and does not need repeating here. But since in Section 1 of this chapter Visual Dictation 2 was only mentioned briefly, it can be added that teachers will find in the pages of Primer 3 plentiful examples to guide them in their choice of sentences that can be constructed as each new word chart is introduced and added to the previous

[1]Illustrated on page 192.
[2]This does not apply to the Mute r Edition of Words in Colour.

charts on display. After a selection of sentences has been visually dictated with the pointer on the charts and worked out in class, pupils can be asked to study the corresponding pages in Primer 3.

4. The five worksheets 8–12 are designed to complement the use of the word charts, the Word Building Book and Primer 3. With the exception of page 3, which still enquires about the meaning of some words, these new worksheets take pupils deeper into their awareness of the sounds and spellings of English. They provide new games calling on different qualities of the mind from those exercised so far.

Page 1

WORDS IN COLOUR   *Worksheet No. 8*

© C. GATTEGNO, 1962 Pilot Edition 1962. First Standard English Edition 1965.

1. A number of signs in the following words have the same sound. Show which they are by marking them in the same way.

	(i) judge	*(ii)* done	*(iii)* walk
	general	blood	fall
	soldier	does	bald
	page	up	smoke
	giant	young	smile

How many are correctly marked?......................................

Page 1 of Worksheet 8

On page 1 of each of these five worksheets the same question is asked, but about three different sets of words. These sets of words present, in black and white, either the same spellings for different sounds or different spellings for the same sound. The learner is asked to identify like-sounding signs.

Such an exercise is a test for the third phase of the programme when varied spellings are met, and should be used for this purpose.

Considerable freedom in the manner of answering the test is left to the pupils. Within some of the sets of words chosen there is occasionally more than one relating factor, a feature which represents a departure from the strict stimulus-response type of test used earlier, trust now being placed in the initiative of the learners.

Indeed this is the value of such tests in this programme. Since multivalence and autonomy of learning are cultivated from the beginning, attempts must be made to develop these aptitudes through the exercises that are offered either for practice or for testing the work done.

5. On page 2 of the worksheets pairs of words are given in which certain signs or sequences of letters are underlined. Reflection is required before one can decide as asked whether such spellings, different or identical, correspond to different or identical sounds.

Page 2

2. Can you say whether the sounds one must make for the signs underlined in the following pairs of words are the same (*s*) or different (*d*)?

john	food	singer	real	wood
joan	flood	finger	false	cool

s, d   *s, d*   *s, d*   *s, d*   *s, d*

How many are the same?............................

How many are different?............................   How many are correctly marked?............................

Page 2 of Worksheet 8

One has to know the particular sounds to produce in response to seeing each printed word concerned and, in listening to one's voice, be able to discern whether like sounds occur in each member of the pair spoken with respect to their underlined portions.

This test is, therefore, one of recognition of the ambiguities encountered in written English; in other words, it is a test of spelling. Together these five worksheets provide a good coverage of the power that, once acquired, makes someone proficient at spelling.

It is advisable for teachers to wait until Worksheet 12 has been completed before they conclude that any particular individual is not able to spell. It is most likely that pupils returning to the word charts or to pages of Primer 3 will establish the criteria necessary for a decision to be made to categorise the sounds as the same (s) or different (d) in a pair under consideration.

There are four possibilities to this game played with written words:

—spellings of signs may be the same, with sounds for them different or the same

—spellings of signs may be different, with the sounds for them different or the same

And the game can be played orally. Four possibilities are also open with pairs of words spoken aloud for consideration as to the *spelling* of particular elements in them:

—Like sounds can be spelt: alike
                                    or unalike

—Unlike sounds can be spelt: alike
                                    or unalike

The table below shows various pairs of words illustrating all four different pairings possible in the game played either visually or orally, with results for each version tabulated. In two of the pairs the results are the same in both forms of the game, in the other two they are not.

		Results	
		Visual game	Oral game
pairs		sound	spelling
pat	cat	s	s
pat	what	d	s
pot	what	s	d
pot	cat	d	d

Scoring full marks is not hard. Further evidence from a number of classes playing this game will establish whether it is helping the development of an awareness of the relation of sound to sign.

6. On pages 4, 5 and 6 of Worksheet 8 there are examples of exercises with signs having two or more sounds.

Page 4

4. Draw a line under all *s* signs that sound as in *is* and one above all those that sound as in *us*.

sings	pets	dolls	birds
sits	things	dad's	pups
binds	winds	tops	months
roses	losses	lessons	lions

How many sound as in *is*?............................

How many sound as in *us*?............................   How many are correctly marked?............................

Page 4 of Worksheet 8

On each of the three pages sixteen words are given and in each of the words a particular sign occurs. The pupils are required to decide, on listening to the sound of their own voices reading the words aloud, which of these signs sound alike and which do not. They are asked to indicate their decision by marking like sounds consistently in one way and unlike sounds differently. Anyone familiar with the words chosen and who can listen to his own voice will score one hundred per cent success, but with learners this very simple game is found to present a range of problems.

Correcting work can be carried out in a number of ways, of which the following could be one sequence:

(i) The teacher may first ask the pupils who state that they have gone through pages 4, 5 and 6 to form pairs. She then asks, in turn, one member of each pair to give his answer, and the other whether he accepts or rejects it. Should the pupils agree that the work was done properly, or even if they should entertain certain doubts,

(ii) the teacher could form a group, of which she may herself be a part, to listen to the sounds made by individual pupils each in turn reading a word from the list and waiting for the group to respond with its judgment. This procedure relieves the teacher from having to be the sole and final arbiter and gives the pupils an opportunity to develop the criteria that enable one to be sure of one's answers.

7. Alternative ways of playing such games are found on page 4 of Worksheets 9-12. Pupils are asked to rewrite words from given selections, grouping together those in which the same sound occurs, whether or not the corresponding signs are spelt the same. The form the game takes is altered slightly from one worksheet to the next in order to indicate that there are a number of ways of presenting the

---

Page 4

4. Rewrite in groups the words in the following list in which you think the sign *ou* sounds the same.

tough	trough	troupe	courage	mouse	hour	your
trouble	loud	cough	soul	group	four	double

How many groups have you found?.................................

Page 4 of Worksheet 9

rules. Nevertheless, all the variations of the game serve the one purpose of making pupils aware that in English each word learnt must be known for itself—known 'personally' as it were. This intimacy with words creates fondness for their 'personality' and prevents resentment and impatience from developing in face of the multiplicity of spellings. Playing such games will also naturally yield evidence that words are accurately known.

On pages 5 and 6 of Worksheets 9–12 many of the more difficult spellings have been collected together. After working on the word charts in class, followed immediately with reading the pages of words and sentences in Primer 3, pupils will find these exercises helpful with the words that usually present most of the spelling problems. It is expected that the variety of ways of working as well as the gamelike nature of the activity involved will remove the doubts that cause spelling difficulties. Since at any given stage the worksheets are the last of the various materials to be worked on by the pupils they will test just this.

---

5. Write down in groups the words in the following lists whose underlined signs you think sound the same.

(i) mauve   laugh   maul   laughing   paul   overhaul

(ii)· trial   carriage   marriage   pliable

(iii) friend   lie   field   relief   pie

(iv) field   would   could   shield   should

How many groups have you found?   (i)..

(ii)..

(iii)..

(iv)..

Page 5 of Worksheet 9

6. Put a line below the signs *ed* that sound as in *finished* and one above them if they sound as in *rolled*.

wedded	married	stopped	backed
rented	hired	linked	salted
punched	robbed	cluttered	polished
stoned	priced	pegged	stroked

How many sound as in *finished*?.............................

How many sound as in *rolled*?............................. How many are correctly marked?.............................

Page 6 of Worksheet 9

8. On page 7 of these worksheets there is a Visual Dictation 2 exercise in black and white. The words chosen are short and simple, the emphasis having now shifted from spelling to the education of inventiveness. What is involved here is to convey the understanding that words are 'multivalent units' that can be used in a variety of different sentences having very different meanings. At the same time, pupils learn

—that sentences have structures;

—that the position of words in sentences is not arbitrary;

—that clauses may be linked together to form longer sentences;

—that meaning can be conveyed by different means—i.e. with fewer or more words.

Page 8 takes the challenge one stage further. Here pupils are asked first to choose twenty-five words from among those already met on the word charts and in their primers and to make sentences with them.

7. Make sentences out of some of these words. You may use the *s* to make plurals.

we	to	a	fat	stop	house	do	he	's
is	late	not	has	at	thin	as		
salt	man	his	does	go	little	s		
and	it	dog	she	tom	left	have		

How many have you made?......................................

Page 7 of Worksheet 8

The first part of the exercise brings out the capacity of pupils to discriminate between

a. words that are highly specialised and those that are common;

b. words that are compatible and those that are mutually exclusive.

The second part is similar to the exercise on page 7. But since the responsibility for the choice of the words is left to the learners the outcome of the combinations may be very different indeed in the worksheets of different pupils. It may happen that because of a particular choice of words not a single sentence can be formed. Such an occurrence will sharpen the pupil's awareness of the function of words in sentences and will pave the way for the study of sentence structure and grammar that is to follow.

9. The next two pages, 9 and 10, in the five Worksheets 8—12 relate the work done on words to the final tables of the Word

8. Choose 25 words from anywhere in your Books 1, 2, and up to page 9 of Book 3 and write them here.

Now make sentences out of some of these words.

How many have you made?..................................

Page 8 of Worksheet 8

Building Book. Since the programme is still concerned with the study of spelling, questions are asked that relate the signs that form words to the sounds they are supposed to convey. But the questions are really about a comparison of two tables of signs (i.e. the signs the pupils have met and known, and the signs as presented in the table of the Word Building Book in question, and in the exercise on page 10). Yet another ability is therefore required and the extent to which this has been developed is revealed in the answers given to the exercises on these two pages of the worksheets. So again the worksheets test ability and knowledge.

The main difference between pages 9 and 10 is obvious. On page 9 it is left completely open to the pupils to see which signs are new and which they have already studied. On page 10 signs to be considered are to be found in the words presented, and unless these words are known it may be very difficult to 'disentangle' the signs from each other. This is why allowance is made for pupils' not knowing some of the words.

179

9. In your Word Building Book Chart No. 12 you see new signs; some may correspond to new sounds and some to sounds you already know. Write down those that correspond

(i) to a new sound

(ii) to a sound you already know

How many new signs have you written down?

(i)............................ (ii)............................

Page 9 of Worksheet 8

10. Up to page 10 of the worksheets the study of words and sentences that has been followed from the beginning has been adhered to. The importance of listening, of watching and of making images of words has been stressed, and as a result more conscious spellers will be formed and people more aware of words.

Although this is a valuable contribution to education, there are further aspects of communication through words which make demands on other qualities of the mind. It is to exercises developing or testing these qualities that the last six pages of the five Worksheets 8–12 are devoted.

11. Page 11 of the Worksheet 8 presents a twelve-word sentence; the corresponding sentence in Worksheet 12 has twenty-nine words. In each case pupils are first asked to reduce the number of words in the sentence but without altering its meaning. There may be several solutions and pupils are encouraged to offer as many of these as possible.

10. Which of these words use any of the signs introduced in Word Building Book Chart No. 12? When you think they do, draw a line under each word that does use one of the signs and a line over each word that does not.

If you do not know put a cross near them.

often	should	apostrophe
could	calf	ark
tomorrow	few	beer
rough	near	taxi

How many lines under?..

How many lines over?..

How many crosses?.. How many have you marked correctly?..

Page 10 of Worksheet 8

In the second part of the exercise new sentences are to be formed, involving changes in position of the words and hence of the meaning of the sentences produced, but the words themselves may not be changed.

In this play on the two variables of *means* and *meaning*, stress is placed on accuracy, economy of words, and adequacy of expression; and from this stage of learning pupils are made aware of style insofar as it is the outcome of choosing a small number of words or many adjectives.

12. In the exercise on page 12, Visual Dictation 3 is in effect introduced. The elements now to be combined are sentences. The six sentences provided do not form part of the same story if read in just any order. But if some are omitted and the order of others changed, something new appears: an overall meaning emerges from the sentences where each contributes more than the meaning it has when considered alone.

11. Can you write the following sentence leaving out some words without changing the meaning?

the large black cat jumped into the narrow road behind the shop

Write your sentences here.

Now use the words to form new sentences with different meanings.

How many answers have you got?..

Page 11 of Worksheet 8

Through this exercise it is possible to discover something more about 'words in time'. Time is needed not only for words to be uttered, and again for the meaning that is the outcome of a sequence of words to be conveyed, it can also make something be felt that neither each word nor each sentence can by itself provide. This cumulative meaning, which is already well known as an attribute of speech, is now a special awareness that can be considered and worked on with regard to the written word.

13. On page 13 the study is of whether word sequences make sense or not. Words can naturally be said one after the other, but the sequence thus formed can

—evoke a reality
—be in agreement with one's experience, or contradict it
—evoke puzzlement
—evoke rejection.

12. Which of the following sentences can go together and be part of the same story if read one after the other?

    1. dad's toes are large

    2. most of us like fresh water

    3. the path was hard and he got tired

    4. the well is full after the storm

    5. we can drink now

    6. his shoes hurt his left foot more than his right

Which goes with which? ....

(Give the number of the ....

      sentences) ....

How many different stories have you made?......................

Page 12 of Worksheet 8

The question: 'Which of the following sentences make sense and which do not?' is asked in such a way as to allow development by teachers. For while knowledge is wanted of whether the pupil's reaction to each sentence is indicated in any one of the categories above, all that is asked is whether the sentences make sense or not. Of course, *her finger was looking* (Worksheet 8) could be construed as making sense by someone whose imagination is wild, but for others it could not. This lesson therefore cannot satisfactorily end with the simple 'yes' or 'no' answer requested. Some elaboration is required.

The lesson could begin with one pupil writing down a sentence he has thought of. Then one word in it could be replaced by another, to generate contradiction, puzzlement, or rejection as nonsense.

Suppose a pupil wrote:

The snail moves slowly

The teacher could replace 'moves' with 'springs' or 'jumps'. Puzzlement is the reaction of those who have never seen a snail do anything

13. Which of the following sentences make sense and which do not?

1.	he was falling walking	yes	no
2.	her finger was looking	yes	no
3.	the ink bottle was full of blood	yes	no
4.	the soldier told the general off	yes	no
5.	strong hooks are made of soft wood	yes	no
6.	the singer rings the bell	yes	no

Where necessary, alter the sentences above so that they all make sense.

How many have you altered?.............................

Page 13 of Worksheet 8

other than crawl; but to those who know nothing about snails the idea now conveyed may still be regarded as a possibility. Or if, instead of altering 'moves', the teacher had replaced 'snail' with, for example, 'satellite', then those who know that for a satellite to remain in orbit speeds which on earth are considered very great must be maintained, will normally find the statement absurd, or at best true only if qualified by certain other statements.

On the other hand 'the *statue* moves slowly' could generate a feeling of awe, or stimulate the imagination in various ways, while 'the snail moves *bulldozers*' might rouse a feeling of disbelief and even an assertion as to its impossibility resulting from a simple comparison of sizes. When the question: 'Does this statement make sense?' is asked and the answer 'no' is marked beside the sentence to which it refers, this fuller treatment can be regarded as providing a sufficient answer.

Any number of such statements can be looked at in this manner until the class realises that there are very few cases in which the whole of one's mind or all minds together would choose to classify a statement as nonsense.

What has been acquired here is the experience that words as a *medium* of communication are not the message, while feelings, for instance, are both medium and message for each individual. Thus one may be sad and know it, and yet still say 'I am gay'. This important attribute of words, which is little pondered on by their users, will be best recognised in the statement of the French diplomat Talleyrand: 'Words have been given us so that we disguise our thoughts'.

It does not seem too early to introduce this property of words at this stage in the learners' development, when learners are once again becoming aware of words and their behaviour, as they did earlier in learning to talk.

Truth is to be known beyond words, from the message words convey or fail to convey. That one can know oneself as capable

—of reaching truth directly and knowing it through inner criteria

—of testing whether or not the medium used carries it

is without a doubt a happening whose implications should be seriously considered by all.

14. The exercise on page 14 tests yet another power of the mind. Here the pupil is guided by an arbitrary selection of words, being asked to produce a story of up to a certain length incorporating them. What is left variable is the sort of images the words are to evoke and how these are to be framed in statements that are linked together in sufficiently clear a fashion as to suggest to readers that one has conceived of a coherent whole in which the words occur.

For example, in Worksheet 8 where the words are he, sun, wet, not, hot, with, was, in, after, a child might write:

> I went to the lake *with* Tom.
> The *sun was* very *hot*.
> *After* swimming I went *in* as I *was* too *wet*.
> But Tom *was not* very wet so he stayed outside.

This type of writing both assists and challenges writers. The assistance is found in the fact that pupils are not left with nothing to start them off or nothing to stimulate them. But there is also a con-

14. Write a story of up to four sentences that includes the following words:

| he | sun | wet | not | hot | with | was | in | after |

Can you write other stories of up to four sentences which include all the above words?

How many stories have you written?.................................

Page 14 of Worksheet 8

siderable challenge in meeting the requirements in four sentences or fewer. Whenever teachers find that their pupils would prefer to write more than four sentences they should allow them (once they are satisfied that they have produced a story of some kind) to alter the word 'four' to any number they wish.

One day, perhaps returning to the challenge, a pupil may wish to meet it as proposed. The number four is only there as it seems reasonable to require this much from writers of this age. But such opinion may have to be revised in the light of experience.

Pupils will provide a variety of solutions. These could be collected by the teacher and kept for use in stimulating their own ability to follow the challenge presented by such opportunities.

15. Now that the emphasis has shifted from reading to writing, and that pupils have been made more aware of their own creative powers in the use of words both as tools to express themselves and to guide their imagination, a look can be taken at the writing of others and its

relation to one's own achievements. This is begun on pages 15 and 16 of Worksheets 8–12 through a study of certain stories in the Book of Stories, and is taken much further in the whole of the remaining two worksheets, which are considered in detail in the next section of this chapter.

It will be found that the texts referred to in the Book of Stories contain words not yet met. Thus the stories help to increase one's vocabulary. But a text should not be looked at only for what is felt to be lacking in one's experience. What is understood is as important and as good a measure of one's actual state, since the sets of words *understood* and *not yet mastered* are complementary.

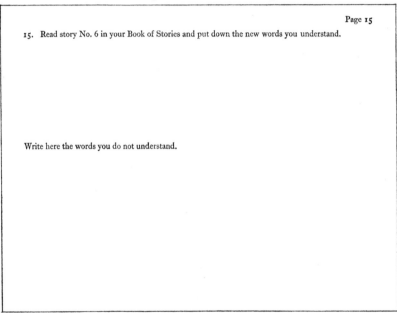

Page 15 of Worksheet 8

Very often the meaning of an unknown word can be deduced from the meaning of the whole, or context of the passage. This technique, which everyone has the right to employ, should be made clear from the start since it has in fact been used from the beginning of life in making speech a possibility.

On page 15 of the worksheets one of the stories in the Book of Stories is referred to. Pupils are asked first to write down the words they understand and secondly those they do not, the words concerned in each case clearly being 'new' words met in the story. On page 16 the pupils are invited to carry the story on, writing further sentences of their own. In this second exercise their acquired writing skill is related to the writing of others in yet another way. Each story in the Book of Stories already has a final paragraph. The form existing endings such as these take is the privilege of an author but the choice made is in a sense an arbitrary one open to examination. The stories to be studied are part of the programme as

---

Page 16

16. Write out more sentences to add to story number 6.

How many have you written?.................................

Now add up your scores. This is your total score for Worksheet No. 8.

Date

Published by Educational Explorers Limited, Reading, England.
Printed in England by Lamport Gilbert & Co. Ltd., Gun St., Reading, Berks., England.

Page 16 of Worksheet 8

---

a whole and were so written originally as to lend themselves to being continued in the manner suggested in the exercise. In extending the stories on their own, the pupils are encouraged to see the future as being as open as it really is, and may at the same time note how their imagination is variously stirred by their involvement in an event or by their relating of an event.

As the stories incorporate references to various aspects of life it may be hoped that diverse sensitivities of the pupils will be struck resulting in a wide range of answers revealing to the teacher more about the creative potential of children.

16. In this fourth section of this chapter the worksheets have been discussed in greater detail than Primer 3 which also forms part of the present study. The main difference between the primer and the worksheets is that the first is a complete unit intended to take pupils stage by stage through a programme of work, while the others, as open books, are to be tackled at different stages of maturation as the work proceeds and as insights in oneself and in the language increase. The primer can be completed but work on the worksheets may always be resumed. And the book, which is a test of the scheme as a whole and of its soundness as a teaching medium, relates in its contents more to teachers and to the language than do the worksheets, which test rather the extent to which the pupils' powers have been taken into account.

The last pages of Primer 3 can be seen to be different from all that has gone before so far. Here is stated what has been achieved by the programme and for the learners, not what the learners have actually achieved. Pages 36 and 37 of Primer 3 are reproduced below:

—we can now read almost all words of the english language

—many of them are not easy to spell because each sound may have so many forms and each form so many sounds

—we have met about three hundred and thirty forms for forty-nine sounds

—we can imagine the colour for each special sound whatever the form, as we have met each sound associated with one colour all along in our work with the charts

—in our word building book we have found how to put together the various forms that make one sound; we separated the vowels (which have sounds of their own) and the other signs that form syllables with the vowels. these last signs we call consonants because they need vowels to form sounds

—we found twenty-one sounds for the vowels and about one hundred and seventy forms for these vowels differing in shape or colour

36

—we found about one hundred and sixty consonants and twenty-eight sound groups among them

—the english language which we speak makes use of all the signs that we have found in these books, in the charts and in the word building book

—to write the english language as we should, we must practice reading aloud to see if we can give the right sound to the various shapes we look at

—the better we can do that the easier it will be for us when we want to write what we are thinking about

—the second visual dictation game we played showed us how many more sentences we could form than seemed possible at first

—in this way we learned to write new things until we could write anything we wished

—when we can read and understand all texts and write whatever we think so that others know what we mean, we say that we have a good knowledge of english

—this is what we have tried to achieve in this work

37

Pages 36 and 37 of Primer 3

These results will have been achieved by everyone who has followed the course as indicated.

17. Some of the conventions of written English still remain to be presented. Two of these are given on pages 38 and 39.

Study of all the signs on the Fidel phonic table reveals that a limited number of constituent units, or letters, are used to construct its 284 signs.[1] Such units, when arranged in a conventional sequence, form what is known as an *alphabet*. The English alphabet contains twenty-six letters, and these and their names are given on page 38.

<table>
<tr><td colspan="2">names for the shapes of letters or
alphabet</td><td></td><td colspan="2" align="center">CAPITALS</td></tr>
<tr><td colspan="3">read the part of each word that is underlined and
you will find the name given to each of the 26
letters of the english alphabet.</td><td>a</td><td>A</td><td>n</td><td>N</td></tr>
<tr><td></td><td></td><td></td><td>b</td><td>B</td><td>o</td><td>O</td></tr>
<tr><td></td><td></td><td></td><td>c</td><td>C</td><td>p</td><td>P</td></tr>
<tr><td></td><td></td><td></td><td>d</td><td>D</td><td>q</td><td>Q</td></tr>

</table>

names for the shapes of letters or alphabet				CAPITALS		
read the part of each word that is underlined and you will find the name given to each of the 26 letters of the english alphabet.			a	A	n	N
			b	B	o	O
			c	C	p	P
			d	D	q	Q
a is called eight	b is called bee		e	E	r	R
c „ sea	d „ deal		f	F	s	S
e „ eve	f „ effort		g	G	t	T
g „ gee	h „ eightch		h	H	u	U
i „ I	j „ jay		i	I	v	V
k „ kay	l „ elephant		j	J	w	W
m „ empire	n „ end		k	K	x	X
o „ oh·	p „ pea		l	L	y	Y
q „ cube	r „ are		m	M	z	Z·
s „ esteem	t „ tea					
u „ you	v „ veal					
w „ double you	x „ extra					
y „ why	z „ zed					
38						

All the signs of the word building charts can be put in the form of capitals by using the corresponding capital above *as the first letter* of the word. For example for pat write Pat.

39

Pages 38 and 39 of Primer 3

In addition to the form so far encountered of the letters, each has another shape associated with it known as its *capital*. In a number of instances this second shape is exactly the same as the *lower case* form used up to this point, except that it is larger (C, O, P, S, V, W, X, Z). For another group the capital is related in shape to the lower case form and is readily recognisable from it on sight (J, K, U, Y). The remaining signs—excluding *I* which has already been met—

[1]There are 380 signs on the Mute r Fidel.

require special introduction, for which a single lesson should prove sufficient (A, B, D, E, F, G, H, L, M, N, Q, R, T).

One way of introducing the letters in this third group is to give each in turn in a word containing two of the capital letters that have been recognised. Here is a sequence among thousands that are possible:

T	in	POT	G	in	EGG
A	in	CAT	H	in	HIS
B	in	TUB	M	in	MY
L	in	LOTS	N	in	MAN
E	in	TELL	R	in	RUN
F	in	OF	Q	in	QUICK
D	in	LID			

The conventions governing the use of capital letters are many and it is as well to let the pupils know this. The most important require that capitals be used

a. at the beginning of a sentence;

b. for proper names—whether of persons, places, geographical entities, days, months, specific holidays, nations, races, languages, eras, or for titles, epithets, nicknames, trade names and so on;

c. for certain derivative adjectives for some of the proper names above.

Each of these points could be stressed as the occasion arises—this is to be preferred to giving the conventions as a set of rules. Now every time a text is looked at it provides an opportunity for noting which words have capitals and for determining which of the three categories above applies.

Just as it seems important to teachers that pupils master the uses of capitals in written English, it is important to pupils that teachers do not repeatedly put questions to them that have ceased to present a challenge. Hence teachers who watch their pupils absorb the easy rules of capitalisation through observation of case after case will know how to avoid unnecessary testing.

18. Primer 3 concludes with a short text for continuous reading. This is a letter, so written as to include practically all the different

punctuation marks. Here all the conventions of written English are being observed.

In this passage the sanserif italic type used previously and elsewhere is dropped. Now normal Roman print appears, found commonly in everyday life and adopted for the later stories in the Book of Stories—as well as having been used all along in the instructions given in the worksheets. This change of typeface is to indicate that by the time pupils have completed Primer 3 they have had sufficient experience to meet this challenge without any trouble, and it also prepares them for reading anything they wish.[1]

It is to be noted that the longer statements on pages 36 and 37 of Primer 3 still remain separate statements, differing from those met earlier in the primers only in the number of their words. The letter, on the other hand, is a narrative conveying one message and requiring that words be put at the service of an idea. The completeness of the letter is equivalent to the completeness of transmission of the idea. A letter is not a story and though no question is asked in the worksheets about it, teachers may naturally wish to use the reaching of this stage to induce their classes to take up letter writing —letters could be written for any of a number of reasons; festivals, such as Christmas, Easter, New Year, special holidays, birthdays and so forth. This part of the study of writing is left to teachers to include or develop as they wish.

*

---

[1]Teachers will find it very simple at any time from this point on to introduce two additional conventions in a few lessons:

   (i) *diacritical marks* needed to use a dictionary—relating these to the Fidel.

   (ii) *rules for dividing words* governing how words are split when a word will not fit fully on one line and has to be completed on the next—(these rules are somewhat different from those for syllabication in speech).

Dear Daddy,

   Thank you for your letter and your lovely present. I am sorry you are still travelling. Come back soon.

   My birthday party next Sunday is going to be very gay. I asked a number of my friends from school and their parents have accepted and will bring them.

   Oh, Daddy, it is so nice to think of what they will bring with them, what we shall give them in return and how to arrange the table around the birthday cake. Don't you think so?

   I shall have a notebook for everyone and a ball point pen and a coloured balloon (each a funny shape to make us laugh) and a bag of sweets with a little bar of chocolate. Do you think they will all like that?

   We shall play games indoors if it is raining and in the garden if it is fine.

   Daddy, please don't tell me I am dreaming and that this is too expensive; please don't tell me to think of all the little children in the world who need food and clothes. I know you are right and that it would be better to forget about my birthday party, but since it comes only once a year, please let's be gay then and think of sad things the other days! Do you agree, Daddy?

   Come back soon.

             With much love from your daughter

                 40

Page 40 of Primer 3

Since the manuscript for this book was written a number of teachers have sent the author some of the material produced by their pupils while learning to read and write. An outstanding example is Sister Mary Leonore Murphy R.S.C. of Sydney, Australia, who, as has already been mentioned, has communicated to her colleagues through the book *Creative Writing* all that her classes using *Words in Colour* have been able to achieve—and indeed in a very short time.

V.

Book of Stories and Worksheet 13

1. The Book of Stories was specially written for this programme. There are forty stories covering a hundred printed pages. The eleven illustrations were inserted in the text because they bring in something words cannot convey: the uniform evocation of the seven characters, and elaboration of some other key aspects of the stories.

The stories cover subjects that could be of interest to learners of any age, though mostly to young ones.

The removal of age as a criterion for vocabulary limitation makes it possible to maintain a 'way of talking' that is appropriate to the subject considered and to the purpose in mind; thus these stories may also be an enriching experience for the reader, or descriptive of any complex situation, or a form of poetic expression.

2. The first story is no story at all. Six sentences very similar to those in Primer 2 do not appear to be linked until Story 2, in its first sentences, recalls the names of the characters mentioned in Story 1 and provides the thread that did not previously exist in the story. This applies also to Story 2. Both these stories can be read at the same time as the pages of the primers are read. In fact all the stories can be read sentence by sentence. What each sentence leaves in mind forms a fabric which is experienced as something additional and is rendered by the word 'story'.[1]

Writer and reader of a story have opposite functions. The writer looks for words that render a thought he has; the reader from these

[1]For text and fuller discussion of first three stories see pages 117-119

words draws a thought which may be akin to the one the writer had at the beginning.

The need for naturalness in reading has been insisted on in order to help learners reach meaning more readily and hence permit enjoyment of the experience conveyed by that reading.

As the stories advance, the characters become more precisely delineated. There has been an effort at maintaining consistency between the short passages. While there is a kind of common background to the forty stories, they are also independent entities and can be read in almost any order.

3. The stories provide an enormous increase in the written vocabulary of learners. Some of the different episodes have been deliberately written with this purpose in mind.

For example, Story 14 contains two statements which refer to the kitchen and food, but the words they contain are presented not as a vocabulary list but as the appropriate words to create this story. The particular passages concerned are underlined:

> - *"not yet," said mum.*
>
> - *"well, may I prepare them?"*
>
> - *"do you know how to do it?"*
>
> - *"I put water in the saucepan and place it on the stove, turn the knob round to light the gas, and when the water boils I put the eggs in it and let them stay for a while."*
>
> - *"good boy," said mother, "go ahead and prepare the eggs."*
>
> - *while sam was doing that, mother asked him, "do you know how to prepare a french dressing for the salad?"*
>
> - *sam said, "I know that you put in oil and vinegar, salt and pepper, but I do not know how much of each nor in what order."*
>
> - *"well, we shall do it together when we have finished what we are doing."*
>
> 22

Page 22 of the Book of Stories

Another example is in Story 18. The beginning of this story is re-produced here, and the passages containing the new vocabulary are again underlined:

18

- the other day a van stopped at the door and a big cardboard box was brought in.

31

- the man asked mum to sign a paper and then he left.

- "what is there in this box?" asked pat and tom at the same time.

- mum said, "I do not know, daddy ordered it and did not tell me."

- "can't you open it and let us see?"

- "no," said mother, "it is dad's order and he must be here to open it and see if he wants it."

- mum left the entrance hall and went to the kitchen.

- the five children stood in front of the closed box and were very curious.

- sam pushed it a little and saw how light it was.

- "such a big box and so light, what can be inside?"

32

- they all started guessing: "not a washing machine," said pam, "not a refrigerator," said sam, "not a stove," said pat, as all of them remembered that these arrived in crates the same size as this carton.

- "could it be a rug?" asked tim.

- they all stopped talking, thinking whether it was possible.

- sam said, "let us roll up the rug in the front room and see if it is as light as this carton."

- they rolled up the rug but the five of them could barely lift it.

- they unrolled the rug and put everything back as it was.

- tom said, "let us go around the house and see everything we have and think of it put into a cardboard box."

33

- 'good idea' said sam 'let us go.'

- they looked at chairs, armchairs, cupboards, blankets, sheets, curtains and most of the things around but none would fit the two things they knew about the box, its size and its weight.

- while they were still studying the items in the house, dad came in and said 'oh! this wretched thing has at last arrived.'

- they all ran to him and asked together 'what is that wretched thing?'

- it is a surprise for you: a flamingo like the one you saw at the zoo the other day, but this one is stuffed with rubber foam.

An extract from Story 18

4. A study of the words used in this book will show that
   - —all prepositions and conjunctions are learned naturally in context;
   - —verbs are used in all moods and tenses, irregular and regular verbs being treated as equal in status;
   - —adverbs, pronouns, adjectives and nouns—along with the above —form between 1000 to 1500 words spelled in the forty contexts of the stories so that many areas of experience may be opened up to expression.

The total number of words used in this programme easily exceeds the 2000 level.

Since exercises have been suggested to fortify the closer examination of words, teachers will expect that their pupils' spelling (i.e. the writing down of the word and not necessarily the naming of its component letters) will be accurate more often than not.

There are of course greater chances now of providing a good background for spelling since the teacher will know what to ask of her pupils. She will also know that in order for her pupils to be impressed by the singular outline of words, and to be able to evoke this outline, the examination of words in isolation should be separated from reading and comprehension. The vocabulary met in the Stories may already form part of the spoken speech of the reader. If so, he has now to concentrate on the physical appearance of words so that he may be able to put them down spontaneously as they should be— that is, in perfect conformity with the models provided by the English language as conventionally written.

Where the words are new, reading will produce an increase in spoken vocabulary as well. Often the context explains one or other of the meanings of a word. For some pupils there may be need to use objects, drawings, or pictures to make the meanings clear. But the first attempt to get assistance is more advantageously made through asking for contributions from classmates who may already know the set of meanings covered by the word. Teachers may be able to learn from some of their pupils how to reach others. Though teachers may also need to remove some general misunderstandings of some words, by becoming acquainted with these misunderstandings they will gain insight into their pupils' minds.

5. In addition to this exposure of learners to a large number of words related within a specific situation, and for which page 15 of Worksheets 8–12 is a test,[1] each story deepens the learner's experience. What is intended by 'depth' is a variable awareness of situations in which one is involved with other people, in mystery, in social conventions, with right and wrong, with imagination and aesthetic experience. These aspects are examined more closely below.

Involved with other people This is a quality of most of the stories, but some stories emphasise interpersonal relations to raise issues for discussion in class. Stories 6, 12, 14, 15, 29, 31 and 40 can all be treated as opportunities to learn from the pupils their individual views about the matter debated in each story.

By inviting pupils to express themselves, the teachers, if they refrain themselves from judging or taking sides, will learn much that they need to know about the ethical sense of their pupils. The author believes that the issues raised are real and important ones that need thrashing out among young as well as older learners, in order to develop the sense of 'the other', or to stress distinctions sometimes neglected in certain environments.

Involved in mystery Some of the situations that make up the stories have been designed to encourage attitudes of mind in the learners that will foster reverence for what is still unfathomed in the universe. Stories 11, 16, 21, 33, 34 and 37 are examples of such situations, and appear to the author to have a perennial appeal to the human mind.

Involved in social conventions These conventions are not discussed as such. They are the subjects of the stories and the readers will feel the significance and value of some of the conventions by reading about them. Stories 9, 12, 17, 22, 28, 30, 36 and 38 are examples in which the behaviour of socially conscious people is used naturally and leads to better understanding.

Cultivating the imagination Such situations are found in Stories 8, 10, 13, 18, 19, 24, 26, 38 and 39 which also involve aesthetic components. These could lead the pupils to attempt to produce their own versions of their own experience in some medium other than words.

6. The purpose of reading is to permit one *to gain experience by proxy*: that is, experience which one has not personally lived through, but

[1]See page 187.

which someone else has gone through and which is offered to all through the medium of words, films, or some other artistic production.

Most people would be very poor if not enriched by experience-by-proxy. The proportion of direct experience to experience-by-proxy diminishes quickly if one reads more and more, but the validity of the experience read about can only come from direct experience. The author therefore attempted to find 'cores of direct experience' around which the expanded experience could be provided. Drama is part of direct experience as much as mishaps or joys or adventure.

By going through the stories, teachers will see that no restriction, other than that of decency, has been put upon the choice of topics included. They will find that 'out of nothing' a story can be made by simply analysing happenings, feelings, wishes, moods so that only by successive approximations a more precise experience emerges. This is one of the vital contributions of the reading of the Stories, and care was taken by the author to cover a sufficient spectrum and to avoid ever making the text too heavy, so that when the book was finished the reader might wish to turn to it again for the abundance of life it contains.

7. At the same time the author had to keep in mind that these stories might be read during school hours. At school, people study in order to become (1) clearer in their minds about their environment, (2) more aware of themselves functioning in relationship, which means also (3) more aware of the language heritage of their group or society.

8. So far the worksheets have referred to the Book of Stories for vocabulary and to stimulate the learners to think of endings to the stories. Now Worksheet 13 sets out to examine a selection of sixteen stories in the Book of Stories, from the point of view of analysing content, human beings and feelings.

Naturally one may have experienced much of what is covered by a story and yet not be able to express it in words. There are different types of questions on each page so that teachers may observe how each individual attacks each set of questions. Teachers may note

—who prefers matter-of-fact questions
—who is disturbed by certain experiences, and by which ones

—who needs time to formulate, in a way satisfactory to him, what has been evoked in his mind

—who is stimulated by what, and to what extent

WORDS IN COLOUR   *Worksheet No. 13*

© C. GATTEGNO, 1962. Pilot Edition 1962. First Standard English Edition 1965.

1. Read story No. 10 in the Book of Stories. Then answer the following questions

   (i)   who is aunt rachel?

   (ii)   how old is she?

   (iii) what does aunt rachel do at home?

   (iv)   name a few of the garments she has embroidered

   (v)   why does aunt rachel not visit the girls at home?

Page 1 of Worksheet 13

Teachers may feel that questions other than these should be asked about the content of these stories, or that other stories should have been selected. But if pupils find exercises such as those in Worksheet 13 profitable and enjoyable they will wish to do more of them. It then becomes possible for the teacher to propose others. She can for instance:

—add her own questions to the six the author has given on each of the sixteen stories

—ask for questions from her class and select those which evoke the most interest

—leave each pupil to prepare six or more questions on the story or stories he likes best

Classwork can follow this individual work since the various answers to the same questions can be read aloud for all.

Much more work could be done on the Book of Stories. But this text has already served, among other things, as

—a continuous reader for practising reading at the speed of speech
—a source of enjoyment in varying degrees according to the content
—a source of experience by proxy
—a challenge relative to the expression of feelings, to the analysis of impressions, and so forth
—a contributor to vocabulary
—a source of word images leading to correct spellings
—a source of ethical, social, and personal issues which involve one at both theoretical and practical levels.

9. In the next chapter the same texts will become a source of structural and grammatical awareness, to which Worksheet 14 is mainly devoted. And in that chapter, in addition to a further consideration of the Book of Stories, the use of the last type of material forming this programme is considered—the Word Cards.

10. The present chapter has been called the *meeting of spellings*, but obviously much more has been covered than this. In particular, attempts have been made to involve pupils in activities from which a deeper awareness of oneself in relationship could emerge.

It follows that the programme is concerned with educating the person in every learner while obtaining mastery of spelling as a by-product. This is deemed to be very important in the world of today where we are asked to conceive of a complex reality, and to work in harmony with it while acting on it to change it and ourselves.

Chapter Four

A STUDY OF STRUCTURES

THE PREVIOUS CHAPTERS of this book discussed the use of the material of *Words in Colour* to overcome the difficulties of learners who must move from spoken speech to written speech. It can now confidently be assumed that the pupils can make sense of every page of written English using words and expressions within their hearing and speaking vocabulary.

Nevertheless the language they are using has more to it than the mere value of a vehicle of communication. As an 'object' developed over the centuries, it encloses a number of interesting aspects which have been the constant concern of linguists. The modes of thought of peoples find their way into the languages, mould them, and in turn the language-users mould their own thought using their own language. The result is that it then becomes natural to express one's thought in the mother tongue but far less so in 'foreign' languages.

A number of tasks therefore still remain after the techniques of reading and writing have been made available to the pupils. Among them is knowing how language behaves when it renders thought. This includes grammar as one of the awarenesses reached ultimately in the process of becoming conscious of oneself talking or writing.

Since writing is more tangible than speech, the one being in space and the other in time, these tasks will naturally be undertaken on the written material; later on it will be noticed that the observations made apply to both forms.

In this chapter we shall still remain within the material created for this programme when it was first initiated. In particular the pack of Word Cards and Worksheet 14 will be used. But before this material is reached the role of dictation and writing in the study of the structure of English will be briefly considered.

I.

Dictation and Writing

1. Dictation, both visual and oral, has been used all along to promote flexibility in the study of words and sentences. One can now consider more closely what it can do for pupils if it is recognised that in oral dictation for instance, the pupil's memory is called in to perform a special job.

Indeed, if the author's proposal is recalled of saying a sentence once only, with intonation and at the actual speed of the speech related to the content, it can be seen that when the teacher embarks upon such a dictation she is drawing pupils' attention to the meaning involved, and recognising that this particular meaning is rendered by *this* set of words in *this* order and with *this* intonation and no other.

Hence dictation is a tool which on the one hand permits an entry into this study and on the other ensures that both pupils and teacher have material available in any amount needed for working as equals.

2. This tool can be used in a number of ways:

(i) It is possible to utter a sentence once and ask the pupils to indicate that they have received it as uttered, either

  a. by saying it
  b. by finding it with the pointer among the words on the word chart[1] (or later on the word card sheets on the wall) or on the Fidel
  c. by putting it down

In the first two cases only one pupil at a time can give the indication; in the third the number participating is immaterial—thus a good reason for having it written instead of uttered.

(ii) It is possible first to read a succession of sentences linked by a meaning that is meaningful to the pupils, and then to utter the sentences one-by-one—but as complete units with the intonation and speed required by the meaning—leaving no time between the sentences beyond what is needed to put them down. In this way

[1]See page 59.

writing is linked with whole statements retained because of their meaning and because a particular language has been chosen to render it.

(iii) It is possible to start with an existing text recognised as something that can be read and understood. (This could be given through visual dictation on the word charts, or later on the word card sheets, as well as read from a printed page.) To commit such a text to memory is to be able, after looking at it, to utter it again or to put it down. Hence the mental activity preceding writing is not very different from that preceding uttering.[1]
When we are aware of holding the words rather than the meaning, we talk of memory; but when we are aware of holding the meaning rather than the words we talk of understanding. *Both* memory and understanding reinforce each other and can can be cultivated by dictation.

3. Statements used in dictation for the purpose of making people aware of structure and the way in which it supports memory and understanding will naturally vary a great deal from simple phrases to quite long sentences. Teachers who already know their pupils' competence can short-cut the sequence and start at a point that adequately challenges them. Here are graded samples to exemplify this suggestion:

—The man met his death by drowning.
—The return trip was very sad as they had to take the body back to their home town.
—In the convoy there were his widow and their two children, his friends, and his dog which seemed to be feeling the grief more than anyone else.
—It had all happened during the holiday. The family had gone on a long journey to a warm isolated beach where for a fortnight they would be far away from their strenuous occupations.
—The place they had found was ideal from every point of view. Everyone was as happy as could be, running on the soft sand along the shore, splashing in the shallow water, feeling the cool sea breeze after a swim.

[1]See page 60 et seq.

—On one day they were tempted to try out a new part of the beach where the surf looked so inviting. No-one suspected that the ocean at this point was treacherous and that below the surface of the water the ground fell away sharply.

—The dog, sensing the danger, barked, and scratched the mother and the daughter. It made a nuisance of itself, refusing to go into the water or to let anyone else in; it left the beachball to float away rather than rush out to fetch it as on the previous days.

—When the man and his friend and his son went into the water they shouted and laughed happily, calling out for everyone to join them, and pushed forward to challenge the waves with their chests, getting thrown off their feet every time.

—But then all of a sudden all three felt the ground sliding away under their feet as the swell of the water caught up with them. The son, who was agile and not so far out as his father, kept his balance and turning around managed to struggle against the current and reach safety. The friend, a grown man, fought and fought for his own life but was unable to do anything to prevent the other man from drowning, whose efforts to save himself proved puny against the power of the sea.

—It had taken a team three quarters of an hour to bring his dead body ashore.[1]

4. The sequence of sentences above makes a story and can therefore be remembered because of the feelings and experiences it evokes. But in order to remember each word and each sentence exactly as they are it is necessary to concentrate not on the feelings or the events but on each of the expressions used by the author. For this the text must be broken down into short statements and pupils allowed to receive them, both as specific sequences of sounds and as feelings. Because it is the purpose of the exercise to make people note words and their relationships and put them down as they are found in correct English, everyone will insist on conformity in this type of work since flexibility and freedom would not achieve this purpose. Discipline then is the requirement.

[1]Adapted from C. Gattegno, *Short Passages* (part of the *Silent Way* programme for teaching English as a second language), Educational Explorers, Reading, 1968.

5. The discipline of a language is its grammar.

To study grammar one analyses what one writes or says, or what others write or say. An interesting way of doing it will form the substance of the next section.

For most beginners speech is an automatic function of the mind, and to learn to watch oneself using speech is not an automatic activity. Writing is also automatic for those who have mastered it and know their language. But because signs must be put on paper, it takes longer to write than to talk. Hence a little more time is available for considering what is being done. It is therefore sounder to look at written forms for a study of grammar than to examine the fleeting oral speech in spite of their close correspondence.

II.
GAMES WITH WORD CARDS

1. The Word Cards in this programme are a set of over 1200 words printed in black on various colours of cardboard. The colours chosen correspond to grammatical categories as follows:

green	for	*nouns*
salmon	for	*verbs*
yellow	for	*adjectives*
blue	for	*adverbs*
ivory	for	*conjunctions*
gold	for	*interjections*
grey	for	*pronouns*
pink	for	*prepositions*

A full list of the words on each colour of cardboard—arranged in alphabetical order within each colour grouping—is given in Appendix 4.

2. The material presentation of the Word Cards is in the form of sheets of perforated coloured cardboard. The perforations enable the sheets to be transformed into packs of loose cards.

It is recommended that one set of these words be kept in the form of sheets for use on the wall in the games with the whole class, or a large group in the classroom, and that as many packs be prepared from another set of sheets as are necessary to relate to the number of small groups of learners often working together.[1]

The printing of the words, in view of the use of a machine for perforation, has forced a choice of location of words mainly according to their length, though it can be seen that an alphabetical order was originally chosen.

3. As these sheets are to be introduced all at once, the teacher will not be able to learn the location of words on them as she did on the word charts—where these were introduced one after the other and with the pupils; she must therefore spend some time in becoming familiar with them. For a while she will need to have them on display where she can look at them frequently and take in their content and the location of words on the sheets, and see how to distinguish sheets by the words they carry as well as by their grammatical function, since there are often a number of sheets of a single colour.

One way of overcoming these difficulties is by placing all the sheets on a wall, reserving areas for those of the same colour so that, in columns, they display their content by length of the words from left to right. If there are more sheets than can fit in one column, a double-column can be formed. The small but useful sets of conjunctions, prepositions, interjections and pronouns can be placed together in an accessible area—perhaps between the nouns and the verbs or the nouns and the adjectives which form most of the words in the set.

4. The teacher in the beginning will be leading the games described below. Once she looks at the display she will find it easy to select words that form a sentence. These words will be of necessity on a number of different charts—and most frequently on charts of different colours—since sentences use words with different functions.

The pointer may now be used to touch these chosen words in an order which creates a sentence (in a new version of the Visual Dictation 2 which was used earlier on the word charts).[2] This

[1]Since only one set of Word Cards is included in a Classroom Set of materials, teachers will probably wish to obtain a second set.

[2]See page 41 et seq.

could generate, for example, *it is* or *it is my father* or *who was this man?* Teachers practising the game—here the proper movement of the pointer among the proper charts to generate the sequence wanted—will do well to recognise that practice will create the desired familiarity. It is helpful to make sure of where some very useful words are by involving them in a large number of different sentences. These sentences will show where to find key words, and where those needed to complete other sentences are to be found.

it is

becomes

   —it is us
   —it is not me
   —it is not my dog
   —it is a cat
   —it is dark
   —it is a black cat
   —it is a black cat moving
   —oh, it is a black cat moving in the dark
   —oh, it is a black cat moving quickly in the dark because it is cunning

The last sentence, which involves all eight categories of functions, shows that at one stage or another in the evolution of this series some criteria related to the various functions will have to come to consciousness. From then on it is these deeper insights that will organise the bulk of the material so that it is possible to move immediately from one function to another as the sentences are formed one after the other.

It may be of help to write down the sentences produced after they have been found, and then the next day, from looking at the written record, try to find them again with the pointer on the sheets on the wall. Since the positions of the words on the sheets are arbitrary, it will require either a photographic memory or the necessary practice to retain them.

5. Once the teacher has established her familiarity with the words she will be able to use these materials with her class. When the following games are part of the total programme called *Words in Colour,* they are played at the end. (With other classes—say between

the ages of eight and ten—these games can be used at any time if the children are able to read the words.)

Game 1

The teacher points at some of the words as described (Visual Dictation 2), and the class utters the sentence indicated. The rules are the same as for the Visual Dictation 2 met with the word charts. That is, first slowly—and even word by word if necessary—the teacher points at what is to be decoded, speeding up as the class competence permits. The pupils are not introduced to the significance of the colour of the background and should never be. It is the goal of these games to bring to the students' awareness the structure of English; to tell them anything about the colour would remove most of the enjoyment and most of the value of the exercise.

This game can go on for as long as it is useful. It is advisable to increase the challenge slowly by gradually extending the sentences to include all the coloured areas and more words in each colour-group, thus making longer and longer sentences which demand all the attention of the pupils. Naturally all this is done silently, and the pupils are left to judge whether or not the volunteer performers are right.

Game 2

The teacher gives a sentence orally and the pupils must point to the matching words on the sheets in the correct order.

Here the difficulties are greater than with the Visual Dictation 2 practised earlier on the word charts because a word may appear more than once on charts of different colours. Thus it may be necessary to reject a solution offered because the colour of the background to some words has not been taken into account.

Pupils may not accept that they have chosen the wrong word if they do not as yet consider the colour. Even if the teacher points out the same word on a sheet of another colour, the reason may still be unclear to the pupil if he is not yet aware of grammatical function. In order to help pupils develop criteria of function, it is profitable, when playing Game 1, to introduce particular sequences of example sentences. These will be such that in one sequence a certain word will recur but with a different function in each sentence. To reconstruct the sentences from the Word Cards pupils must select this word on different colour cards each appropriate to the function it has in the sentence concerned. Additional example sequences may also be taken up in Game 2. Some examples are:

let us form a line	and	*what is the form of this line*
people like him	and	*people like him are odd*
I said that that man was dead	and	*that man I touched was dead*
he had to inch away	and	*he had a two inch escape*
this cup is full now	and	*he paid in full*
do not cross this line	and	*this cross is of gold*
	and	*it is cross-stitched*

The number of such exercises is left to each teacher who will find from the feedback in each group of pupils how many will be needed.

Game 3

One pupil shows in silence a sentence of his own and the class writes it down. If there are no objections to what he has done the teacher asks the pupils to extend this sentence each on his own paper (using words available on the sheets). Then the pupils take turns in showing their extended sentences using the pointer on the sheets. The class writes down each proposal so that the result can be discussed later on.

Obviously Game 3 is both a mixture and an extension of Games 1 and 2. The teacher will get confirmation of improved familiarity with the materials as well as of the extent of the imagination developing in various pupils. The class as a whole, by pooling experience, will make greater progress in this extension of sentence power.

Examples from the author of this text will not help since classes behave very differently. All experience shows that pupils enjoy this game once they have sufficient knowledge of the new materials and are not in doubt about the rules of the game.

6. The packs of cards formed from separating the words on the sheets and classifying them according to colour and length may now be considered. A small number of pupils can use one full pack kept in a box.

Game 4[1]

One pupil, after thinking of (but not saying) a sentence, places any one word from it on the table, or in a slot on the board.

Next to this word someone else in the group places another word linked to it in some way in a sentence he has in *his* mind. This is continued by a third student and then by a fourth and so on—each adding a word that is linked in his mind to the words already put in position by others.

It is natural to say 'pass' when no sentence comes to mind and thus to give up one's turn. The game is over when no-one can extend the set of words into yet another sentence.

After the game has been played a few times, this rule is added: only sentences that are totally new in this game can be used. The teacher may then ask each pupil to put down the sentence he is thinking of before he adds his word card to the set. When the game is over, each pupil in turn reads his sentence or sentences so that the whole fabric of the game is made clear to all.

Here, except in the case of the pupil starting the round of games, no-one is completely free to think of anything that comes: servitude and constraint increase steadily and the game stimulates the imagination in requiring pupils to integrate what is offered by others while adding something personal.

The colours of the cards introduce their further constraints; and no card can be added until the pupil knows in what part of the pack to look for it, since the length of a word determines fairly closely the size of the card. If this is too difficult, the game will die, and the teacher will have to intervene by suggesting either that the number of cards in the pack be reduced in quantity or that some cards showing words used very frequently be placed face up on the table for quick reference.

Another mode is to give each pupil a certain number of words to form a personal pack while retaining a group pack open to all. There are enough nouns, verbs, and adjectives in the complete pack to permit, even at random, a sufficiently even distribution of word

[1]The numbering indicates that this game could come after those dealing with the Word Cards on the wall, but this is not a firm rule. Teachers can learn something new if with some pupils they start with the packs of loose cards rather than with the sheets.

cards to create a feeling of fair competition, to challenge players, as well as to nourish the game for a little while.

It is clear that this game forces the players to notice the place of words in a sentence and to put each new word in a special location so that whatever one is seeing at any instant does not clash with a feeling of what is right in the linguistic experience of one's own language. As the sentence becomes more and more complex this feeling becomes more precise, to the point where one can formulate rules of structuration of sentences. If the name of the colour of the cardboard is known by the pupils, these rules can be seen and hence can at the same time be expressed. The blue cards are always in a certain relation to the salmon cards; the white are never found at the beginning or end of a true sentence; the yellow always precede the green if they come together; and so on.

After a few such observations are made and the game continues to hold some interest, it is recommended that teachers tell the class the customary words that grammar books have used over the centuries for what here are colour names.

The teacher might say:
—'Name a word that is on a green card' (Example: island)
—'This is called a . . .' (the teacher may say *noun* or point to this word on the green sheet of words)
—'Can you give me three nouns that are among your cards?'
A similar procedure can be followed for giving the conventional names for all the other parts of speech.

An obvious transfer could be obtained by taking any one of the sentences in the Book of Stories and asking pupils to say
—on what colour card each word would be found (assuming it were in the pack)
—which of the newly met conventional names would be given to each word in the sentence

For example:
sam had vaguely heard tim cry and the next morning he asked him if he had
can be answered:
green salmon blue salmon green salmon white yellow yellow green grey salmon grey white grey salmon
or:

noun verb adverb verb noun verb conjunction adjective
adjective noun pronoun verb pronoun conjunction pronoun verb

7. Of course this is only a beginning of the study of the language.
This is only naming the words according to some attribute that seems
to belong to them. But words gain functions with respect to each
other; nouns seem to order verbs or to be ordered by them. For
example:

> *sam heard* and
> *someone touched mum*

give different impressions.
'Sam' is the subject—that is, he initiates the action; 'mum' on the
other hand is called the object because 'someone' initiated the
action.

Hence there is a whole new field of experience opening up to the
learner with this new sensitivity to the function of words one with
respect to the other. It is not possible in a course for beginning
readers to go all the way in making this happen. But some of it can
be attempted leaving the boundary of this new field to be placed
by the learners themselves.

8. This is achieved partially through a new game.

Game 5

Here the game opens with a long sentence made from the cards.
Words are taken away one by one but in such a way that a sentence
always remains.

This game was discussed earlier when the eleventh page in
Worksheets 8–12 was described.[1] Now it is played with the Word
Cards in order to reach a different awareness. What had been
under consideration before was the alteration or preservation of
meaning by the removal of some words. Now the object is to establish which are the functions carrying the essential meaning.
Obviously the degree of constancy with which a coloured card
appears in the coloured images of the sentence will lead to this new
awareness. Pupils will soon see that there is a hierarchy of importance
among the functions of words—that some only qualify others and

[1]See page 182.

add precision upon precision, while others can be eliminated without removing the essence of the thought.

9. What has been learned with these games can be summed up as follows: In speech, and so in reading which is written speech, communication is the aim. We talk to convey meaning.

In the preceding games this was left in the background; words were worked on, and their various links with each other as they carry out the job of conveying meaning—maintaining either the sense of a sentence or just some meaning which has grown with the habits of speech. How this was done was inquired into, even when only superficial answers could be obtained. In every case it was at least recognised that there exists a certain dynamics behind speech that can be described, yet it has been seen that transformations of this dynamics that are compatible with meaning are possible.

The transformations studied are:
—extensions and contractions of sentences
—alterations of meaning by changes in the order of words or by removal of key words
—maintenance of meaning by some change in the order of groups of words

Structure has indeed been reached as a reality as easily manipulated intellectually as are sounds to create words. At least children will know that they are as free to let their minds entertain them as they have been when they played with words.

10. An additional insight is generated by the coloured cards when these are fully taken into account.

There are sometimes two, or even three or four, salmon cards following each other. This tells something about the structure of verbs and how speakers render their consciousness of time in English. Events referred to in speech either have happened, are happening, or will happen. To convey this knowledge the proper mood and tense automatically come to mind. Use of the tenses is obviously still more subtle than this, and yet five-year-olds can already convey shaded meanings by *using different sets of words* just as adults do when they talk. The cards are useful in bringing all of this to consciousness since pupils will ask themselves or the teacher why this happens on some occasions and not on others.

The teacher could answer this best via other questions, such as:

—'Why do you think the words *will* or *shall* (or *would* or *should*) have been used?'

—'When do *you* use each?'

—'When do you know that you are talking of something past?' complemented perhaps by

—'Would it sound right to you if I said:

yesterday I will go on vacation

tomorrow I left with him

went now (as an order)

yesterday I have come walking from his shop

are they coming from Mexico last week?'

Rightness of sound goes with correctness of form, and they translate each other in spoken and written speech through the grammar of the language. From the gross incorrectness made by foreigners to the subtle distinctions accessible only to cultured native adults using their own language, there is a whole spectrum into which the capabilities of one's pupils will fall. Teachers may find it useful to enquire more closely into their pupils' sensitivity to the shades of meaning verbs can affect. They can best do this by refraining from correcting and by challenging pupils with exercises such as the following:

How does the meaning shift in the sequence of statements below:

—I say goodbye . . .

—I come to say goodbye . . .

—I have to come to say goodbye . . .

—I have had to come to say goodbye . . .

    or

—I said goodbye . . .

—I came to say goodbye . . .

—I had to come to say goodbye . . .

—I had had to come to say goodbye . . .

    or

—I shall say goodbye . . .

—I shall come to say goodbye

—I shall have to come to say goodbye

—I shall have had to come to say goodbye

    or

—I would say goodbye if . . .

—I would come to say goodbye if . . .
—I would have to come to say goodbye if . . .
—I would have had to come to say goodbye if . . .

III.
Worksheet 14

1. Although each of the worksheets used so far has had a contribution to make to the study of English as a language in contrast to knowing how to use it correctly, it is in Worksheet 14 that steps are taken to test structural awareness, and awareness of word functions.

In the previous two sections of this chapter, lessons have been sketched which will give the adequate background to learners so that they can be thought of as sensitised to grammar and interested in looking at sentences in order to find something that will justify the use of the particular words to communicate a meaning in mind.

2. *Page 1*
This is a test of those criteria that would permit pupils to dis-

---

Page 1

WORDS IN COLOUR   *Worksheet No. 14*

© C. GATTEGNO, 1962   Pilot Edition 1962.   First Standard English Edition 1965.

1. Which of the following sentences are in the present tense?

in the garden we have a tent	yes	no
sam has many books and likes to read late	yes	no
when it is warm we may sleep in the tent	yes	no
dad tells us stories in the house, in the tent or on the sand	yes	no
mum often asks pam and pat to clean the house with her	yes	no
a red apple from the top rolled down and fell in the gutter	yes	no

---

Page 1 of Worksheet 14

tinguish the present tense from the others. Six sentences are chosen, though a number from the Book of Stories could serve the purpose equally well. Some are straightforward and should not create a problem for learners. But one is more subtle. It says:

when it is warm we may sleep in the tent

The request here is to answer only 'yes' or 'no'. It may take no more than a few moments to complete this page and the two following. If pupils are already beyond this stage, sentences using tenses, which may be called present, past, and future—though not so immediately recognisable—could be proposed by the teacher; the example above shows this type of subtlety.

Pages 2 and 3

These follow the same pattern as page 1 and can be treated also as tests. When it is clear that learners are beyond this stage, new challenges should be offered by their teacher.

3. Pages 4, 5 and 6

If these are applied as tests without prior preparation, they will not prove much. The teacher must make sure, before giving the test, that the words *conditional* (page 4), *negative* and *affirmative* (page 5), and *interrogative* (page 6) are fully understood and can be used freely by her classes. This can be done by generating a situation actually involving objects, and using speech naturally with it. She should then ask someone to say what was said again and to relate the words to the meaning. The teacher will get the point across more easily if she uses wrong tenses or wrong forms to generate the shock that will move consciousness to note what *is* relevant in the situation. Only after an adequate number of examples will the teacher put into circulation the labels 'conditional' and so on. This is then followed by exercises giving opportunities to the teacher or the class to ask whether or not the statement is about some condition, question, negation or affirmation.

If the worksheet pages are given a few days after all of this, they can be used to test the familiarity of the pupils with these new ideas and with the translation of meaning into moods or forms that will conversely convey the wanted meaning when read.

4. Which of the following sentences are conditional?

if I had given you one, you would have eaten two and I one	yes	no
sam looked at his arms and thought: I would like to be as strong as him and have a pneumatic drill to handle	yes	no
why did you go to look for him, when he knows the way home	yes	no
mum knew that they could do nothing now to make tim not dream	yes	no
he would show him the next day that he too could be tough	yes	no
miss dunn would be pleased if she knew	yes	no

Page 4 of Worksheet 14

4. *Page 7*

In the previous section it was mentioned that words printed on the same colour cardboard can still be distinguished by a secondary attribute that was exemplified on nouns. A noun can be a *subject* or *object*.[1] When pupils understand this distinction, it is possible to introduce additional perceptible clues on the cards by taking, for example, two of the packs of cards and marking nouns with a special sign that from now on refers to this second attribute. Objects can be further distinguished according to whether they are *direct* or *indirect*; for example, in,

—*every living man has a body*

'body' is the direct object of 'has'; in,

—*this woman asked her child a serious question*

'child' is the indirect object of 'asked' since 'question' is the direct object.

Additional markings can now be applied on those noun cards already marked as objects, in order to make this third attribute clear.

[1]See page 212.

7. Which of the following sentences have a direct object (d) or an indirect object (i)?

under the tap there was a bucket and water was dripping slowly into it	d	i
I would prefer sugar cane to tooth paste to keep my teeth healthy	d	i
mum has a dentist friend whose name is mister brown	d	i
the five children sat on the carpet around the armchair in which dad was sitting, waiting for them	d	i
he loves books and especially travel stories	d	i
dad showed a map to the children and explained how they will go there in two weeks' time	d	i

Page 7 of Worksheet 14

Again if pupils quickly become conversant with these distinctions, teachers can make the exercise more testing by continuing to give examples which extend their capacity to observe words and find in them the distinctive attributes.

5. *Page 8*

This test is concerned with the notion of a clause in a sentence. The awareness of a clause is reached very soon if sentences are considered as they are uttered. Good reading does not usually break the flow of words just to allow breathing. Instead the pauses are linked with clauses, which one recognises to be the real units of meaning in written material.

Only the scrutiny of the number of verbs (or compound verbs) in a sentence will give the final count of clauses, assuming it is recognised that sometimes a verb is dropped because its meaning is understood without its being there.

6. *Pages 9 and 10*

These pages are self-explaining and should not present any

8. Which of the following sentences contain more than one clause?

the journey to the vacation home was long and tiring but nothing special happened on the way   yes   **no**

first by car to the station, then by train for three and a half hours, then by car to the house, in all over five hours' journey   yes   **no**

tim slept all the time in the train and did not see the many tunnels that they went through   yes   **no**

when he returned to the house breakfast was ready   yes   **no**

they had to put their slippers out there to change footwear when coming and going   yes   no

9. Change each of the following sentences into the plural.

he ate with good appetite and had two fried eggs on toast

each in turn drank from the jar and expressed his or her pleasure at the freshness of the water

the miller answered that he could grind all the grain of his own fields in one day

Pages 8 and 9 of Worksheet 14

problem for those who know the meaning of the words 'plural' and 'present tense'.

The inclusion of such material in the tests provides a smooth transition between the types of games played all through the programme and classical education which proposes exercises mainly of this kind.

7. *Page 11*

The exercise on page 11 concerns the Book of Stories, with which pupils are becoming more familiar as a literary work every day.

Page 11

11. Are there stories in your Book of Stories that are told:

    (i) in the present?   (give their numbers)

    (ii) in the past?   (give their numbers)

    (iii) in the first person plural?   (give their numbers)

    (iv) by a narrator?   (give their numbers)

Page 11 of Worksheet 14

Here the test is much more one of maturity, confidence and self-reliance than of scholarship.

The exercise requires that this book be viewed as a whole and the stories be classified according to four criteria. Though the criteria are by now familiar, it is a new exercise to use them as tools for classification. Any pupil who can complete this task in a time comparable to what the teacher would take in this final test of the programme deserves recognition of his progress.

8. *Page 12*

This page places further demands on the student. Can he recast a story from one type of presentation into another? He has knowledge of the existence of the types and can recognise them when he meets them. But can he perform such a transformation? Can he do it from beginning to end consistently and correctly?

His success here is certainly another proof that he has been made aware of subtle and often hidden attributes of the written language and that he is beginning to act beyond linguistic boundaries and is reaching new literary regions.

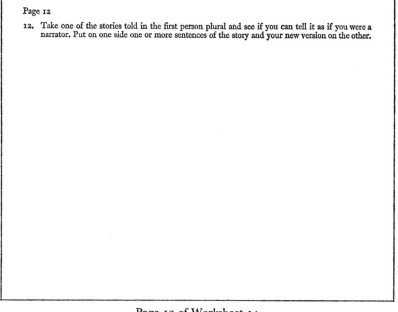

Page 12

12. Take one of the stories told in the first person plural and see if you can tell it as if you were a narrator. Put on one side one or more sentences of the story and your new version on the other.

Page 12 of Worksheet 14

9. *Pages 13 and 14*

These pages take this opening into literary regions a little further. The questions are wholly unstructured and concern judgments of

13. What do you like about:

sam

pam

tom

pat

tim

14. Which of the stories do you like best?

Give their numbers and for each of them say why in a few words

Pages 13 and 14 of Worksheet 14

taste, of introspection, and of feelings which on the whole are left to take care of themselves because teachers believe that young children do not look at themselves enough to reach them. Observers of young children disagree on these matters. The tests are included here because the whole programme can reveal that children are unknown to those who teach them and that they are much more competent than anyone ever suspected.

Thus, in a way, the exercises test the preconceptions of adults as well as the capabilities of children.

10. *Page 15*

The simple example presented on this page has been added in order to communicate to teachers that there may be many additional openings that can be exploited from the content of some of the stories.

Page 15

15. Do you collect postage stamps?   Give the name of a few countries from which you have stamps.

Would you like to collect stamps?   Why?

Do you know the difference between state, county, province, country, continent? Give examples of each.

Page 15 of Worksheet 14

Here collecting stamps has been used to show the relationship of all that has been done to the study of English and the social sciences. Clearly, if words differ, they may somehow refer to different experiences, notions, entities, while a consideration of them may suggest that our world has an existence of its own where continents can be noticed. The subdivision of the land into countries, states and counties is only one of the possibilities. The rest is the opening that has been mentioned. Examples are demanded only for definition purposes. But much more may follow from this, and perhaps should.

11. *Page 16*

This page sums up the progress achieved in working through the programme. Though this page may represent weeks of work, its inclusion is a sign that students can be trusted to keep all their experience present in their mind in so far as the skill is concerned. And because of the cumulative effect of learning, a review of each of the completed worksheets will provide immediate evidence of the mastery that was the constant aim of the programme; and with this evidence will come the extension drawn from it: the recognition of what one can oneself achieve. It should not be

---

Page 16

16. Go over your worksheets and find out if you can do some of them and increase your score now.

	Old Score	New Score		Old Score	New Score
1.			8.		
2.			9.		
3.			10.		
4.			11.		
5.			12.		
6.			13.		
7.			14.		

Now add up your scores. This is your total score for Worksheet No. 14.

[   ] Date

Published by Educational Explorers Limited, Reading, England.
Printed in England by Lamport Gilbert & Co. Ltd., Gun St., Reading, Berks., England.

Page 16 of Worksheet 14

forgotten that reading has been considered to be a skill. But it is a complex skill based on a number of others, awakening new powers and new possibilities.

Because of this viewpoint the learners have been challenged and challenged again, always being taken to a higher level of competence through the exercises confronting them, and are hopefully performing with greater and greater effectiveness.

12. The worksheets have been used as tests of the programme, hence of everybody involved in it—the author and the teachers as well as the learners. Although the learners are the recipients of the programme, their taking the tests—rather than the teacher or the author—is merely a convenience. It is not an indication of a belief that they alone, with their qualities and their achievements, are being tested.

Some teachers will start with the thought that the hurdles have been made too high and that very few pupils will achieve anything like the results which seem to be expected. Experience will teach them, as it taught the author, that whoever has been able to mobilise the needed intellectual powers demanded by the learning of one's own family's spoken speech has far more power available then even these supposedly hard tests can test.

We can say that we have learned to work with children only when we are certain of avoiding the confusions we may create and so are always in contact with their mental powers. The tests then are a method of getting feedback that our vision of these powers is not too wrong.

These tests are moreover merely samples of what could be done to ensure that the teacher-programme-student relation is continually reviewed. This will then increasingly become the process by which each student reaches autonomy and independence with respect to the language. And at the same time he will feel his intellectual muscles well trained and working smoothly.

IV.

Conclusion—Self and Speech

This programme began with the claim that it is easy for most people to learn to read and it ends with another claim: that it is possible to make people aware of many dimensions of spoken and written speech which previously were considered the preoccupation of specialists.

In the few years since this programme was published many teachers who have used it have found from their experience that the claim was justified that children learn to read much better and much faster than had previously been believed possible. They also constantly report amazement at the ability of children to show interest in aspects of language that had always remained beyond them until teachers gave this programme a fair and full trial.

The reaction appropriate to something extraordinary in life is usually amazement. In the present case, ignorance even by linguists of the challenge the language poses leads to the belief that the performance of children is indeed outside the ordinary. The familiar, on the other hand, passes unnoticed until one becomes sensitive to what it *is*. What linguists study is in fact accomplished by everybody: that is, everyone can and does master a new language—which might be any language—competently and automatically, and very early in life. This is the language that happens to be the language of the environment, which becomes the mother tongue. The proper observations of how language behaves must have been made by the speaker for it to be used like everyone else uses it. And he must have been equipped with all the mental tools in order to make sense of speech so early in life.

Does anyone know what the equipment required for such a task is? Linguists are passionately seeking understanding of it and to describe it.

What can be learnt from the success of this programme is that if anyone challenges small children (around four years of age) with problems calling on the use of the same tools as were required for the decoding of the spoken speech of the environment, these children respond by showing as great a competence in making sense of the new challenges. For instance, they learn to read with as much understanding as they showed in learning to talk. But still more may be demanded, so that they play games of transformation which may look incredibly difficult to teachers and psychologists.

It may be that one of the most important findings to emerge from this approach is that no-one can really do anything of value for himself unless he notices the transformations compatible with what he is doing.

Time is obviously consumed in living; obviously everyone has learned from the start that everything has an infinity of appearances linked together by transformations that integrate change and produce permanence. Without any number of samples to represent it, no noun can exist as a noun. Nouns are concepts and as such cover classes. The link between the elements of a class is their equivalence through one or more attributes in common, even when many other quite different attributes can belong to some of the elements. Pronouns replace nouns and provide one of the transformations without which no-one can talk. A change of system of reference from one speaker to another is needed in order to make sense of the fact that 'my nose' can be described by another person as 'your nose', and by another as 'his nose' and so on. This sense of relativity with respect to many systems of reference is a precondition of speaking any language. This is another set of transformations everyone has had to acquire at around the age of two, and may have been prepared for much earlier.

It is therefore felt that truth and reality are more closely approached, that more insight into what happens is shown, if any challenges can be presented as related to some transformation, or several transformations, and if fragmenting and distorting supposedly for the sake of simplicity are rejected.

What may be simple for children may be what is as complex as reality.

To learn to do in every direction what is proposed here for reading is, in the opinion of the author, the challenge of education for the future. To be correct in any educational situation consists in taking reality into account, not just one's preconceptions. The self is capable of generating the components of speech and specialising its production finally to show ownership of speech as it is used in the environment. But the self does more than talk or produce speech. Some clues for the understanding of speech and how one practises as a speaker may be found in some other study of the functioning of the self. Conversely, if a true observation has been made concerning the speaker in the individual, this may help throw light on other functionings of the individual.

If the many muddles created by specialised and fragmented views are to be avoided, much larger chunks of reality should be considered than have been suggested by Descartes (1637) and by others since. That this idea is now current among educators is one of the achievements of this programme. Through developing the ability to encounter, and work on, complexity, the programme has in addition shown that it is possible to eliminate a number of pseudo-problems clogging education—among them the idea that reading is hard—and has opened up vistas which renew hopes about the future while showing how an attack can be initiated on apparently insurmountable obstacles.

The day is not far off when adults will be seen who have retained intact the zest they had as small children, and who behave with respect to reality as people who know what it is or can be.

This programme began with people and their powers and led them to solving their problem of reading. It ends with people more conscious of their power and their functioning.

Examples of 6-year-olds' writing

Keith.

Once upon a time their lived three little men and they went to a cave it was dark in the cave but they had a torch they went throw lots of passengers then they saw a hole there is the gold in there a man said yes said sam it is the hole with the gold in good they got the gold and ran out of the cave they whee rich. the cave was on a cave and it was a long way down.

Graham porter

Once upon a time some men went to the moon they saw tenhundred craters. they walked to the black side of the moon. they fownd some tresares. and then they saw a dragon heading towards them.

wendy

I went to the sea-side with daddy and I went on to the san and I made a sand castle an so did daddy Made a sand castle and then we went into the sea to play and I met Pat and ron and samt

VIVIENNE

one day a rabbit was lost in the woods and he dinnol no wear to go but he saw a prth so he went down the prth and he saw a log so he went on the saw a log a wolf came it said to the rabbit I am going to chase you little rabbit so he did the went so fast that the rabbit she dyded but then a gilcame she saw the rabbit she rock it came rabbir to no srabell but the the mate he there.

Claire

once upon a time a little bird wos bon in summer time and its mother wood bring it some food to atfi. one day the wind wos clowing and the baby bird. fell out of his nest. and a boy wo, comeing alog the rede and he cach he and he toc he home augen

penny

One day a Littel girl
called Janet went
to the circas they
saw Some clowns
and horses the clowns
where funny Janet
Liked it very much
She claped a longtime
then she went home
to bed she sleeped
a long tinne in bed

Lynne

We went to neks dors bon fire and me and
Kay mad a little Gay and We took lo,
Sparklers with aut my sisde and my
sparklers, suisefall We Went t the
bon fire and We col the flams bon-
fire We Went to let of the sue vaeus
and We lib the sparklers.

Hilary

once upon a time There
lived a witch who
had a cat
one day the witch
went out into the
woods and as she
and her cat
went along The
road They met a
lady who was
carruing a baby
just what They
were looking for
and when the lady
saw the witch
she droped her baby
and ran away
Then the witch saw The baby

Philip

once they were six Robbers that lived
in a hause. when it was night they went
into each hause and stole about ten pounds
each night, one night they came and stole
to pounds from the king the next morning
king asked for his girl his men went to get it
But when they got to the Tower the box was gone
wen the men told the King that it was gone he was very
angry he called all his men to look for it soon they found
up that night the Robbers came back and put the
coce of money back

Jacky

One day Jane Julie Elizabeth
and Angla went to the zoo
together because they met down
the lane and the zoo was
very near the lane. So the
four of them went to the
zoo together But Befour
they went to the zoo
they told their mummys
their mummys said yes But
Janes mummy said No you can
not go so Julie Elizabeth
and Angela kood not
go because Jane kood
not go and Jane vas
their frinds So they
played at home
Angela asked her mumm
kood Julie and Elizabeth
come to bec
in the garden play games
to hey played
Hunt the
slipper he

Luke

once upon a time
some men went
to the moon saw Two me-
haloa craters They
wakld The black side
of The moon. The
craters They f arnt
wine The craters

230

APPENDIX 2

A. *Description of materials*

For the teacher

Reading with Words in Colour (1969)[1]

For the class

21 word charts in colour
Fidel (a set of eight charts)
Word Cards (sheets and packs)

For the pupil

(i)   Primer 1—The First Certificate
Primer 2—All the Sounds of English
Primer 3—All the Spellings of English

(ii) Word Building Book, used with the worksheets (see below)
(The last table corresponds to the Fidel used in the classroom)

(iii) Book of Stories (forty stories for continuous reading)

(iv) Worksheets 1–7 (complementary to Primers 1 and 2)
Worksheets 8–14 (complementary to Primer 3 and Book of
Stories.)
The Worksheets are published in the form of 14 booklets
(16 pages in each) and are for use with the Word Building
Book.

Supplementary items

Introductory set of 14 coloured chalks
Pointer for visual dictation

[1]This text.

I. CHALKBOARD

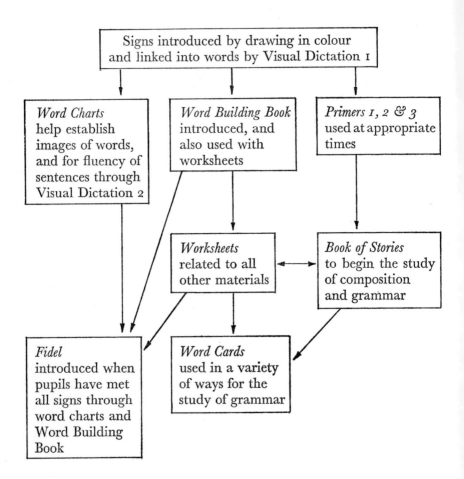

(Note: This first teaching sequence is the one developed in detail in this book.)

2. PRIMERS 1, 2 AND 3

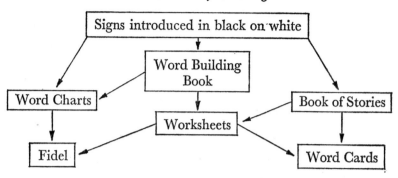

3. WORD CHARTS

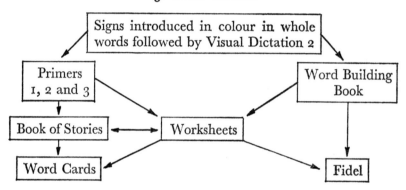

4. WORD BUILDING BOOK

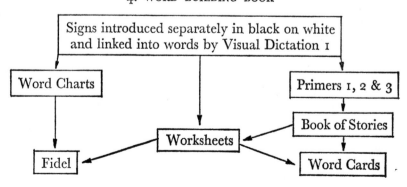

APPENDIX 3[1]

Analysis of links-by-transformation between words on
Word Charts 3, 4, 5 and 6

This section has been placed in an appendix so that teachers new to the programme can choose *not* to look into it if it is not helpful to them when they begin.

It has been found in many cases that teachers who continue to work with Words in Colour are newly fascinated each day by the discovery of many varied ways of introducing each new chart through the links-by-transformation its words have with those on preceding charts and with one another. A summary of some of these connections between words is presented in the diagrams that follow.

Teachers may also find these diagrams helpful in alerting them to the numerous solutions for the Game of Transformations. The diagram relating to Word Chart 6 in particular shows a number of interesting things:

1. the introduction on this chart of the *l* sign that adds the schwa sound to the usual sound of that sign,[2] and

2. the introduction of: three spellings for one sound at one time (*k, ck, ke*);
   two new spellings for another
   (*I, y, i*);
   and a second sound for the sign *i*,

These links require that the rules regarding equivalences be used fully for the first time in analysing transformations.

---

[1]Prepared by Dorothea Hinman.

[2]Mute **r** Edition only.

For example:

$$\text{stri}p \xleftarrow{\quad s \quad} \text{stri}ke$$
$$\text{stru}ck \xleftarrow{\quad s \quad} \text{stri}ke$$
$$\text{sick} \xrightarrow{\quad i \quad} \text{si}lk$$
$$\text{mill} \xrightarrow{\quad a \quad} \text{mil}k$$

In summary, the four operations of transformation are as follows:

pat $\xleftarrow{\ s\ }$ sat	substitution	reversible, shown with
pat $\xleftarrow{\ r\ }$ tap	reversal	a double-headed arrow
pat $\xrightarrow{\ a\ }$ pats or spat	addition	irreversible, shown with
pat $\xrightarrow{\ i\ }$ pant	insertion	a single-headed arrow

The broken arrows in the diagrams indicate some other transformation, or combination of transformations, allowed in Visual Dictation I but not in the Game of Transformations.

Words in parentheses do not appear on any chart but are included in the diagrams since they are useful and can be readily derived from the words that do appear on the charts. The other words not in italics appear on a chart other than the one being analysed.

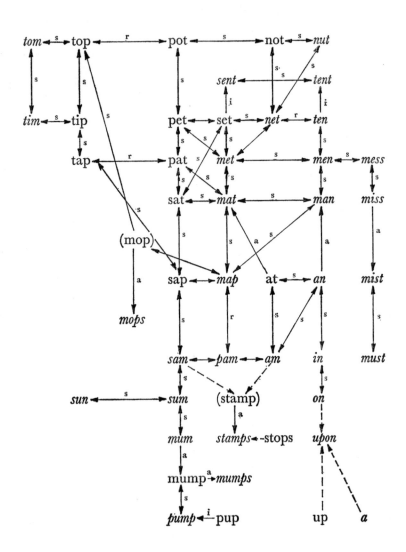

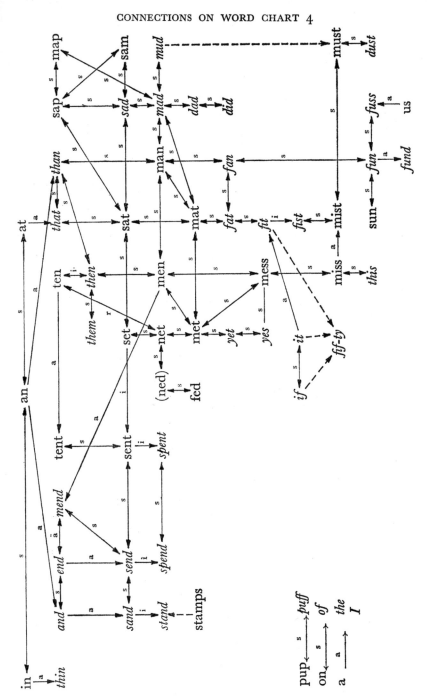

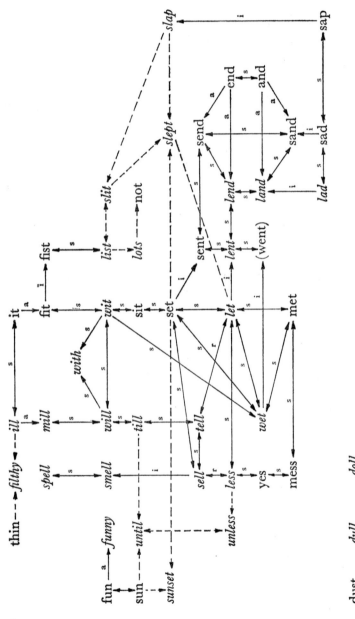

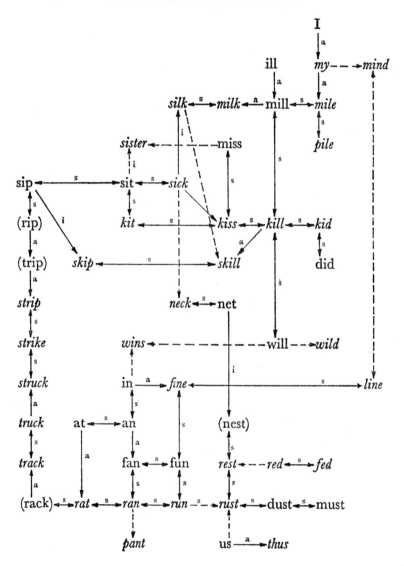

APPENDIX 4

action	breakfast	count	drink
age	bright	couple	drop
aim	brow	court	duty
answer		coward	dwarf
ant	carol	cross	dye
apple	case	crown	
april	castle	cunning	ear
area	cat	curtain	earth
arm	chance	cut	east
art	change		echo
asia	character	dance	edge
axe	charm	dark	education
	chest	date	effect
baby	choir	day	eight
back	chop	dead	election
bandit	circle	dear	elevator
bank	climate	deep	end
basin	cloth	deer	engine
bear	clothes	degree	england
beat	cloud	difference	english
bed	clue	difficulty	enough
black	coal	distinction	equal
blessed	coat	doctor	europe
blood	coffee	dog	eve
blue	colour	dot	eye
body	comma	double	
book	common	doubt	fact
box	compass	dozen	fair
brain	concern	draft	faith
brake	contrary	dream	fall

fancy	fun	honour	land
fantasy	fuse	hope	lass
farm		horse	laugh
father	garage	hose	laughter
fault	garden	hospital	layer
feast	gas	hour	lead
february	general	house	leap
fellow	girl	hundred	length
ferry	globe	hurry	lid
field	glue		lie
fifteen	god	ice	life
figure	gold	idea	light
find	grace	image	lightning
fine	grammar	indian	list
finger	green	invalid	lord
finish	guest	invention	lot
fire	guide	iron	love
fit	gulf	island	
floor	gymnasium		man
flour	gypsy	jacket	mark
flow		jail	market
flower	hail	jam	marriage
flute	hair	job	may
fly	hall	journey	measure
foam	hallelujah		metal
focus	hand	kerb	middle
folk	harbour	key	mill
foot	hat	kid	million
force	hate	kiln	mine
forecast	head	kind	minute
form	heap	king	miss
four	heart	knee	monday
fox	help	knife	money
french	hem	knock	monkey
friend	hen	know	month
front	hero	knowledge	moon
fuel	hiccup		mother
fullness	home	lad	mountain
		lady	

mud	period	reason	set
mule	person	record	seven
	photo	red	shade
nail	physician	region	shadow
name	pianist	reply	shame
nature	piano	restaurant	shape
navy	picture	rhythm	sheep
need	piece	ride	shelf
news	pig	ridge	shoe
night	pill	ring	shop
no	pilot	roast	shot
nose	plane	rod	shoulder
note	plate	roof	show
nought	play	root	shred
noun	pleasure	rope	sick
november	plenty	rule	side
nurse	pocket		sieve
	point	sail	sign
object	police	sake	signal
ocean	post	salt	silk
october	potato	sand	silo
offer	present	sap	silver
officer	pupil	sauce	sir
one	pussy	saw	sister
order		scene	six
	quantity	school	size
pain	quarrel	science	skill
paint	quarter	score	skin
pair	queen	scot	skull
palace	question	scream	sky
past	queue	screw	slack
path		sea	slate
patient	rabbit	season	slave
pay	rage	second (2)	sleep
peace	rain	self	slice
pen	rash	sense	slide
pencil	rat	sentence	slip
penny	ray	sergeant	snail

NOUNS – GREEN CARDS

snake	storey	tense	unit
soccer	storm	tent	up
sock	story	thanks	use
soldier	strain	thing	
solid	straw	thirty	valve
son	strike	three	verb
sorrow	stroke	throat	view
sort	study	throw	villain
soul	subject	thursday	visit
south	sugar	time	vocabulary
space	suit	tip	
spade	sunday	tire	war
speed	sunset	tomato	water
sphere	surprise	ton	wave
spirit	sweat	tool	way
spoon	sweet	tooth	wednesday
spring	swing	top	week
spy	syllable	total	wind
square	syrup	town	wine
stable		toy	winter
staff	table	trade	wood
stalk	tailor	traffic	work
stamp	tan	transport	worth
stand	taste	treasure	wrist
star	tax	true	
station	taxi	tube	year
steam	tea	tuesday	yes
step	teacher	tunnel	yesterday
stomach	team	turn	youth
stone	tear	two	
stop	teeth		zero
store	ten	umbrella	zoo

ADJECTIVES – YELLOW CARDS

a	alone	another	back
able	american	anxious	basic
all (2)	an	any	better

big	each (2)	forward	just
bigger	easy	four	
black	effective	fourteen	keen
blessed	eight	fourth	kind
blue	eighteen	frank	
both	either (2)	free	large
brave	equal (2)	french	last
broad	elder	full	late
brown	eldest	funny	latter
busy	eleven	furious	least (2)
	empty		left
clever	english	general	less
close	enormous	good	light
common	enough	gray	like
complete	excellent	great	little
considerable	extraordinary	green	long
contrary	even		longest
coward	every	half	lost
cunning		happy	loud
	faint	hard	low
dark	fair	heavier	lower
dead	faithful	heavy	
dear	false	her	mad
decent	fancy	high	many
deep	far	his	mean
definite	farther	holy	middle
different	fast	honest	more (2)
difficult	few (2)	horrible	most
dim	fifteen	huge	much
direct	final	human	
dirty	fine	hundred	near
discreet	first		neither
disgraceful	fit	impossible	next (2)
double	five	indian	new
drunk	foreign	intelligent	no
dry	former	invalid	none
due	foremost		north
dumb	forty	jolly	nice

ADJECTIVES – YELLOW CARDS

nine	remarkable	some	twentieth
nineteen	remote	sore	twenty
number	rich	sorry	
numerous	right	special	ugly
	rough	stupid	unequal
off	rude	such	unique
old		sudden	upper
one	sad	superior	upright
only	same	sure	useful
open	scarce	sweet	usual
opposite	scotch		
orange	second	tall	vain
other	self (2)	tender	various
our	seven	tense	vast
out	sharp	tenth	very
own	sheer	that	visual
	short	the	
pale	shy	their	weak
plenty	sick	these	well
plural	silly	thin	what
poor	simple	third	which
possible	singular	thirteen	white
	six	thirty	whole
quiet	sixteen	this	wide
	slack	those	wise
ready	slow (2)	three (2)	wrong
real	small	tidy	
red	smooth	top	yellow
regardless	soft	two	young
regular	solid	twelve	your

ADVERBS – BLUE CARDS

about	ago	already	apart
above	all (2)	also (2)	around
across	almost	altogether	as
after	alone	always	aside
again	aloud	any (2)	away

ADVERBS – BLUE CARDS

back	fine	nearby	so
because	first (2)	neither	suddenly
before	foremost	never	sure
behind	forth	next (2)	
below	forward (2)	no	that
beneath	from	none	then
better	full	nor	there
between		not	thereby
but	hard	now	therefore
by	hardly		though
	here	off	through
close	high	often	to
	highly	on	today
dear	how	once	together
deep	however	only	tomorrow
direct	huge	opposite	tonight
down		otherwise	too
due	just	out (2)	twice
easy	last (2)	perhaps	under (2)
either	late		underneath
else	least (2)	quickly	up (2)
enough	less	quite	
equally	little		vastly
especially	long	rather	very
even	low	ready	
ever			well
exactly	more	same	when
	most (2)	seldom	where
fair	mostly	since	while
far	much (2)	slow (2)	why
farther		slowly	without
fast	near (2)	small	
			yet

PREPOSITIONS – PINK CARDS

a	above	after	along
about	across	all	amid

246

PREPOSITIONS – PINK CARDS

among (2)	down	like	than
an			through
around	except	near (2)	till
at		next (2)	to
before	for	of	under
behind	forth	off	underneath
below	from	on	until
beneath		opposite	up
beside (2)	in	or	upon
between	into	out	
but			with
by	less	since	without

PRONOUNS – GREY CARDS

another	he	much	same
any	her	my	she
as	him		so
		neither (2)	some
both	I	none	such
	it		
each			that
either (2)	me	one	their
every	mine	other	theirs
	more	our	them
former	most	ours	these

PRONOUNS – GREY CARDS

they	we	which	you
this	what	who	your
those	whatever	whom	yours
	where	whose	
us			

ah!   oh!   so!

VERBS – SALMON CARDS

accept	bury	die	fancy
act		differ	farm
aim	came	dim	fasten
am	can	direct	feast
answer	carry	discuss	figure
are	cease	do	find
arise	chance	does	fine
arrive	change	done	finish
ask	charm	dot	fire
avail	close	double	fit
avoid	cloud	doubt	fix
awake	chose	draft	floor
	coat	dream	flow
back	colour	drink	flower
bank	comb	drop	fly
be	come	drunk	focus
bear	compass	dry	follow
beat	complete	dye	foot
become	concern		forbid
been	conquer	earth	force
begin	could	eat	forget
begun	couple	echo	forgot
being	cross	educate	forecast
better	crown	eliminate	form
bless	cut	empty	found
book		end	fox
born	dare	endeavour	fulfil
brave	date	equal	
break	deal	except	gauge
bring	defy		gave
brought	deny	fail	give
burn	depend	faint	given
burnt	did	fall (2)	get

248

go	last	object	ride
goes (2)	lead	obtain	ring
going (3)	leap	occupy	rise
gone	learn	open	roast
got	learnt	offer	run
grow	leave	order	rush
guide	led	own	
	left		said
had	let	paint	sail
hail	lie	pass	sat
halve	light	pay	save
happen	like	pick	saw
has	list	play	say
hasten	listen	pocket	scare
hate	live	point	score
have	long	pray	scream
head	look	present	screw
hear	lose	purr	second
heard	lost	put	see
held	love		seek
help		quarter	seem
hold			seen
hope	made	raise	seize
house	make	ran	set
hurry	man	read (2)	sew
	mark	reason	shake
imagine	market	receive	shall
invent	may	record	shave
iron	mean	refill	shoot
is	meant	reflect	shop
	might	refrigerate	shot
keep	miss	regard	should
kept	move	remain	show
knew	must	remember	shown
knock		remove	shrink
know	name	reply	shut
	need	request	sing
lake	nurse	respect	sit
		rid	

249

VERBS – SALMON CARDS

speak	stride	tend	wait
spell	strike	thank	was
spelt	stood	think	wash
spin	stop	threw	waste
spoke	study	throw	wear
sleep	subtract	time	went
slice	succeed	tire	were
slide	swim	told	will
slow	swing	took	win
smell		top	work
soften	take	toss	worry
spare	taken	touch	would
squeeze	takes	turn	write
stamp	talk	use	d (27)
stand	taste	used	ed (21)
star	tear		ing (9)
step	tell	visit	

CONJUNCTIONS – IVORY CARDS

after	either	now	that
although	except		though
and (4)		once	till
as	for	only	
		or	unless
because	if	since	
before		so	while
but	neither		
	nor	than (2)	yet

APPENDIX 6

The content of the set of word charts arranged in alphabetical order
The numbers indicate the charts on which the words occur

3 a	9 bigger	11 catch	17 daughter
12 able	7 black	10 channel	14 day
20 adieu	21 blithe	11 character	20 debt
12 adjective	11 blood	10 charm	20 diaphragm
14 aged	18 boar	10 cherry	4 did
20 aisle	18 board	10 chicken	9 dirty
11 all	8 bone	10 child	12 do
3 am	18 bored	10 children	10 does
21 amoeba	19 borrow	10 chill	9 dog
3 an	19 bough	10 chin	5 doll
4 and	11 box	10 china	10 done
12 animal	18 boy	10 chips	15 door
19 anxiety	16 break	10 chorus	17 doubt
8 any	7 brick	10 church	5 dull
9 april	18 broke	21 clique	15 dumb
2 as	7 brother	18 cloak	4 dust
2 at	18 buoy	21 clothes	9 duty
12 ate	7 burden	11 clutch	
21 awkward	17 bury	14 conceit	
21 azure	15 business	14 conceived	
	15 busy	14 cool	16 ear
7 back	7 but	19 cough	12 education
9 bankrupt	16 buy	13 courageous	8 egg
7 bat	11 by	19 cramp	18 eight
21 bathe		11 crime	18 eighty
13 be	21 cage	11 criminal	17 either
17 beauty	11 call	11 cry	13 elephant
17 because	20 calm	21 cube	4 end
13 been	19 calves		15 england
13 between	11 capable	4 dad	19 examination
9 big	11 cat	8 date	19 exist
			14 eyes

11 false	4 fuss	7 his	5 lad
12 family		8 home	15 lamb
4 fan	11 garden	14 honey	5 land
11 fantastic	12 gem	7 horror	8 late
10 far	12 generation	9 horse	17 laugh
15 fast	8 get	9 hose	17 lawn
15 fasten	20 ghost	7 hot	16 lead
4 fat	8 girl	10 hotel	16 lead
8 fatal	9 give	13 hour	8 leg
12 father	8 globe	13 house	17 leisure
4 fed	8 go	9 hundred	5 lend
13 feet	10 goes	9 hungry	5 lent
14 field	9 gold	20 hymn	5 less
4 fifty	9 gone		15 lesson
5 filthy	8 got	4 I	5 let
6 fine	14 gray	4 if	15 lie
14 finished	16 great	5 ill	8 like
8 fire	14 greyhound	7 impossible	6 line
9 firm	20 guarantee	3 in	5 list
8 first	20 guard	20 indict	15 listen
4 fist	9 gum	2 is	7 little
4 fit		18 isle	19 loaf
9 five	19 half	2 it	19 loaves
7 flat	21 hallelujah		12 look
18 flowers	19 halves	12 jack	9 loss
18 flown	7 has	21 jewel	5 lots
12 fool	7 hat	12 joan	
13 foot	8 hate	12 john	4 mad
10 for	10 have	12 judge	8 made
18 freight	8 he		17 mail
20 friend	16 hear	6 kid	17 maintain
7 from	16 heart	6 kill	8 make
9 front	15 height	6 kiss	8 male
18 fruit	15 heir	6 kit	3 man
4 fun	7 her	16 knee	3 map
4 fund	16 here	16 knew	3 mat
5 funny	19 hiccup	16 know	11 match
6 fur	14 high	16 knowledge	14 may
8 fuse	7 him		21 mayor

8 me	15 ocean	7 promise	18 saw
17 measure	4 of	20 prosaic	21 scheme
3 men	9 off	21 psalm	21 schist
4 mend	18 oil	4 pup	12 school
3 mess	3 on	3 pump	20 science
3 met	15 once	2 pup	20 scissors
10 michigan	15 one	15 push	20 scythe
6 mile	10 or	15 put	13 see
6 milk	11 orchestra		20 seize
5 mill	13 our	21 quay	5 sell
6 mind		11 question	4 send
3 miss	17 paid	21 queue	3 sent
3 mist	3 pam	11 quickly	20 service
19 mix	6 pant	17 quiet	2 set
18 moist	2 pat		9 seven
14 money	17 paul	6 ran	18 sew
3 mops	17 paw	6 rat	10 shall
8 more	16 pear	17 raw	10 she
12 mother	16 pearl	20 receipt	10 shell
4 mud	21 pension	6 red	10 ship
3 mum	15 people	21 region	20 shoes
3 mumps	2 pep	20 reservoir	10 shop
3 must	2 pest	6 rest	10 shot
6 my	2 pet	21 rhythm	14 should
	13 photograph	16 right	10 shred
	11 phrase	21 righteous	10 shut
6 neck	13 physics	9 robe	6 sick
3 net	6 pile	15 rolled	20 siege
16 new	2 pit	6 run	20 sieve
16 news	17 plateau	6 rust	15 sigh
11 next	21 pneumatic		6 silk
14 night	17 poor	4 sad	7 simple
8 nine	2 pop	17 said	13 sing
8 ninety	17 pore	3 sam	2 sips
9 no	2 pot	8 same	6 sister
10 nor	12 potato	4 sand	2 sit
8 nose	17 pour	2 sap	7 skill
3 not	14 prayers	2 sat	6 skip
3 nut	14 prey	14 saturday	5 slap

13 sleep	18 sweet	5 till	16 weird
5 slept	5 swim	3 tim	5 wet
5 slit	16 sword	2 tip	13 when
11 small	16 sworn	21 tissue	13 where
5 smell		12 to	13 who
9 so	15 talk	15 told	13 whom
18 soar	2 tap	3 tom	13 whose
9 sold	17 taught	12 tomorrow	13 why
12 soldier	19 taxi	12 too	6 wild
7 son	16 tea	12 took	5 will
18 sore	16 tear	12 tooth	6 wins
7 sorry	16 tear	2 top	10 wish
13 soup	5 tell	2 toss	5 wit
18 sow	3 ten	2 tot	5 with
18 sow	3 tent	19 tough	8 woke
2 spat	2 test	6 track	19 woman
5 spell	4 than	17 treasure	19 women
4 spend	9 thanks	21 trekked	14 wood
4 spent	4 that	6 truck	7 word
3 stamps	4 the	19 true	7 work
4 stand	16 their	12 two	7 world
2 step	4 them		7 worry
2 steps	4 then	8 unite	14 would
2 stop	7 there	5 unless	16 write
15 stopped	17 therefore	5 until	16 written
2 stops	13 these	2 up	16 wrong
20 straight	14 they	3 upon	
6 strike	15 thigh	2 us	20 yacht
6 strip	4 thin	9 usable	4 yes
6 struck	9 thirsty	8 use	4 yet
7 suddenly	9 thirty		20 yield
15 sugar	4 this	21 vision	13 you
18 suit	19 thorough	21 vulture	13 young
18 suite	19 though		13 your
3 sum	19 thought	15 walk	13 youth
3 sun	19 through	4 was	
5 sunset	19 thursday	11 watch	18 zero
15 sure	6 thus	17 water	18 zip
19 swamp	9 tiger	8 we	18 zoo
		19 wednesday	

BIBLIOGRAPHY

Armington, David, Sally Kirsdale and Lee Switz. *Right to Read: A Pilot Program in Adult Literacy.* Cleveland, Ohio: PACE (Program for Action by Citizens in Education), 1965. (Out of print.)

Armington, David. *The Words in Color Remedial Reading Project Central Junior High School,* (September 16–October 27, 1965). Mimeographed report. Cleveland, Ohio: Cleveland Board of Education, 1965.

Baily, Carolyn. *A Comparison of the Effectiveness of Two Reading Programs and a Language Development Program with Culturally Disadvantaged Children.* Unpublished doctoral dissertation. Nashville, Tennessee: George Peabody College for Teachers, 1966.

Bentley, Harriet. "Words in Color", *Elementary English.* Champaign, Illinois: National Council of Teachers of English, May, 1966.

—— "Words in Color A Reading Program?!!," *Issues and Innovations in the Teaching of Reading,* ed. Joe L. Frost. Glenview, Illinois: Scott, Foresman and Company, 1967.

Curtis, Olga. "The Rainbow Road to Reading," *Empire Magazine,* (April 4, 1965). Digested for the *Catholic Digest.* Denver, Colorado: *The Denver Post,* 1965.

Defner, Hilda and Lee Temkin. *A Unique and Exciting Action Program.* Adult Literacy Program, Report of the Fourth District of Wisconsin Congress of Parents and Teachers, Milwaukee, Wisconsin: Annual Meeting of National Congress of Parents and Teachers, 1966.

Dodds, William J. *A Longitudinal Study of Two Beginning Reading Programs: Words in Color and Traditional Basal Readers.* Unpublished doctoral dissertation. Cleveland, Ohio: Western Reserve University, School of Education, 1966.

Dulcina, Sister M., C.PP.S. "Words in Color: Excerpts from a First Grade Teacher's Diary," *The Community Post,* (September 29–December 23). Minster, Ohio: 1965, ten articles.

Fowles, Mary. *Rainbow's End,* a third monograph in a series on *Words in Colour in the Classroom.* Educational Explorers Limited.

Gallagher, Joan. *With the Five-Year-Olds,* a fourth monograph in a series on *Words in Colour in the Classroom.* Educational Explorers Limited.

Gattegno, C. *La Lecture en Couleurs: Guide du Maître.* Neuchâtel, Switzerland: Delachaux and Nièstle, 1966.

—— *Metodo Morfologico-Algebraico,* Segunda edicion, completamente revisada. Madrid, Spain: Cuisenaire de España, 1961.

—— *The Morphologico-Algebraic Approach to Reading and Writing,* ed. D. Hinman. Mimeographed by the Student Government of the San Francisco State College Center. Santa Rosa, California: 1959.

—— *Notes on Words in Colour,* Pamphlet, Reading, England: Educational Explorers Limited.

—— *Report on One Month Experiment in Public School 113 in New York City.* Mimeographed. New York, New York: Schools for the Future, P.O. Box 349, Cooper Station, 1966.

—— "Short Passages". Part of the *Silent Way for Teaching English As a Second Language.* Reading, England: Educational Explorers Limited, 1968.

—— "The Subordination of Teaching to Learning," *Teaching Foreign Languages in Schools*. Reading, England: Educational Explorers Limited, 1963, Ch. 1.

—— "Teaching Reading: An Indefinitely Renewable Problem," *Spelling Progress Bulletin*. North Hollywood, California: 5848 Alcove Avenue, 1964.

—— *What Does Words in Color Demand of Us?* New York, New York: Schools for the Future, 1966.

—— *Words in Color—Background and Principles*, revised edition of *The Morphologico-Algebraic Approach to Reading and Writing*. New York, New York: Learning Materials, Inc., Xerox Education Division, 600 Madison Avenue, 1962.

—— *Words in Color—Classroom and Pupil Materials*, revised edition. New York, New York: Learning Materials Inc., Xerox Education Division, 1962–63.

—— *Words in Colour: Further Reading*. 3 vols.: (1. The Eastern Beam, 2. The White Canary, 3. The Magic Forest and Other Tales). Reading, England: Educational Explorers Limited, 1968.

—— "Words in Color—The Morphologico-Algebraic Approach to Teaching Reading," *The Disabled Reader: Education of the Dyslexic Child*, ed. John Money. Baltimore, Maryland: The Johns Hopkins Press, 1966, Chap. 11.

—— *Words in Color—Teacher's Guide*, revised edition, New York, New York: Learning Materials, Inc., Xerox Education Division, 1962.

Hinds, Lillian R. *An Evaluation of Words in Color or Morphologico-Algebraic Approach to Teaching Reading to Functionally Illiterate Adults*. Unpublished doctoral dissertation. Cleveland, Ohio: Western Reserve University, School of Education, 1966.

Hinman, D. "The Current Status of Words in Color in the United States," *The Disabled Reader: Education of the Dyslexic Child*, ed. John Money. Baltimore, Maryland: The Johns Hopkins Press, 1966, Addendum to Ch. 11.

—— *Questions Frequently Asked About Words in Color*, pamphlet. New York, New York: Learning Materials, Inc., Xerox Education Division, 1962–63.

—— "Words in Color," *Current Approaches to Teaching Reading*, ed. Helen K. Mackintosh. Elementary Instructional Service Leaflet. Washington, D.C.: Chief Elementary School Organization Section, U.S. Office of Education, EKNE Department, National Educational Association, 1965.

Holland, Allan R. *A Comparative Study of First Grade Reading Programs: Initial Teaching Alphabet, Words in Color, and a Traditional Basic Reading Approach*. Unpublished doctoral dissertation. Cleveland, Ohio: Western Reserve University, School of Education, 1967.

Holland, Merry. *My Experience Teaching Words in Color in a First Grade*. Unpublished master's research project. San Francisco, California: San Francisco State College, 1966.

Hopkin, Brenda. "Eight Hours to Literacy," *School and College Journal*. England: 1964.

Jones, Gretchen H. *An Experiment Evaluating the Words in Color Method of Teaching Reading to Fourth and Fifth Grade Pupils*. Unpublished master's research project. Deland, Florida: Stetson University, 1965.

Lee, Terrence. *Writing the Talking*. Report by County Borough of Rotherham Education Committee, England: Schools Psychological Service, 1967.

Leonore (Murphy), Sister Mary, R.S.C. *Beginning to Read: A Report on Teaching of Reading, Writing and Spelling in the Infant School*. Reading, England: Educational Explorers Limited, 1964.

—— *Creative Writing*, a first monograph in a series on *Words in Colour in the Classroom*. Educational Explorers Limited, 1966.

—— *Douglas Can't Read*, a second monograph in a series on *Words in Colour in the Classroom*. Educational Explorers Limited, 1968.

—— *To Perceive and to Write*, a fifth monograph in a series on *Words in Colour in the Classroom*. Educational Explorers Limited, 1969.

"Reading by the Rainbow," *Friends*, (October, 1966). Detroit, Michigan: Ceco Publishing Company (Chevrolet), 1966.

"Reading by Rainbow," *Time*, Vol. 83, No. 24, (June 12, 1964). Report on Dr. Gattegno's demonstration at the U.S. Office of Education, (May 26–28, 1964). New York, New York: Time-Life, Inc., 1964.

Spaulding, Robert L. *Report of the Durham Educational Improvement Program—A Project of the Ford Foundation*. Durham, North Carolina: Duke University, 1966.

Steele, Jeremy. *A Solution for Secondary School Non-Readers*. Reading, England: Educational Explorers Limited, 1965.

"Words in Color," *Current Approaches to Teaching Reading*. Washington, D.C.: National Education Association Journal, December 1965.

Films and Filmstrips

Gattegno, C. *Words in Colour*. Training film, color, 16 mm, 39 min. Educational Explorers Limited, 1965.

Words in Colour. 32 mm filmstrip of 29 frames showing each of the 21 Word Charts and the 8 Phonic Code Charts.

INDEX